THE BASICS

Jazz: The Basics gives a brief introduction to the history and repertoire of jazz. It is ideal for students and interested listeners who want to learn more about this important musical style. The heart of the book traces jazz's growth from its folk origins through early recordings and New Orleans stars, the big-band and swing era, bebop, cool jazz and third stream, avant-garde, jazz-rock, the neo-conservative movement of the 1980s, and the polystylism of the 1990s.

Key figures from each era including: Louis Armstrong, Benny Goodman, Charlie Parker, Miles Davis, and Wynton Marsalis are highlighted along with classic works. A list of recommended recordings highlights essential listening for anyone who wants to learn more about jazz.

Jazz: The Basics is an excellent introduction to the players, the music, and the styles that make jazz an enduring and well-loved musical style.

Christopher Meeder is a graduate of the Master's program in Jazz History and Research at Rutgers University, Newark. He is also an active freelance musician in jazz, classical, and rock contexts.

You may also be interested in the following Routledge
Student Reference titles:

BLUES: THE BASICS
Dick Weissman

FOLK MUSIC: THE BASICS
Ronald Cohen

JAZZ: THE BASICS
Christopher Meeder

OPERA: THE BASICS
Denise Gallo

WORLD MUSIC: THE BASICS
Richard Nidel

JAZZ
THE BASICS

christopher meeder

Routledge
Taylor & Francis Group
NEW YORK AND LONDON

First published 2008
by Routledge
270 Madison Ave, New York, NY 10016

Simultaneously published in the UK
by Routledge
2 Park Square, Milton Park, Abingdon, Oxon OX14 4RN

Routledge is an imprint of the Taylor & Francis Group, an informa business

Typeset in Aldus and Futura by EvS Communication Networx, Inc.

Printed and bound in the United States of America on acid-free paper by Sheridan Books, Inc.

Library of Congress Cataloging-in-Publication Data
Meeder, Christopher.
Jazz : the basics / Christopher Meeder.
p. cm.
Includes bibliographical references (p. 264), discography (p. 256), and index.
ISBN 978-0-415-96693-1 (hardback) -- ISBN 978-0-415-96694-8 (pbk.) -- ISBN 978-0-203-93145-5 (ebook) 1. Jazz--History and criticism. 2. Jazz musicians--United States. I. Title.
ML3506.M38 2008
781.6509--dc22
2007041685

ISBN10: 0-415-96693-0 (hbk)
ISBN 10: 0-415-96694-9 (pbk)
ISBN10: 0-203-93145-9 (ebk)

ISBN13: 978-0-415-96693-1 (hbk)
ISBN 13: 978-0-415-96694-8 (pbk)
ISBN13: 978-0-203-93145-5 (ebk)

CONTENTS

INTRODUCTION AND ACKNOWLEDGMENTS

This is by no means the first single volume devoted to providing an introduction to the history and appreciation of the jazz tradition. Since jazz is still an active and constantly changing part of musical culture, a new volume must be written every few years to place past events in context, evaluate the present jazz scene, and provide some indication of current trends in the music. What has not changed over the last thirty years or so is the need for such a formal introduction to jazz. Jazz occupies a peculiar place in American culture. Audiences since the 1970s have changed drastically, and while they are growing, they are doing so from a recent low point. But while the likelihood of a live recording from the Village Vanguard becoming a smash hit is low at best, jazz still permeates popular culture through film, television, and the occasional significant compact disc. To consider jazz history is to look at twentieth century American culture as a whole (with brief but significant glances towards Africa and Europe).

One of the greatest difficulties facing someone who is learning about jazz for the first time is the difficulty of developing a fundamental definition of jazz. Most of us have some idea about what to expect when we are about to listen to a jazz performance, but those ideas are vague at best—if a single word can be used to classify the music of Fats Waller, Dizzy Gillespie, and Chick Corea, vagueness is that word's best asset. Often, the only commonality between two recordings of Miles Davis is that Miles Davis was somehow involved in both of them. The fact of the matter is that the word "jazz" is more of a social descriptor than a musical one. While there are significant musical elements common to many different kinds of jazz, the largest determining factor of whether a specific work can be called jazz is that the recording is filed in the jazz bin at a record store, or discussed in a jazz magazine, or made at a jazz club. As a social term rather than a musical one, then, a full understanding of the music at the center of jazz requires a fairly detailed treatment.

It is my hope that this book will provide at least a rough treatment. It was written with the intent of providing the jazz neophyte with a general technical understanding of the mechanics of a jazz performance, as well as historical context for any jazz recordings or performances that might be encountered, whether in a university classroom, jazz club, or record store. In addition to discussing the musical aspects of any particular artist or style, I have made an effort to discuss major controversies and conflicts that arise (they do so frequently). While I have done my best to provide both sides of any disputes, I have no doubt that my own opinions and biases are clear, and I hope you take any such statements with an open invitation to disagree and form your own opinions.

There is always a danger in treating jazz history (or the history of any of the Fine Arts) as a clear, teleological progression of ideas towards an aesthetic ideal. All too frequently, jazz is taught as a clear path from ragtime to New Orleans to swing to bebop, etc. For the sake of clarity, I have distorted the complicated history of jazz into a neat list of styles, and I have emphasized novel artists for the sake of brevity. It should be clearly understood that a graphic depiction of jazz history would not be a straight line, but rather a massive and steadily growing pile of parallel lines. Stylistic change in the arts happens additively, and the music discussed in the context of 1917 is still being performed, often quite brilliantly, at the same time as any other style. While I argue that jazz sub-styles, fragmented after the first generation of bebop musicians, emphasized individuality and personal style, it should be understood that the co-existence of multiple styles of jazz at any given time in jazz history was the norm. By the time the Original Dixieland Jazz Band released what is conventionally considered the first jazz recording, they were already controversial among midwestern jazz musicians, and popular songwriters, stride pianists, and proto-swing dance bands were already developing in different directions on the East Coast.

I place a heavy emphasis on the history of sound recording in this book. While jazz is live music at its core, our understanding of its history comes primarily from recordings, and jazz developed largely in parallel with recording technology. The first jazz recordings appeared on the market shortly after the first affordable phonograph, and, as studio technology developed and new formats became available, they had an immediate and important impact on how jazz musicians played.

One of the distinguishing characteristics of this book from other similar introductions to jazz is that the standard anthology of jazz recordings on which most books are based, *the Smithsonian Collection of Classic Jazz*, has gone out of print. Since its first pressing, the *Smithsonian Collection* has served as the standard general collection of jazz for use in classrooms, and as such the collection has gone a long way towards establishing a canon of classic jazz recordings. At the time of press, the Smithsonian Collection is undergoing significant revisions before it will be re-released, and nothing currently available exists to adequately replace it. Still, it is pointless to discuss music without being able to hear it. Whenever possible, I have drawn examples that are available on the four CD set *Ken Burns Jazz: The Story of America's Music*. The phenomenon of *Ken Burns Jazz* has caused controversy since long before any television episodes or compact discs reached the market. The controversy is discussed in Chapter 22 of this book. In the meantime, while I strongly recommend that you acquire a copy of the CD set to illustrate much of the music discussed in the first half of this book, you should be aware that the conservative bias espoused in nearly every thing with the phrase "Ken Burns Jazz" associated with it make the set problematic for illustrating jazz recorded after around 1957. What is included on *Ken Burns Jazz* fits in with the greatest recordings in American history, but it is by no means a complete and thorough anthology.

Jazz: The Basics was written at the suggestion of Richard Carlin, who was at that time an editor at Routledge, and I was suggested as the author by Lewis Porter, who was my advisor in the Master's Degree program in Jazz History and Research at Rutgers University, Newark Campus. I am indebted to both of them for the opportunity to contribute this text. I have also received invaluable assistance from my present editor at Routledge, Constance Ditzel, and her assistant, Devon Sherman.

Many of the ideas expressed in this book were formed under the direct influence of the faculty at Rutgers-Newark—Lewis Porter, Henry Martin, Evan Spring, and Bill Kirchner have provided a great deal of guidance for which I am grateful. My colleagues at Rutgers have also been of tremendous help in sharpening my arguments through passionate discussion. All deserve mention, but Scott Carter, Kevin Frey, and Bob McMahon showed special patience with my often heated method of discussion.

Public thanks are also due to a number of friends who

have helped me with this book by proofreading, discussing my problems, and otherwise showing support and patience with me as I wrestled to complete it. Chris Hamilton, Zoe Milgram, Dan Jones, Caleb Burroughs, Jesse Rakusin, and Kevin Shea are among them. There are surely others, and I apologize for their omission as I endeavor to thank them privately.

Finally, I have received support on every level from my family, especially my brother Jonathan, my sister-in-law Jessica, and my parents, Phil and Judy. I dedicate this book to them.

1

FUNDAMENTALS

As a precursor to dealing directly with the history and repertoire of jazz, it is important to be familiar with some of the concepts and ideas that will come up again and again in this book. As the Introduction indicates, a one sentence, or even one chapter long definition of the music is impossible, or at least narrow-minded. However, it is, more or less, a single tradition that is under discussion, and as such, most of the following will be a part of most of the music in the following chapters. Some of the ideas presented in this text generally apply to all music from the West, and some of it is specific to jazz. All of it is subject to different opinions, definitions and interpretations.

IMPROVISATION

Improvisation is one of the most frequently mentioned and heavily emphasized aspects of jazz performance practice in discussions of the music, and for good reason. With only rare exceptions, jazz musicians do much of their work spontaneously, allowing their environment to have an influence on what they play. Details about timbre, rhythm, even what notes to play and when are left to the discretion of the individual performer, and vary from performance to performance, to a degree far greater than is found in classical music, rock, and just about any other Western musical tradition.

Of course, it would be incorrect to assume that John Coltrane's *A Love Supreme*, for instance, sprang fully formed from the imaginations of the players at the moment the record button was pushed. What is left undetermined until the time of performance is far from the full story of what makes jazz sound like jazz. A great deal of time is spent by jazz musicians preparing for a performance, both in individual practicing and rehearsal. Compositions are chosen or written, arranged and rehearsed to varying degrees before the performance. Furthermore, different players rely on their improvisational skills to different degrees, and it is difficult to tell from the way they play how much time has passed between coming up with a phrase and playing it. It has been a problematic issue for jazz scholars in the past—the 1925 recording of Louis Armstrong's "Cornet Chop Suey," for instance, was lauded as a particularly fiery and well-formed improvisation on Armstrong's part until it was discovered that he had applied for copyright for the solo, written out note for note, some two years earlier.

The only surefire way to determine the degree to which a performance involves improvisation is to compare multiple performances of the same tune by the same musicians. When the advent of the compact disc expanded the standard duration of recordings (previously, LPs would contain around thirty-five to fifty minutes of music; now CDs can be 80 minutes or longer), the inclusion of "alternate takes," or previously unreleased renditions of a work, became the standard for filling out older recordings to make them worth the money.

With all of this in mind, the fact remains that a B-flat is a B-flat whether a musician decides to play the note at the performance or twenty years earlier. Although improvisation is a very important part of jazz from the player's perspective (and fun and interesting to explore through comparing takes), it does little to add to the experience of the audience to know when someone is playing prepared music and when s/he is improvising. Over the course of this book, little attention will be paid to this aspect of performance practice.

INSTRUMENTATION AND ITS ROLE WITHIN FORM

Jazz can be and has been played on just about any musical instrument, from egg shaker to bagpipes. It can be performed solo, or by a large orchestra, or any size group between. While some instruments, like clarinet and tuba, go into and out of fashion, the most common instruments in jazz are trumpet, trombone, saxophone, piano, double bass and drum set. Slightly less used, but still quite common, are guitar (electric guitar was commonplace as soon as it was invented), violin, vibraphone, clarinet, and tuba.

While there is a great deal of variance with the roles of each instrument over history and among different playing styles, a few general descriptions can be made here. Since jazz is more or less homophonic music (in which a melody is supported by harmonic accompaniment), it is an easy task to differentiate between melodic instruments (often simply called "horns," but to avoid confusion with the instrument commonly called French horn but more properly called simply horn, this book will refer to "winds") and accompanying instruments, collectively called the "rhythm section." The work of the winds in jazz is, at its base, to play the tunes and solos.

The rhythm section generally contains piano, bass and drums. Often, guitar will join in as well, and in early jazz recordings, tuba and banjo were common substitutes for

COMMON JAZZ WIND INSTRUMENTS

Trumpet and **trombone** are both brass instruments, meaning that they are essentially brass tubes, played by buzzing the lips together into a cup- or funnel-shaped mouthpiece on one end of the instrument. Pitch is partly determined by the length of the tube: on trombone, the length is changed by extending a sliding portion of the instrument, while a trumpet player opens and closes valves that divert the air to different lengths of extra tubing. Important trumpeters include Louis Armstrong, Dizzy Gillespie, and Miles Davis. Trombone soloists are somewhat more rare than trumpeters, but include Jack Teagarden, J.J. Johnson, and Roswell Rudd.

The **saxophone** is a reed instrument, played by passing air over a thin reed strapped to a mouthpiece. Saxophones are actually a family of related instruments specified by pitch, but all usually made of brass, roughly conical, and pitched by opening and closing holes in the side of the instrument controlled by keys. From highest to lowest, the most common saxophones are the soprano, alto, tenor, and baritone saxophonists. Many saxophonists play two or more different instruments from the saxophone family, and a few also play **clarinet**, which is another reed instrument – older than the saxophone, and usually made of wood and more cylindrical in shape than the saxophone. Grouped by instrument, some important saxophonists include: soprano – Sidney Bechet, Steve Lacy, and John Coltrane (on occasion); alto – Johnny Hodges, Charlie Parker, and Paul Desmond; tenor – Lester Young, Coleman Hawkins, and John Coltrane (most of the time); baritone is generally secondary, background instrument, and Gerry Mulligan was a rare example of a baritone specialist in a solo context.

bass and guitar. The instruments in the rhythm section work together to provide accompaniment for the horns, and each instrument tends towards a specific role. Like rock, but unlike the classical tradition, percussion serves a structural role in the jazz performance, driving the ensemble and articulating important structural moments. The bass serves as timekeeper in most performances, providing a steady articulation of the beat, while the pianist provides harmony. The piano's traditional role of providing harmonic background to a soloist is often called "comping."

Of course, these are the broadest generalizations. It is absolutely common for any of the rhythm instruments to take solos, and some drummers, such as Max Roach, Shelly Manne and Joey Baron, have been known to carry the tune themselves. In fact, among common performing groups, the trio of piano, bass and drums has a lauded position somewhat akin to the string quartet in classical music. And the converse of the traditional horns/rhythm relationship is an occasional occurrence—Lee Konitz's alto saxophone comping behind Sonny Dallas's bass solos on his 1961 album *Motion* is one clear example.

Jazz is primarily an instrumental music, or at least it has always had a peculiar relationship with singing. Singers have always played an active role in jazz. In the 1930s, when jazz was pop music, every self-respecting big band had a full-time vocalist or two among its ranks. But with only a few exceptions, jazz singers have been stylistically, socially and otherwise separate from the mainstream jazz tradition. To date, scholars still tend to specialize in either instrumental or vocal jazz, at the expense of a full understanding of the other. The present author is not excluded, and jazz singers and singing styles will be only briefly and occasionally addressed in this book.

RHYTHM AND MELODY

One extremely simplified definition of jazz is the synthesis of African melody and rhythm with European harmony and instrumentation. Like any aspect of American culture, jazz is much more complicated in its origins and materials than that, but it is a fairly good starting position. A working knowledge of some basic ideas of western music theory and common ways in which jazz deviates from the classical tradition is necessary to facilitate any kind of detailed discussion of jazz. The reader is strongly encouraged to consult a basic text on music theory, which is not nearly as difficult to grasp as it seems, but some basic concepts of harmony, melody and rhythm follow for now.

Jazz is essentially tonal music, which is to say that one note is more important than the other notes. As a result of repetition and emphasis, this important note, called the tonic, feels like home in the context of a specific work of music. Just about any simple song you can think of to sing—"Happy Birthday," "Home on the Range," "Anarchy in the U.K.," etc.—ends on the tonic, and ending on any other pitch feels uncomfortable to the listener. The tonic is just one of many notes, usually seven, that contextualize the tonic into the tonality, or key, of a piece of music.

The notes are named after the first seven letters of the alphabet, and the key is named after the tonic. Since there are twelve notes to the octave in Western music (an octave being the name for the distance of a note and the next higher note that sounds the same—more easily heard than described, but, for instance, women and children tend to sing an octave higher than men when groups sing together), pitches between C and D, for example, are indicated with the modifier "flat," meaning lower, or "sharp," meaning higher. So between C and D lies a pitch that is called either "C sharp" or "D flat." They are the same pitch. For example, if you sing "Happy Birthday" so that the last note is F, you would be singing in the key of F, or more simply in F.

The distance between two different pitches is called an "interval" and is named for the number of notes in the scale that must be traveled from one note to the next, counting the first note as "one"—so the interval between C and D is a "second," between C and E a "third," and so on.

Playing three or more notes at the same time results in a chord. A chord, at its simplest, is described in different ways by classical and jazz musicians. In classical music, a chord might be tonic, reinforced by the fifth scale degree, and colored by the third scale degree, which would be either major or minor. In jazz, chords are usually conceived and described as stacked thirds. In both cases, the chord would be the first, third and fifth scales degrees played at the same time, but in jazz, it is much more common to continue the pattern to include the seventh, ninth, eleventh and so on, without changing the function of that chord. A chord can be built on any scale degree, and is named by the roman numeral that represents that degree in the scale. I, ii, iii and IV, in the key of C Major, represent chords built on C, D, E and F respectively. The use of upper and lower case roman numerals indicates whether the third of the chord is major (upper case) or minor. It is the chords, their durations and relationships that are held constant in a jazz performance and upon which solos are built.

The "blue note" originates from the blues. This is a note, usually the third, fifth or seventh, which is lower than it usually occurs in the scale. In most instances, a blue note moves in pitch and cannot be played on the piano. Pianists, who cannot bend notes, will frequently play "crush tones," the notes on either side of where a blue note usually lies, in order to simulate the effect.

RHYTHM

Rhythm refers to the way music deals with the passing of time. We can use the term to describe any aspect of this— the frequency with which chords change, for instance, is called harmonic rhythm—but most frequently, we use the term to describe the smallest level on which music marks and measures time: the points in time at which a sound occurs, and its relationship to other such points in time. As a concept, this is fairly abstract and difficult to grasp, but in practice, musicians need to be organized in order to play together, and certain conventions apply that are easily understood.

Most music, and especially most jazz, is played in relation to a steady beat. We can define a beat as a regularly occurring moment of emphasis—the moment that you tap your foot. The rate at which beats occur is called the tempo, and we measure that in beats per minute. In jazz, tempos can have quite a range, from forty beats per minute in a ballad to over 300 beats per minute in a heated post-bop performance.

Beats are grouped, as in poetry, in small groups of repeating patterns of emphasis. In jazz (as well as rock, European art music, and all other western music), it is most often a pattern of four beats, with the second and fourth beats weakest, and the first the strongest. Each group of beats is called a measure, or a bar, referring to the use of a vertical bar drawn between measures in musical notation. The first, strongest beat of a measure is called the "downbeat," or the "one."

We describe the duration of a note by the amount of a measure of four beats that it would occupy, regardless of the actual meter. Thus, a note that is one beat long is a quarter note, one that takes half a beat is an eighth note, one that is four beats long is a whole note, etc. There are two important caveats. In notation, a dot following a note increases the length of that note by half, so a dotted quarter note occupies as much time as three eighth notes, and so on. Also, since most western music is in duple meter (which is to say, the beat is subdivided by two—a common alternative is triple meter, in which it is subdivided by three), durations are always described this way. In other words, there are no "12th" notes. We would refer to such as notes as eighth notes, and in that case, a note that is one beat long is a dotted quarter note. This system of nomenclature greatly simplifies musical notation, but it can sometimes be confusing in other cases. Generally, I will refer to a note that takes up one beat as a "quarter note," and if a beat is divided by three instead of two, I might refer to three notes that occupy one beat as "triplets," which name is also common and conventional.

Jazz frequently makes use of syncopation, in which an unexpected emphasized note played on a weak beat or off the beat altogether. For those unfamiliar with the term, it is quite helpful to hear a melody played squarely on the beat, followed by a syncopated version to get a clear understanding of the feel; most musicians could do this without practice. Another common rhythmic technique in jazz is called "double time," in which the rhythm section suddenly behaves as if there were two beats where one previously prevailed, although the harmonic rhythm in most cases remains what it was.

FORM

In jazz, the emphasis for the listener is not on large scale structure, but on moment-to-moment detail. Because of this, the vast majority of jazz follows the same form on the largest scale. In the European art music tradition, where the structure of an entire work is more varied, most jazz works would be said to follow a Theme and Variations form, in which a short and memorable tune (the theme) is played repeatedly, each successive repetition somehow embellished or transformed (the variations).

In jazz, things are a bit more specific, and the language is a bit different. The Theme is called the head, and is generally played by the entire ensemble (sometimes after an introduction). The variations are called solos, and are usually played by one person with accompaniment from the rhythm section. The variations are almost always melodic in nature. This means that the harmony, duration, tempo, etc. of the head is repeated basically unchanged, while the soloist plays a melody of his/her own invention that fits. Each repetition of the cycle is called a chorus, and a solo might be one chorus, or two, or eight, or fifty-eight. It might even be half a chorus in a ballad. Often, during the last chorus or two, the soloist will "trade" with the drummer or bassist, playing four or eight measures and then allowing the drummer to solo in response for the same amount of time. The last chorus of the performance is most often a direct repetition of the head.

A typical jazz performance might be as follows: The pianist plays a short introduction. The rest of the group joins in for the head, then the tenor saxophone player solos for three choruses, the trumpet player for two, then the trombonist solos one chorus and trades fours with the drummer for a chorus, and the band comes back in to play the head one last time, "and out." This will work for a mid-tempo or fast tune, but it might take a half hour or more to play out in the case of a ballad. So the number of choruses is fairly indeterminate, and it is not uncommon to allow a soloist who is playing particularly well to take as long a solo as he wants. And conversely, a good, slow ballad might only be one or two choruses in its entirety.

The Theme and Variations form is so common in jazz that it is simply assumed. So when jazz people discuss form, they are not discussing the large scale, like a classical musician would, but the structure of the heads themselves. There are a few common forms in jazz, and two of them comprise about 85% of the jazz repertoire.

Borrowed from the American Musical Theater that provides many jazz standards, 32-bar AABA structure is about as accurately named as it could be. A tune is thirty-two measures in duration, and divided into four eight-measure phrases. The first, second and fourth phrases are identical, or nearly so. The third, which is usually called the bridge, but might be called the channel or release on occasion, tends to be more harmonically active than the A section, and serves to build tension and provide contrast before the return. This is more easily heard than described. Good examples of this structure include "I've Got Rhythm," "So What," and "My One and Only Love." Of course, there are other forms common in both popular music and jazz melodies, and the method of description for many of them is the same as is used for 32-bar AABA structure. Identifying phrases with a letter of the alphabet, one can find many examples of ABAC, AABC, and any other number of forms, in any number of durations (although 32 measures is the most common, as it creates a balance of eight-measure phrases that are conventionally comfortable to Western audiences).

The 12-bar blues is a distinctly American structure (and probably a twentieth century one at that), which is unusual in western music for its asymmetry. It is important to make the distinction between the word "blues" as it is used in this formal sense and as it is used to describe the American musical genre. While much blues uses a twelve-measure structure, there is tremendous variety and flexibility in blues music, and this structure seems to have been formalized in jazz. A 12-bar blues consists of three four-bar phrases with a specific harmonic content.

It is easiest to understand the 12-bar blues structure in relation to vocal blues, since the form is common and recognizable when sung. The first two phrases are usually melodically quite similar. The first iterance would be based entirely on the tonic chord. It is then repeated, while the harmony changes to IV for two measures, then back to I for the final two. The third and final phrase of the chorus serves as an answer to the question posed in the first eight measures. Harmonically, it is some variance of a traditional cadence. When sung, the first two phrases would be a repeated set up—"I woke up this morning, and my baby's gone away"—and the third phrase would be the punch line: "Don't know what to do to make a good woman stay." So although the harmonic structure prevents a 12-bar blues from being described as an AAB structure, the melody (and nearly always the lyrics) do maintain that structure over a shifting harmony. Examples of 12-bar blues tunes include "One O' Clock Jump," Chick Corea's "Matrix," and the theme to the 1960s television series *Batman*. Many of the best examples of the use of this form, however, do not even have a title attached. Since the form is so specific and well-known, it is a common occurrence at many jazz performances for the band leader to simply call for "Blues in B-flat," or whatever key, in which case no specific head is used, or needed.

It is important to note that, although these structural ideas apply to most jazz, pop forms like 32-bar AABA structures were not really a part of the music at first. By the end of the 1930s, they are ubiquitous. But trying to hear these forms in the music of Scott Joplin, for instance, can be very frustrating. The 12-bar blues, however, was already a common form in jazz by the time the first jazz recordings were made.

EXAMPLE: JONES-SMITH INCORPORATED, "OH, LADY, BE GOOD!"

Ken Burns Jazz, Disc 2, Track 13

As an example of a standard approach to a jazz performance, "Oh, Lady, Be Good!" is fairly straightforward and easy to navigate. At a tempo of approximately 96 beats per minute, each chorus is about 40 seconds long, and each section of the 32-bar AABA head clocks in at about ten seconds. Like many jazz performances, this recording speeds up slightly as it goes on, as a result of the pulling against a steady beat that results in swinging performances. As it has been mastered for *Ken Burns Jazz*, this recording also serves as an example of the hissing and popping of early jazz recordings – something that must be endured at first, but can be ignored fairly easily with some acclimation. In this and all detailed descriptions throughout the book, timings are approximate and might be a second or so off from what your CD player will display.

0:00   This performance dispenses with an introduction, and the main melody is played (with some ornamentation) in the highest notes of the piano.

0:10   The second A section of the main melody begins. With repeated listening, the similarity to the first eight measures of the performance should become apparent.

0:20   The B section (or bridge, or channel) of the head.

0:30   The final A section of the melody.

0:40   A solo for two choruses by the tenor saxophone begins. While the saxophone plays an entirely new melody, the harmonic structure is repeated from the first 40 seconds of the performance.

1:21   The second chorus of the sax solo begins.

1:33   In the beginning of the second A section of this chorus, the saxophone repeats the tonic several times. Even with chords shifting beneath him, the repeated note still serves as a "home" and the tonality of the performance is based on this pitch.

2:02   A trumpet takes over to play a solo for one chorus. Note that the saxophonist still plays accompanying figures, once again emphasizing the tonic.

2:45   Somewhat unusually, the first 16 measures of the head are omitted in the final chorus of this performance. The piano solo begins directly on the bridge.

2:55   The rest of the band joins in for the final A section of the performance.

"SWING"

Swing is a particularly problematic word, because it is used in at least three distinct ways when talking about jazz. The 1930s and early 1940s are often referred to as the "Swing Era," and the popular music of the big bands, exemplified by Benny Goodman, Jimmy Lunceford, *et al*, is often called swing. In another sense, swing is the uneven division of a steady beat. Rather than chugging along, machine-like, musicians frequently will play the first of two notes within a beat longer than the second; this technique is used in many traditions, including the European art music tradition most commonly taught in schools—although calling it "swing" originated in jazz, and classical musicians have only picked up the term for themselves in the twentieth century.

The third musical definition of swing is rather subjective and requires a bit more discussion than the previous two. In essence, swing is that aspect of a good performance which makes physical movement irresistible for the listener. Of course, this could mean different things to different people, and the whole concept can and does bring about arguments among fans and performers. The techniques by which this sensation is accomplished are several and subtle. Indeed, many consider this sense of swing to be indescribable—if you have to ask, you'll never know. But such an approach simply exchanges critical thinking for the opportunity to reserve jazz enthusiasm for an elite group of initiates. In jazz, this sense of swing is accomplished by allowing performers to toy with a steady beat, sometimes rushing ahead and sometimes lagging behind.

None of these senses of swing is common among all of the music that we consider jazz. Of course, this would be a very different book if jazz were limited to the music of big bands of the late 1930s and 1940s. And there are plenty of examples of jazz that use straight eighth notes; certainly since the 1970's, when the steady rhythms of rock became a strong influence, but also among Latino and Latin-influenced musicians in the 1940s and among Swing Era musicians like Raymond Scott. The third definition is a little vaguer, and so harder to argue. Many jazz scholars cite the music of the New York free jazz scene as not swinging because of the lack of a steady beat. But a steady tempo need not be explicitly played in order to bring a swinging feel to music, and I would argue that Charles Tyler, for instance, swings beautifully. There are several perfectly good examples of jazz that do not swing, though. Much of the music of Stan Kenton, for instance, works in spite of a lack of swing feeling, and the music of the Chicago avant-garde of the late 1960s often deals with different senses of time that do not allow for the possibility of swing.

JAZZ IN SOCIETY

From its very beginning (and before that), jazz has been a chink in the armor of the highbrow/lowbrow divide with which we tend to view culture. The first generation of jazz musicians earned reputations as degenerates contributing to a morally lax society, while simultaneously earning praise as creators of the future of music among the elite of the art music world. This ambiguity has been a part of jazz's place in culture ever since, and for everyone that applies the phrase "America's Classical Music," there is someone to argue the fallacy of that phrase. Jazz musicians generally reside in the territory between culture and Culture happily, and draw materials from all over the map, whether it be Beethoven or Sly and the Family Stone, without regard for the cultural implications (or because of them—many musicians consciously play with audiences' tendency to pigeonhole in mind).

RACE

Nothing American in origin comes without the history of race relations. Questions about race, power and cultural ownership arise from the beginning of any discussion of jazz. There is no doubt at all that many aspects of jazz, both technical and cultural, are African American in origin. However, there is also little doubt that whites were involved in jazz from almost the very beginning. Indeed, racial tension, as much as black or white culture, has continually been a driving force in the formation of jazz and jazz culture.

At the core of any discussion of jazz culture is the question of whether jazz is black music. There are persuasive and passionate arguments on both sides—one can easily point to the majority of the greatest innovators in the music, and then counter with the majority of the audience. This book brings up the issue when it arises, but draws no conclusions. One point worth making, though, is that skin color is no more audible than hairstyle, and the recorded repertoire of American music is full of examples, from Jimmie Rogers through Charlie Pride to Eminem, that one of the driving forces behind racial politics is the fascination that people of one race have with those of another, and that many artists can rise to the top of their genre regardless of the race most often associated with that genre.

LISTENING TO JAZZ

With its emphasis on improvisation and formally indeterminate duration, jazz is music best experienced in person. Our understanding of, and appreciation for, jazz history is wholly dependent on audio recording technology, since the music is almost never fully recorded in notation. Nevertheless, limitations on what technology can record places limitations on what musicians can play on record. The abundance of three- and four-minute performances from the years before the long playing record, when commercial recordings were only capable of holding about four minutes of music, can not give a proper impression of what went on in ballrooms, when musicians soloed for twenty minutes or more.

There has always been a social aspect to jazz performances. Until the 1940s or so, jazz was mostly accompaniment for dancing, and performed in ballrooms, hotel lounges and smaller clubs. Since bebop, it has become less likely to find dancing at jazz performances. The area in front of the stage at most jazz clubs is filled with seats and small tables, or auditorium seating. But it is still somewhat rare to find a venue for jazz performances that does not serve at least alcoholic drinks, and formal concert settings tend to be reserved for star attractions and living legends.

2

PRE-JAZZ

Jazz does not have a clear and direct origin or inventor. Like many other American cultural phenomena, jazz resulted from the synthesis of many predecessors of various origin—some African, some Latin American, some European, and many, by the time the music started to take shape, uniquely American. Rather than attempting to deduce a direct story with places, names and events that brought about the first jazz performance, this chapter will look at many musical styles and trends that had some role in shaping jazz. This is a much more complicated affair than it first appears—jazz might well be considered the beginning of post-modernism in Western artistic movements. It has always been a part of the jazz tradition to beg, borrow and steal any musical influences that are available. It is notable that in most accounts of the beginnings of jazz, the crucible was the city of New Orleans—a cultural center for white Americans, freed slaves, Latin Americans and Creoles (blacks born free and held as a distinct social and racial class), among other ethnicities. As an example of the cultural gumbo that allowed the first jazz musicians from a wide variety of influences, New Orleans is apt. But even if New Orleans was a primary location for the development of jazz, cities such as Chicago (an important and convenient destination for successful

New Orleans musicians), New York and Baltimore also played important roles.

Since the recorded history of jazz necessarily begins with the first jazz recordings of 1917, it is general convention to begin the history of jazz then. Doubtless, music existed before this that could be called jazz—indeed, recordings and player piano rolls from earlier years exist that might blur the lines significantly—but it is fair to say that the beginnings of jazz coincide roughly with the beginnings of World War I.

AFRICA

It is doubtful that the first jazz musicians had much direct familiarity with the music of Africa. The slave trade was outlawed in the United States 1808, 75 years or more before the first generation of jazz musicians was born. And while slavery itself remained legal until the end of the Civil War, and an illegal black market for new slaves still existed, African-American culture had already had a good 200 years to develop its own distinct characteristics. And unlike European immigrants, who tended to live among others of the same nationality and maintain their cultural traditions, Africans were frequently separated from their families and discouraged by force from practicing their customs, religion and culture as property of white families. The often cited New Orleans tradition of allowing Africans to practice traditional drumming and dancing on Congo Square, though not apocryphal, is historically inaccurate; the gatherings ceased long before it was previously thought, and were certainly over before the turn of the century. While the direct influence of African culture on black Americans might be somewhat exaggerated by some sources, however, it was far from absent, and evidence exists that many aspects of African culture are maintained in America today.

Africa is a very large geographical space with numerous different cultures, and slaves in America came from a number of different backgrounds. Although it is a gross generalization to speak of African music as a single genre, it is universally true that African musical traditions are passed on orally, distinguished from the written tradition of Europe. Of course, one byproduct of oral traditions is a lack of historical documentation, so determining what music that might have survived the slave trade into America is problematic.

There are, however, enough parallels between early African American music and African music that it is fair to assert that certain aspects of jazz can find their indirect origin in African music of the nineteenth century and earlier. The structural importance of polyrhythmic percussion, frequent modulation of pitch and timbre in the melodic line, and a fondness for buzzes added to an instrument's sound through mutes, snares, vocal sounds or moist breath are all common aspects of both jazz and African music.

EUROPE

European classical music, on the other hand, was certainly a large part of American culture, and early jazz musicians had plenty of opportunities to become familiar with it on some level or another. This is especially true of New Orleans, a cosmopolitan town with opera houses, and less racially segregated than most of the United States (although a class structure clearly delineated along racial lines was strictly in force). Any urban musician—however or wherever jazz came to be, it was and remains an urban phenomenon—would have been familiar with at least the popular light classics of the turn of the century, heard through the performances of brass bands, chamber orchestras, and even in opera houses.

The French military band tradition, more specifically as it was interpreted by John Philip Sousa (1854–1932), exerted perhaps the greatest force of influence on jazz. Sousa's band was tremendously popular, and toured incessantly from the 1890s well into the twentieth century. The band featured the finest technical musicians in America, and Sousa's repertoire featured their skills strongly—most of his marches end with a rousing, contrapuntal final strain, in which the melody is proclaimed by trumpets, with a strong countermelody from trombones and ornamental filigree played by clarinets and piccolo. In New Orleans, jazz bands feature a nearly identical horn line (minus the piccolo), with exactly that division of labor, and at least one Sousa-style march, "High Society," is such a standard composition that Charlie Parker could quote it in an entirely different context (though it should be noted that "High Society" was not a Sousa composition, but a college march written by a Yale student in 1902).

AFRICAN AMERICAN MUSIC

In the eighteenth and nineteenth centuries, African Americans, out of contact with their ancestral culture and communities, developed their own music, drawing on elements both African and European in origin. The social context in which music was performed is indicative of a life spent in slavery: documentation of early African-American music consists mainly of work songs and worship songs, mostly sung without instrumental accompaniment.

Early work songs and spirituals certainly maintained a connection with African music—most obviously in the call-and-response structures, in which a song leader sings a passage which is then "answered" by the congregation (or other laborers), and by the development of blue notes. It should be noted, however, that both of these techniques are used in much of the music of poor whites in Appalachia from the same period. And at the same time, European influences, such as the verse structure of hymns and a tendency towards regular, four- and eight-measure phrasing—not to mention the use of the English language for lyrics—were strong in the development of African-American music. This kind of mutual cross-cultural influence is at the root of just about all American music.

MINSTRELSY

For as long as there has been African American culture, there has been a fascination with it among European Americans. This fascination was once epitomized by the minstrel show, which was at once the pinnacle of nineteenth century racism and the birthplace of the American pop song. Traveling troupes of minstrels were very popular, especially in the frontier towns of the west, from around the middle of the ninetheenth century until around 1900. The performers themselves were almost exclusively whites in the beginning, made up in blackface, who parodied African American culture with derogatory humorous stereotypes. But in lampooning black music, minstrelsy introduced African American musical elements and instruments such as banjo and bones (two bones or sticks used as percussion instruments) into the dominant white culture. Eventually, the minstrel show became a viable career for musically talented blacks. Although many of the songs from the minstrel repertoire were so overtly racist that they are best forgotten (one example, "All Coons Look Alike To Me," is not so derogatory in its lyrics, but the title speaks for itself), many others have become classics. And of those classics, some of the most notable were composed by African American minstrel singer James Bland, such as "Oh, Dem Golden Slippers"—"dem" is an example of the lampooning of black speech, replacing the word "those" with "them," and deliberately mispronouncing the first letter of the word.

RAGTIME

Reaching its heyday around the latter half of the 1890s and continuing as a popular music tradition through the 1910s, ragtime is often considered the direct predecessor of jazz. The reality is that the lines that divide ragtime, blues and jazz are blurrier than that—the three genres share many features and probably developed side by side, or at least nearly so. But as written music, ragtime songs and piano works offer a clear picture of American musical trends at the turn of the century.

The earliest ragtime probably arose as a process of improvisation—popular works from the march repertoire and light opera would be ornamented and altered, or "ragged" by the pianist, and the result was a heavily syncopated melody in the right hand over a steady, march-like bass. By the mid-1890s, the process was formalized in the piano works of black composers like Scott Joplin and James Scott, and Joplin's white protégé Joseph Lamb.

For the most part, ragtime takes its form from the march: four repeated "strains" of contrasting material, often featuring a change of key before the last section or two. Ragtime composers, including Joplin, were somewhat looser with form than Sousa. While military marches tend to stay with Intro-AABBCDCD form, in which the last two strains are called the break strain and the trio, respectively, and are almost always in a different key than the intro-

> In ragtime, early jazz, and other western music, a **strain** is a short section of music, repeated immediately before different material is similarly treated.

duction, ragtime tends towards a more casual approach, in which various themes are repeated, but without a stringent requirement about how many strains, repetitions, or key changes.

Evidence suggests that in addition to formalized, written rags by composers like Joplin, ragtime pianists frequently and consistently improvised and played in increasing tempos. Some of this evidence can be found in Joplin's scores, which occasionally contained instructions such as "Not too fast," or "Don't fake." Paired with some of the compositions of Baltimore pianist Eubie Blake, which sound ahead of their time, and with the early material of stride pianists like James P. Johnson, this suggests a possibility that stylistic development among pianists of the east coast led to jazz in a manner rather independent of the New Orleans scene.

BLUES

The blues probably developed as a genre around the same time as ragtime, and shares with jazz predecessors in work songs, spirituals and minstrelsy. While historians have often been eager to look to the solo performances of African Americans in the Mississippi Delta and other rural regions of the southern United States as an origin for jazz, rock and modern blues, it should be noted that it is very difficult to find evidence of such music being made, or at least propagated outside of remote rural communities, before the 1920s. Rather, it was a more formalized, sophisticated city blues that was probably familiar to the first generations of jazz musicians.

The music that has come to be known as classic blues was first recorded in 1920 by Mamie Smith, and sheet music for blues began showing up rapidly just after the turn of the century. It is usually vocal music, with the 12-bar

BESSIE SMITH, "BACK WATER BLUES"

Ken Burns Jazz, CD 1, Track 7

In this 1927 recording, Bessie Smith, perhaps the most popular blues singer of the 1920s, performs a fairly straightforward version of the blues as it was likely heard by early jazz musicians. Accompanied subtly by pianist James P. Johnson, Smith sings about the struggles of a major flood, using the loud, clear half-shouting voice, sliding pitches, and rhythmic variety that typify classic blues.

structure and AAB lyrical scheme described earlier. Most blues singers in the early generations started in vaudeville, and the powerful delivery, sometimes near a shout, was as much of necessity in the days before amplification became available in 1925 as it was aesthetic. The blues singing style is also marked with frequent use of blue notes, sliding pitches, and a loose approach to rhythm—in many ways, the classic blues singers were the first generation of jazz vocalists.

The jazz repertoire drew heavily from blues sheet music from its very beginning. Of the blues composers, the most famous and notable was W.C. Handy. Handy is frequently and inaccurately credited as the inventor of the blues, and many of his works, including "St. Louis Blues" and "Memphis Blues," remain jazz standards. Indeed, the first jazz recording was entitled "Livery Stable Blues."

NEW ORLEANS

Even as musicians throughout the country were developing jazz and jazz-like approaches to music, the most popular and influential jazz musicians in the 1910s and 1920s were largely from New Orleans. The popularity of the New Orleans scene was so great that by the 1920s, the word "jazz" essentially referred to the New Orleans style of ensemble playing, and the city gained the reputation as the birthplace of jazz that it continues to hold today.

By all reports, New Orleans had an unusually vibrant and active musical and social culture, with an opera house, frequent outdoor performances and public events, and neighborhood brass and string bands every few blocks. Additionally, with its unusual topography—New Orleans is basically a bowl-shaped area surrounded on most sides by water—tales of trumpeters that could be heard from miles away are frequently recounted, and probably less exaggerated than they seem. To grow up in New Orleans was literally to be surrounded by music day and night.

New Orleans also has had a rich and diverse ethnic makeup since its earliest days. Large communities of French, Latin and African cultures interacted on a daily basis. Racially, New Orleans was uniquely diverse, and Creoles of color, who were of African and mixed ancestry, were for some time a skilled and educated class with full rights of citizenship. A popular scholarly theory about the creation of jazz is that Creoles of color, with formal musical training, interacted with the folk stylists of the black community. This is probably a bit simpler than the kind of cultural cross-influence that was happening in New Orleans, but it was certainly happening, especially as Creoles of color lost their class status as the Twentieth Century approached.

JAMES REESE EUROPE

In New York at the turn of the twentieth century, conductor and arranger James Reese Europe (1881–1919) led a series of bands with instrumentation similar to John Philip Sousa's,

but with a repertory of popular songs and ragtimes that reflected both his southern African American upbringing and
the ballroom dancing that was a popular pastime. As the
musical director for the popular dance team of Vernon and
Irene Castle, Europe received international attention, and
he is generally credited with combining African American
musical traditions with American popular music to create a
sort of proto-jazz.

The recordings Europe made as a bandleader certainly
bear this assertion out. The strong, busy percussion, constant glissandi (sliding) in the trombones, and occasional
breaks, in which the band stops for a measure or so to allow for a brief solo, are all featured elements of the first
jazz recordings. In fact, the only substantial difference between Europe's recordings and those of the first jazz bands
from New Orleans a few years later is the size of Europe's
band.

LIEUT. JIM EUROPE'S 369TH INFANTRY ("HELL FIGHTERS") BAND, "MEMPHIS BLUES"

Ken Burns Jazz, CD 1, Track 3

This 1919 recording of W.C. Handy's composition conve-
niently presents early classic blues structure, ragtime's syncopated rhythms, and the influence of Sousa's marches combined
into one neat package. While the band is large and features
the instrumentation and strict arrangements of marches, the
similarity of Europe's band to the earliest jazz recordings is
remarkable, from the chattering woodblocks throughout the
performance, to the "stop time" breaks in the final strains (beginning around two minutes into the recording), in which the
band stops for a moment for a brief solo).

BUDDY BOLDEN AND ORIGIN MYTHOLOGY

With origins as murky as those of jazz, the temptation is great to make something up and go with it. Part of the jazz tradition has been to give in to this temptation, and lay all blame for the music on a trumpet player named Buddy Bolden.

He is a convenient suspect. Although he surely lived, and led a small group in which he played trumpet, he never made a recording, nor performed outside of New Orleans. So, in the memories of older musicians, and in the retelling of these musicians' stories, Bolden became the loudest, flashiest, most competent and stylistically cutting edge musician in history. Anyone who was alive at the turn of the century, and a few who were not, claimed to have played with Bolden. Musicians as young as Wynton Marsalis are able to claim authority in describing Bolden's style and contributions in alarming detail without ever having heard a note of his playing.

The fact about Bolden is that there are not many facts. The most thorough biography, Donald Marquis's *In Search of Buddy Bolden: First Man of Jazz*, runs fewer than 200 pages. Although it is likely that he attained a certain amount of fame within New Orleans, his influence outside the city is doubtful, and his playing certainly did not reach the ears of stride pianists in New York and New Jersey.

But as a widely accepted part of jazz mythology, Bolden should not be dismissed entirely. Facts aside, jazz enthusiasts react to the most common explanations, rather than the most accurate. In the case of Bolden, it is a typical origin myth without much consequence (although, with the first acknowledged jazz record recorded by whites, it is significant to choose an African-American as creator), but in other cases, aspects of jazz can be better understood in the context of legend rather than fact. For instance, the origin of the word jazz, while fairly uncertain, is probably not, as is commonly thought among musicians, sexual. But to understand resistance to the word among many jazz musicians (notably drummer Max Roach and the members of Chicago's AACM), it is necessary to assume that the word "jazz" is sexual in nature, and that sexual promiscuity is a negative racial stereotype of African Americans.

3

EARLY JAZZ RECORDINGS

Jazz has always been conceived and worked out as music mostly for live performance. However, without the liberty of time travel, our understanding of jazz history and performance practice comes from recordings. Since the phonograph had only been available to homes for about 15 years when the first jazz recording was released, the impact of recording technology on the changes in jazz styles since the very beginning has been tremendous. Technological limitations have made a difference between the way jazz was most frequently played before the 1950s and the way it is now heard.

One clear limitation put on jazz performance by early recording technology was duration. Commercial recordings for home use were limited to under four minutes per side until after World War II. Because of this constraint, jazz performers had to carefully prepare and perform short versions of tunes that might be played for twenty minutes or more live (editing would not really be possible until the adoption of magnetic tape in sound recording studios in the 1940s). Musicians were under some pressure to present their best work in a limited time frame, so it is likely that early jazz recordings contain far less improvisation than a live performance, in which a musician would have another chorus to make up for a risky idea that did not work.

Additionally, the need for quiet to capture sound in a recording studio eliminates the audience from the dynamic of a live performance. While it would be difficult to quantify the difference between playing in a club for an audience and playing in a studio without one (and impossible to read the mind of the musicians doing so), most jazz musicians agree that interaction with an audience affects what they play. Certainly, the goals of live performance and recording are different. Rather than playing for the immediate gratification of a live and tangible audience, the recording musician is concerned with sonic perfection. Different musicians react to the change in dynamic in different ways. Some thrive in a studio without the distractions of clapping, conversation, attractive people in the audience, etc.; others prefer the instantaneous feedback of a crowd and might be inhibited in a closed room. Of course, live performances in 1925 are not available today, so determining the difference between an individual player's live and recorded work depends on second hand reports and nostalgic interviews, and does nothing to enhance the listening experience.

Many of the successful jazz musicians and bands of the late 1910s and early 1920s started their careers in New Orleans, and followed a similar migratory pattern out of the city by the time they recorded. While opportunities for performance in New Orleans flourished, bigger cities were necessary to gain larger audiences and recognition, and Chicago became the center for New Orleans jazz. As time went on, many of these musicians followed the next generation of jazz musicians to New York. But a large number of jazz records made in the early days were recorded in the Chicago area.

Early jazz generally does not follow the common head-solos-head form that would eventually become the norm. Rather, the most common form was the repeated strains of marches, ragtime, and dance music—three or more themes are played before the first idea returns, in something like AABBCCABC. In fact, the first generation did not usually play solo-driven music at all. The emphasis in early recordings is on ensemble sound. Clarinet, cornet (sometimes two), and trombone play contrapuntally over a rhythm section that contains bass or tuba, banjo, drums and often piano.

Tempos in the music discussed in this chapter are constrained relative to later music. Ranging from around 100 to 200 beats per minute, this is music for dancing. The rhythm section in this music often plays in a two-beat feel, again derived from ragtime. Very occasionally, the bass player

Even without a change in tempo, beat can be articulated with a variety of **feels**. In early jazz styles, the most common rhythmic approach is a **two-beat** feel, in which four-beat measures are played with a heavy emphasis on the first and third beats, as in a march. Later styles smoothed out the emphases, with each beat nearly equal in strength, resulting in the smoother sounding **four-beat** feel. If a group so desires, they might also incorporate a **double time** feel into any performance, in which the tempo seems to speed to twice as fast as it was previously.

might inject a double time feel. More often, rhythmic variety was effected through breaks, in which the rhythm section rests for a measure or two in order to feature a brief solo, or through stop time, in which the ensemble plays only the beats together.

THE ORIGINAL DIXIELAND JAZZ BAND

On February 26, 1917, Victor Records recorded a phonograph of the Original Dixieland Jass Band, performing

"Livery Stable Blues" with "Dixie[land] Jass Band One Step." On March 7 of that year, it was the first jazz recording ever released, and might be the only first in jazz over which there is little dispute.

In most accounts of jazz history, "Livery Stable Blues" is discussed in the context of controversy. The ODJB (they changed the spelling of "Jazz" in their name to match 1918 convention and are commonly referred to by their initials) were a white novelty band, and an especially ostentatious one in their marketing. They proudly and falsely proclaimed themselves the "Creators of Jazz" while African American musicians like King Oliver and Freddie Keppard missed out on international publicity. As a result of this, the ODJB have gained the reputation of culture thieves, more important for their historical fortune than their music.

Dwelling on the racial politics of the ODJB, however, distracts from their musical and historic merits. "Livery Stable Blues" was not only the first jazz record; it was a smashing success. Victor claimed to have sold one million copies, which is surely an exaggeration, but hundreds of thousands of records were spread worldwide, and the question of the geography of jazz's origins became moot as musicians throughout the United States and Europe came under its influence. It is an entertaining record, and the ODJB went on to make better sounding recordings that showed real talent for a certain brand of tightly arranged novelty jazz.

The band formed in New Orleans in 1916 as Stein's Dixie Jass Band, and secured a regular gig in Chicago, where drummer and leader Johnny Stein was eventually fired (or the rest of the band quit), and they reformed under the leadership of trumpeter Nick LaRocca with drummer Tony Sbarbaro, pianist Henry Ragas and trombonist Eddie Edwards. Larry Shields joined the group on clarinet later that year, replacing Alcide Nuñez. In January of 1917, the ODJB secured a gig at Reisenweber's Restaurant in New York.

THE ORIGINAL DIXIELAND JAZZ BAND, "LIVERY STABLE BLUES"

Ken Burns Jazz, CD 1, Track 4

"Livery Stable Blues" is a fairly straightforward 12-bar blues in E-flat with three strains, a four-bar introduction and tag ending. It is played with the large scale form of Intro-AABBCCABC, which is a form that had been used for dance music for hundreds of years and is quite common in works by Mozart, for example. Most surprising for contemporary jazz listeners is a total lack of variation in the repeats, and little change of the arrangement over the years of the ODJB's career (they recorded the tune, re-titled "Barnyard Blues" after a lawsuit, eight times between 1917 and a reunion concert in 1946). The tune is named for special effects featured in the third strain, during which Shields crows like a rooster and LaRocca gives his best horse whinny. Throughout the recording, the ODJB play with what became the classic counterpoint of the Dixieland style, as borrowed from Sousa: LaRocca's trumpet proclaims the melody in straightforward fashion, while Edwards' trombone comments with a countermelody full of glissandi (sliding tones) and references to the harmonic structure, and Shields plays a faster, ornamental part. This kind of scoring—a kind of contrapuntal pyramid, in which lower voices play fewer and longer notes—is the textural basis of most early jazz styles, and the emphasis on these early jazz recordings is more on collective playing than solos.

Beyond the shrill tone of Shields' clarinet that provides the immediate and lasting impression of the recording, a few stylistic attributes of the ODJB are apparent even in the first recording. The playing of both Edwards and LaRocca is essentially "straight," and would not get them fired from a good marching band of the time. When sounds that are

> **Scoring**, also called "orchestration," is the process of determining the instruments used in a performance, and how they are used.

more typically associated with jazz are used, such as glissandi and growling, they come off as special effects, rather than fully integrated elements of technique. Accusations of stylistic plagiarism are probably not far off the mark for this band. Ragas plays piano so busily, with so many elements of both melody and accompaniment, that should the wind players and drummer be caught in a fire, the audience would not notice anything missing. The real joy in these recordings is to be found in Sbarbaro's drumming. For the most part, the percussion parts are strongly reminiscent of the constant snare-drum prattling of the marching band. But within that context, Sbarbaro is able to provide many surprises, from unexpected accents with the bass drum, to brief but bizarrely disjunct fills between phrases.

With the immediate and worldwide success of their first release, the ODJB enjoyed considerable popularity and were tremendously influential, and were instrumental in spreading the new jazz beyond the United States. In marketing, LaRocca could be a particularly brash and confrontational promoter with little questioning of what he said. Self-styled as rebellious anti-musicians, the ODJB certainly appealed to the European sensibilities that also created Dada, the artistic movement of the 1910s that was largely driven by shock and absurdity. There were certainly earlier and better groups, and most consisted of black musicians. But for a time, the only jazz recording available was "Livery Stable Blues," and much of ODJB's repertoire, such as "Tiger Rag," became standards for early jazz, and remain so among Dixieland revivalists today. And they recorded a good variety of novelty styles—some of their best recordings, such as "Palesteena" and "Soudan," explore Middle

Eastern and klezmer music, albeit through the prism of a popular dance band.

For the most part, though, it was not terribly long before the ODJB was surpassed in quality and popularity by imitators and predecessors alike. By the mid 1920s, the band was not able to repeat their success with re-recorded hits, and save a few unfortunate reunion concerts, they were disbanded by 1926.

"JELLY ROLL" MORTON (1890–1941)

Pianist, composer, braggart, pimp, gambler, pool hustler and clotheshorse Ferdinand "Jelly Roll" Morton was the embodiment of all the degenerate, evil elements of society for which early (and numerous) critics of jazz said it was responsible. He spoke proudly of his start as a professional musician in the whorehouses of New Orleans' Storyville district. Most likely, he lied about his age his entire life—there is still some controversy about the accuracy of his claimed birth year of 1895, but recent compelling evidence indicates 1890 as more likely. At the end of his life, he blamed his declining health on a voodoo spell. And perhaps most famously, he claimed proudly and fallaciously that he invented jazz single-handedly in 1902 (impressive work for a 12-year-old!).

Although born and raised in New Orleans (with his given name, Ferdinand Joseph Lamothe), Morton spent the bulk of his early career working outside the city. He traveled throughout the South leading bands, playing solo and gambling to support himself between 1907 and 1914, when he settled for a time in Chicago. In 1917, he began an extended tour of the west coast, and finally settled in Chicago, like so many other early jazz musicians, in 1923. It was in Chicago that he recorded several solo piano works, including "Grandpa's Spells," and the classic 1926 small group recordings with the Red Hot Peppers. By the 1930s, Morton, who chose not to adapt his style to changing times, slipped into obscurity, eclipsed by the swing music that he felt was a gross simplification of the music he invented.

The last few years of his life saw Morton resurging in activity and popularity, spurred on by a series of interviews conducted with Morton at a piano by folklorist Alan Lomax at the Library of Congress in Washington, DC in 1938. These interviews were released to the public ten years later, and contribute greatly to both the appreciation of and misinformation about Morton's life and music.

As a composer, Morton was gifted from the beginning. "Grandpa's Spells," first recorded in 1923, owes enough stylistically to the ragtime from which Morton developed his style that it was surely a much earlier composition, and his "King Porter Stomp" from 1906 would become a swing standard in the 1930s. As both composer and arranger, his music is melodically derived from the blues, but rhythmically and structurally, it owes its biggest debt to the syncopated right hand and steady, chugging bass of ragtime. Still, Morton loosens the time, and is more than willing to stray from the steady two-beat feel of ragtime, in a way quite different from the variations-on-a-theme approach of his contemporaries in the northeast, who will be discussed in chapter 5. Morton famously and cryptically told Lomax that all jazz required a "Latin tinge," and if this is audible in Morton's recordings, it is in the broken rhythms of his left hand.

Morton's brilliance as an arranger for small ensembles is epitomized in the 1926 recordings. With constantly shifting orchestration and textures, each three-minute side contains astonishing variety, never playing more than a strain before radically changing the scoring. But regardless of tempo, the Red Hot Peppers play with a relaxed swing throughout that prevents the arrangements from sounding disjointed. In fact, the band plays with such relaxed vibrancy that the records were frequently thought to be improvisation at its strongest before it was discovered that they are, in fact, carefully and tightly arranged.

JOE "KING" OLIVER (1885–1938)

King Oliver's Creole Jazz Band represented the best and brightest among New Orleans musicians. Although the recording career of the classic lineup lasted less than a year, they were prodigious. And the recordings were milestones, the best of the first generation of jazz recordings, and the recording debut of Louis Armstrong.

Oliver had earned his nickname, and the accompanying reputation as "King" of the cornet players, in New Orleans, where he played around town in various cabaret and dance bands (a cornet is, for all intents and purposes, a trumpet, with a slight difference in shape that results in a very slightly darker and rounder timbre). He had an immediately recognizable sound: dark and somewhat clipped, with a strong attack and heavy vibrato. He was also well known for his skills with the plunger mute—literally, a bathroom plunger, which is held over the bell of the trumpet and manipulated to create a "wah-wah" effect that remains popular in other styles of jazz. If no one is looking, you can simulate the effect by singing "ah" into a drinking glass and moving the glass towards and away from your mouth.

Oliver moved to Chicago in 1918, and by 1922 he was leading the Creole Jazz Band, and sent for his former student Louis Armstrong by telegram. The band consisted of the very best New Orleans players: Honoré Dutrey, trombone; Johnny Dodds, clarinet; Bill Johnson on banjo and double bass; Lil Hardin, piano (from Memphis); and Baby Dodds on drums. With the young Armstrong on second cornet, the band worked steadily in Chicago, and recorded frequently.

The 1923 sides display a wilder, looser approach than can be heard in the ODJB or Jelly Roll Morton. If the ODJB don't swing, and Morton swings comfortably, Oliver's band swings hard. Although modern ears might expect to hear Oliver's cornet featured prominently on these recordings, he solos infrequently, preferring to show off a first rate ensemble. When Oliver does solo, most notably on "Dippermouth Blues," his playing features a concise delivery of related motives and a deliberately small vocabulary; he can make the most out of two or three notes for a full chorus. For the most part, though, the two cornets work together on every tune, either alternating phrases in a call and response, or playing close harmonies on the melody. Oliver's and Armstrong's ability to play in harmony seemed uncanny to their audiences—on record, it is best featured on "Weather Bird Rag"—and in concert, according to Armstrong, Oliver was able to silently show Armstrong a phrase he wanted to play, and Armstrong could harmonize it instantly.

The Creole Jazz Band did not last after 1923. Johnson, Dutrey, and the Dodds brothers left the band, and Lil Hardin famously convinced Armstrong to leave to start his own band in 1924—Hardin and Armstrong eventually married. Oliver continued to lead bands and make several fine records, including two sides in duet with Jelly Roll Morton. Dental problems began to detrimentally effect his playing by 1929 or so, and he played less frequently and, frankly, more poorly (though many of his late recordings are still gems).

OTHER EARLY RECORDINGS

While groups like Morton's and Oliver's were disproving the ODJB's claim that jazz was invented and best played by white people, a number of white bands recorded and found success on the coattails of ODJB's considerable success. The similarly named *Original New Orleans Jazz Band*

KING OLIVER'S CREOLE JAZZ BAND, "CHIMES BLUES"

Ken Burns Jazz, CD 1, Track 6

Armstrong is given two choruses to play solo on "Chimes Blues." By 1923, Armstrong was already developing his own style. "Chimes Blues" demonstrates nicely his softer attack and his fluidity in all registers (sticklers for the importance of improvisation in jazz should note the exact repetition of the first ten measures of the solo in the second chorus).

played in a style nearly identical to the ODJB's, and at least as well. Their two most lasting contributions to American culture were the tune "Ja Da," which became a standard, and the inclusion of pianist Jimmy Durante, whose distinctive voice and nose later made him a pop culture icon. The *New Orleans Rhythm Kings* showed a greater allegiance to the harder-swinging style later exemplified by King Oliver. Among their notable recordings is a 1923 session with Jelly Roll Morton on piano—the first recording of a racially integrated group.

According to legend, the first opportunity to record jazz went not to the ODJB but to cornetist *Freddie Keppard* (1889–1933). Keppard, it is said, turned down the offer out of fear that others would steal his style. Regardless of the veracity of this story, Keppard was a highly regarded player with a rough, dirty, staccato playing style and a particularly fat sound. On record, his playing is best featured on the track "Stock Yard Blues," which also features Johnny Dodds on clarinet.

For the most part, the saxophone was absent from early jazz ensembles, or occasionally used as a novelty. *Sidney Bechet* (1897–1959), who was already an accomplished and successful clarinetist, purchased a soprano saxophone while in Europe and quickly became the only master of the instrument (another would not come along until Steve Lacy in the 1950s), acknowledged and acclaimed by jazz fans and the European art music establishment alike. His is one of the most easily recognized playing styles on record. He used a huge, honking sound with an extremely wide and rapid vibrato, and played far more fleetly than his sound would imply. He made a series of classic records with Clarence Williams' Blue Five between 1923 and 1925, many of which also featured Louis Armstrong. "Wild Cat Blues" from July 1923 features his playing throughout, and his interplay with Armstrong on "Cake Walkin' Babies (From Home)" is some of the best ever captured on record. Bechet enjoyed a long and very successful career, with a hit in 1939 with his recording of "Summertime" and a comeback with the Dixieland resurgence of the 1940s.

4

LOUIS ARMSTRONG

There are a handful of recurring themes and cycling opinions that seem to crop up regularly in the jazz community. Every few years, critics proclaim the death of jazz, and shortly thereafter the music is reaching new heights of popularity. Sonny Rollins retires (again) and comes back a year or so later with a new approach to his music. And Louis Armstrong's legacy alternates between that of either the greatest genius of jazz or a sold-out Uncle Tom who wasted his talent appearing on television variety specials.

At present, current opinion on Armstrong is generally glowingly appreciative, and it might not swing back this time. He has been glorified, sometimes even overestimated (which is difficult) on television documentaries, and imitated by current jazz artists. His 1968 album *What a Wonderful World* was certified platinum thirty years after his death, and the title track reached number 32 on the Billboard pop charts, and number 1 in the UK, in 1988. While the academic community has long struggled to justify his pre-eminence as a jazz trumpeter with his later celebrity as a popular singer and comedic character, a few scholars have been looking seriously at his singing lately, and arguments over his stature as a highbrow or lowbrow artist are dying down.

Regardless of public opinion of his career as a celebrity, Armstrong's stature as the predominant jazz musician of the late 1920s is beyond dispute. His impact on audiences and musicians was swift, strong, and permanent. His virtuosic performances and recordings played a central role in the transition of jazz to a soloist's art. His distinctive sound and extroverted, jovial style, complete with vocal asides, is unmistakable. He played with unprecedented technique. No jazz musician played with his flexibility in all registers, velocity, or ease before Armstrong, and few would for some time after the 1920s.

Armstrong was born an August 4, 1901, in New Orleans, although he preferred to give a more patriotic and rounder birth date of July 4, 1900. His childhood was marked by acute poverty, as well as the near constant exposure to music that every New Orleans musician seems to mention in interviews and autobiographies. His wide grin earned him the nickname "Satchelmouth," which, shortened to "Satchmo," stuck with him his entire life. He was raised by his mother and grandmother, and led a life that has become a stereotype of poor African Americans: no male role model, time spent on the streets, and singing with a quartet on street corners for change.

In 1913, he was picked up by the police for firing a pistol in the street on New Year's Eve, and sent to reform school. It was here that he first picked up the cornet. Playing in the reform school band, he likely became familiar with the cornet work of Sousa's soloist Herbert L. Clarke and the cornet method of Paris Conservatory professor Jean-Baptiste Arban (all still standard training materials for brass instrumentalists). At any rate, the rapid scale runs and arpeggios (runs of broken chord tones) of Clarke and Arban became a feature of his soloing style that was more common among clarinetists than cornetists of his time.

It is apparent that Armstrong took to the cornet unusually quickly. He had a teacher and mentor in King Oliver, and when Oliver left Kid Ory's band in 1917, Armstrong took over and impressed his band mates with his strong playing. A year later, he was traveling on the riverboat circuit and continued to work on cruises and in New Orleans until Oliver's telegram brought him to Chicago and the Creole Jazz Band in 1922.

After leaving Oliver's band at pianist Lil Hardin's behest, and spending a brief time with Ollie Powers' Harmony Syncopaters, Armstrong moved to New York to join Fletcher Henderson's Orchestra in 1925, where he came into his own as a mature soloist. Henderson's group, with

FLETCHER HENDERSON AND HIS ORCHESTRA, "SUGAR FOOT STOMP"

Ken Burns Jazz, CD1, Track 12

Armstrong's soloing in the context of the Henderson Orchestra is a study in contrast. The band tends to romp through its numbers quickly and energetically, but somewhat stiffly, and soloists like trombonist Charlie Green follow suit. But when Armstrong enters to solo, it is as if he were bursting into the room with urgent news. His assertive tone, loose approach to the beat, and willingness to make phrases across the bar almost stand in opposition to the rest of the recording. Like Oliver, Armstrong tends to confine his ideas to a narrow range of notes on these recordings—in fact, his solo on 1925's "Sugar Foot Stomp" is the same as Oliver's on "Dippermouth Blues" as a tribute to his teacher with only a few embellishments— but the confidence and bright, powerful sound with which he plays are Armstrong's alone. While in New York, Armstrong made many recordings outside of the context of Henderson's orchestra, including notable blues records backing up Bessie Smith, and surely his experience in different musical contexts, often requiring strong reading skills, added greatly to his confidence as a soloist.

winds in organized sections and tight arrangements that owe more to James Reese Europe and Tin Pan Alley than Buddy Bolden and New Orleans stylistically, would serve as a prototype for the big bands of the swing era.

By November 1925, it was clear to Lil Hardin, now Armstrong's wife, that Armstrong was ready to become a leader of his own, and again with her encouragement, he left the Henderson Orchestra and returned to Chicago. While there has been considerable discussion among jazz scholars and fans about whether Armstrong bent too easily to his wife's wishes, the opportunities available for a female, African American arts manager were scant in the 1920s. One can easily see an alternate point of view, in which Armstrong was not so much a henpecked husband as someone who married his first manager.

While in Chicago, Armstrong worked steadily with bands led by Lil Armstrong and Erskine Tate, but recordings he made there between 1925 and 1928 as a leader—the group was called the Hot Five or the Hot Seven, depending on the size of the band—made Armstrong a celebrity and form the first indubitably great set of jazz records. It is interesting to note that these groups existed only in the recording studio, and personnel varied. Armstrong continued to play as a soloist for others' bands while he sold records as a leader.

In a way, the Hot Fives and Sevens are a synthesis of the work Armstrong did with King Oliver and Fletcher Henderson. The ensemble—cornet/trumpet (Armstrong switched to trumpet in 1928), clarinet, trombone, piano, and banjo/guitar, with tuba and drums added to fill out the Hot Seven—is typical New Orleans fare, and for the most part, the musicians are ones with whom Armstrong had played while working with Oliver. The repertoire and arrangements, however, owe much to the Tin Pan Alley style of American popular music as Henderson approached it. Generally speaking, the feel provided by the rhythm section is smoother, and closer to a fast four-beat feel than the same musicians provided under Oliver's leadership, and instead of the repeated-strain structures of most New Orleans bands, most of the tunes by the Hot Five and Hot Seven bands follow the repeating chorus structure, with ensemble playing in the first and last choruses and solos in the middle, that would become the dominant structure of jazz from the 1930s forward. There are plenty of exceptions formally, like the brilliant "Cornet Chop Suey" that was apparently written while Armstrong was still with Oliver, but the emphasis on solo playing over ensemble work is present throughout the series.

It is difficult to pick out specific tracks from this period of Armstrong's career as worthy of highlight, because the playing on just about all of them is so creative and technically sure. Armstrong is the not the only musician at his peak. The clarinet playing of Johnny Dodds is consistently creative and exciting, and trombonist Kid Ory epitomizes the tailgate style of trombone (so named because the slide of the trombone had to point off the tailgate of a truck when a band played parades).

With "Heebie Jeebies" in 1926, Armstrong had a smash hit with the first celebrated example of scat singing—the singing of nonsense syllables in a jazz vocal solo. A popular story about this recording is that Armstrong dropped his music halfway through recording and was forced to improvise, but one listen to the record is sufficient to debunk the myth: after singing one chorus with the lyrics, Armstrong takes a second chorus to improvise—if there were a mistake, it could not have been better timed. The lyrics for the one verse sung are pretty insipid, anyway, and there is not much point in elaborating with a second verse.

To speak of this period of Armstrong's career as a whole is not to say that there were no developments in his playing and approach during these three years. By 1928, Armstrong had switched from cornet to trumpet, and his sound became

LOUIS ARMSTRONG AND HIS HOT SEVEN, "WEST END BLUES"

Ken Burns Jazz, CD 1, Track 15

Probably the most discussed single recording of the Hot Fives and Sevens is 1928's "West End Blues." It is also among the slowest tunes Armstrong recorded with this group. It is also one of the most sparsely arranged, and, besides being a magnificent recording deserving close attention, it offers a good opportunity to hear both Armstrong and Hines at their best. It opens with a solo fanfare from Armstrong that has become as famous as it is brilliant, and Armstrong himself played the same fanfare on later performances and recordings of "West End Blues." Following the statement of the melody in the first chorus, a sparse, almost soporific trombone solo is accompanied by tricky woodblock work by Zutty Singleton. The third chorus features Jimmy Strong on clarinet, playing entirely in the *chalumeaux* register (the bottom notes of the clarinet's range, named after an early instrument with a limited pitch range), in a call and response with Armstrong's voice. Armstrong scats as sweetly and purely on this recording as he ever did. The ensemble drops out for the fourth chorus, which Hines plays alone in dramatic fashion, with flurries of notes and wide dynamic contrast. For the final chorus, with the rest of the group playing simple harmonies, Armstrong unleashes eight bars of some of the most effective trumpet playing on record. The first half of his solo consists of a single high B-flat held for four measures. This is no easy task by any stretch, but the technical feat is overshadowed by the tension built before a torrent of descending phrases. A short coda by Hines serves to complete the last chorus before a final cadence by the band, and a satisfying ker-chunk of Singleton's percussion adding a period to the end of the sentence.

somewhat brighter and more forceful as a result. And he was also working with pianist Earl Hines by 1928, whose freer style and looser, less predictable rhythmic approach allowed Armstrong to stretch.

For many jazz purists, the end of Armstrong's small group recordings in 1928 mark the end of Armstrong's significance in jazz history. Certainly, the recordings made Armstrong famous enough that his career made a turn from musician to celebrity. He began appearing in films in 1929, and would not record with a small group again for nearly twenty years. In fact, although Armstrong was probably better known as a comic entertainer and singer than as a trumpeter before long, he remained a startlingly talented player well into the 1960s, which is quite a bit longer than most musicians can handle the physical strain of playing the trumpet. He led a big band from 1930 until 1944, and he adapted to the popular swing style of the 1930s far better than many of his generation. The band was generally fairly sloppy, though (Armstrong was never known as a strong disciplinarian), and its survival was almost entirely dependent on the strength of Armstrong's trumpet and vocals.

After World War II, there was renewed public interest in New Orleans-style jazz, and Armstrong returned to small groups, playing with some colleagues from his past like Hines and trombonist Jack Teagarden, as well as other New Orleans musicians of his generation like clarinetist Barney Bigard. Many of these recordings from the Dixieland revival sound nearly as fresh and inspired as the Hot Fives and Sevens, and although the repertoire and personnel of these recordings must have seemed hackneyed at the time, twenty-first century listeners can enjoy them without feeling unhip.

5

THE 1920S

The second half of the 1920s saw a tremendous amount and variety of jazz styles. Spurred on by the success of ODJB et al., record companies saw fit to release recordings by jazz musicians who took inspiration from New Orleans/Chicago groups, and who continued their own regional jazz traditions. There are important recordings from the 1920s that suggest development of the classic New Orleans style of King Oliver, the popular song style and dance bands of New York, the ragtime and stride piano of the East Coast, and a repackaging of jazz techniques and approaches to European art music. To further confuse issues, often the same musicians could be found on these disparate recordings.

In retrospect, it is tempting to view the 1920s as a time of experimentation, when musicians stretched their styles in various directions until they finally hit on the swing style that would dominate jazz during the 1930s and early 1940s. To do so, however, is to set the trap for the modernist model of jazz history described in the Introduction. Jazz musicians saw themselves as entertainers at least as much as modern artists seeking the next step in their progression (at least until the bebop generation). As such, musicians place less emphasis on one specific style and more on ability to play a gig well; the idea of Louis Armstrong leaving King Oliver's band and spending a year with Fletcher Henderson is less incongruous in this context.

THE CHICAGOANS AND BIX BEIDERBECKE

While Chicago was still the major gathering point of New Orleans jazz musicians, it was only natural that a new scene would develop from the white audiences that heard their music in clubs and on records. The Chicagoans, as they would later call themselves, took as much inspiration from recordings of ODJB, the New Orleans Rhythm Kings, and the sweet dance bands as they did from live performances by King Oliver and Louis Armstrong. The musical result, while not as extroverted as Armstrong, was consistently creative, and innovative in a way that that the white bands from New Orleans did not display. The best players from the Chicago circle, most notably saxophonist Frankie Trumbauer and cornetist Bix Beiderbecke, were cited as important influences by both black and white musicians well into the 1930s.

The Chicago scene centered around a group of high school friends from Austin, an affluent suburb of Chicago. In a time in which jazz was largely considered a decadent music and a bad influence on white American culture, the Austin High Gang—a group of middle-class, white teenagers—became an important source of a new style of jazz. In this respect, they reflected a long-standing American tradition of cultural leadership. Like the Beats, Hippies and Punks after them, the Austin High Gang rejected their privileged upbringing to become a significant voice in American culture.

While the Chicago sound was developed in Midwest area bands like the Wolverines, who recorded a few remarkable sides in 1924 (Beiderbecke's cornet solo on "Jazz Me Blues" has been particularly lauded by jazz scholars), the bulk of their work, and their most influential work, was done in New York. While in New York, the Chicagoans, who included cornetist Jimmy McPartland, tenor saxophonist Frank Teschemacher, guitarist/banjoist Eddie Condon and vocalist William "Red" McKenzie (incidentally, McKenzie is probably the finest soloist on tissue paper and comb on record), worked with musicians that were already part of a vibrant New York scene, like percussionist Vic Berton (whose unusual kit included tympani) and guitarist Eddie Lang.

Among current audiences, the central figure of the Chicago style is Beiderbecke. Born in 1903, Beiderbecke was musically gifted at an early age. His parents, concerned about Bix's interest in jazz and the degenerate lifestyle with which it was associated, sent him to a military academy near Chicago, where he was expelled for truancy after too many trips into the city to hear jazz. His expulsion freed him into full-time work as a musician, and by the time he made his first recordings with the Wolverines in 1924 he was already an accomplished soloist. He joined Jean Goldkette's orchestra in 1926, where he forged a lifelong professional partnership with Frankie Trumbauer, whose virtuosity and angular, sophisticated playing on the C melody saxophone (an instrument rarely seen today, whose range and timbre are squarely halfway between alto and tenor saxophones) matched Beiderbecke's own. Collectively known as Bix and Tram, the pair appeared together on numerous recordings throughout the 1920s.

Beiderbecke's life has been thoroughly romanticized; the end of his career was spent playing, for an excellent salary, with the now much-maligned Paul Whiteman orchestra, before alcoholism ended his life prematurely at the age of twenty-eight. He has been portrayed frequently as if Dorothy Baker's fictionalized account of his life in the sappy, melodramatic novel *Young Man With A Horn* were properly researched biography: a stereotypical mad genius

FRANKIE TRUMBAUER AND HIS ORCHESTRA, "SINGIN' THE BLUES"

Ken Burns Jazz, CD 1, Track 21

The two can be heard to great effect on the 1927 recording "Singin' The Blues," credited to Frankie Trumbauer and His Orchestra. The recording features an all-star cast of white jazz musicians from the 1920s. Besides Bix and Tram, the personnel includes trombonist Miff Mole, clarinetist Jimmy Dorsey, guitarist Eddie Lang, Paul Mertz on piano and Chauncey Morehouse on drums. The recording dispenses with the ensemble presentation of the 32-bar, ABAC tune and focuses, after a brief introduction, on the soloing of Trumbauer and Beiderbecke. Both are in top form on this recording. Trumbauer's typically disjunct, angular soloing takes up the first chorus, played, also typically, with a smooth tone and soft attack that softens what could be jarringly angular lines. Trumbauer's soloing style is nearly without precedent in jazz (although contemporaries, like bass saxophonist Adrian Rollini, imply jazz saxophone was coming into its own with or without Trumbauer), and he is often cited as a prototype for the swing style. Beiderbecke's chorus follows. He plays within a much smaller pitch range than Louis Armstrong, with whom he is frequently and aptly contrasted. Beiderbecke's tone is also generally smoother and darker than Armstrong's, but halfway through his solo on "Singin' the Blues," a roughly attacked note, the highest of the chorus, becomes the central point of a beautifully balanced and well-structured performance. Throughout these first two choruses, the accompaniment provided by Lang and Morehouse is creative enough to merit nearly equal status with the soloists. Lang, particularly, avoids the traditional chordal chugging of jazz guitar an instead provides unique countermelodies to the soloists, and displays a technical skill far above most guitarists of his generation.

who squanders his talents in a sellout band before drinking himself to death. But such attention has distracted from his remarkable musicianship, even while with the Whiteman Orchestra, which has been underrated in many accounts of jazz history.

STRIDE PIANO

While jazz ensembles were developing their tradition from the New Orleans groups, the pop and dance bands of New York, and the interaction between the two styles, a number of pianists, mostly on the East Coast and almost exclusively African American, were developing a nearly independent tradition of solo piano performance. Following the lead of ragtime composers like Scott Joplin, and pianists like Baltimorean Eubie Blake, who improvised in and developed the ragtime style, pianists displayed their virtuosity through increasing tempos, complicated accompaniments in the left hand, and florid melodic work in the right. Stride piano, so called after the constant back-and-forth motion of the left hand, found a cultural center in Harlem, New York. Pianists like James P. Johnson, Willie "The Lion" Smith, and Fats Waller could be heard and seen at rent parties, piano battles, and clubs throughout Harlem, and in the Jungles—the former name of the West Side of Manhattan when it was a working class, African American neighborhood.

By the 1920s, the Harlem Renaissance was in full swing, and music was central to making Harlem the capital of African American culture. It was a competitive scene, and stride pianists fought for attention not just with bold playing, but with ostentatious clothing and attention-grabbing entrances. To stay on top, pianists needed to play the most technically difficult licks, in the most difficult keys, and in several styles.

James P. Johnson was the acknowledged "Father of Stride Piano." Born in 1894 in New Brunswick, New Jersy, Johnson spent most of his career playing at clubs and parties in New York and New Jersey. Like Joplin before him, Johnson often wrote for contexts beyond the solo piano for which he is best known. "The Charleston," his most famous composition today, was written for *Runnin' Wild*, his first of several Broadway musicals, and his 1927 composition *Yamekraw* for piano and orchestra was premiered at Carnegie Hall.

"Carolina Shout" is Johnson's signature stride piano work (Johnson's frequent use of rhythms and titles that reference the South may have been derived from his mother's background, or just as likely from his need to impress an audience that consisted largely of dock workers in the Jungles who had migrated from the Carolinas, but it also reflects his general insterest in black folklore). He recorded it several times, including making two piano rolls in 1918, throughout his career. Formally, the piece is not a rag; it is a set of variations on a chord progression rather than a collection of repeated and contrasting strains. Another contrast from ragtime was Johnson's mastery of back-beating—in which the bass seems to turn the beat around by emphasizing beats two and four of a four-beat measure, much like the syncopation in the right hand, but at one-quarter the tempo (this bears no relation to the backbeat, which is the drum pattern found in most rock in which the snare drum emphasizes beats two and four regularly).

The most famous and successful of Johnson's pupils was Thomas "Fats" Waller. While it is usually a mistake to draw parallels when discussing biographies, it is difficult to miss similarities between Waller and Louis Armstrong. Like Armstrong, Waller studied under the top performer on his instrument and surpassed his teacher in fame. And like Armstrong, Waller was an equally gifted vocalist and comedian, although his humor could often be more subversive than Armstrong's, as he often joked about the quality of the light material he sang. The two also worked together at one point. Waller, a composer of numerous classic tunes such as "Black and Blue" and "Ain't Misbehavin'," wrote the music for two successful Broadway shows, and Armstrong was the lead trumpeter on 1929's *Hot Chocolates*.

Waller was a physically massive man, and his immense hands were a key to his playing style at the piano. With the uncommon ability to reach across twelve white keys with one hand (ten is a stretch for most pianists), Waller frequently played countermelodies with the thumbs of both hands while managing the melody and accompaniment at the same time. Difficult as this is technically, what strikes most listeners about Waller's recordings is the apparent ease with which he played. Where Johnson might drive a performance with complicated rhythms in the left hand, Waller races along with a lighter touch.

Waller was also an adept soloist on the pipe organ, and made several recordings of organ solo. In one sense, Waller was prototypical as a jazz organist, although the Hammond organ that would eventually become a standard instrument responds quite differently from pipe organ. In another sense, however, his organ playing, which contains more drama and weight than his piano playing, shows an allegiance to the theater organ tradition of large movie houses of the 1920s for which Waller had played in his youth.

While both Johnson and Waller made many recordings with accompaniment in addition to solo recordings, neither benefited much from the addition of other musicians. They had developed and worked in a solo piano style, and played most comfortably when they could take up any musical space with their own playing. In the case of Johnson, recordings made in the 1940s added drums in a frankly unnecessary support role, while Waller recorded with full bands, but did not always cooperate well, and his comping sometimes seems cluttered to contemporary ears.

MAKING A LADY OUT OF JAZZ

While jazz recordings captured the attention of musicians and aficionados from all styles and throughout the Americas and Europe, their chaotic approach to music making proved a bit too much for more conservative audiences. The 1920s represents a time of tremendous social and cultural conflict in the view of many American historians. While urban America made its first attempts at adding a new, distinctly American culture to the Western pallet with new approaches to literature, cinema, film, and music, resurgent fundamentalist Christianity and the Temperance Movement fought for the puritanical aspects of America. Although jazz was not necessarily an embattled and oppressed music, it did carry associations with drinking and wild dancing, and for many musicians, the music needed some taming and assimilation with other forms of popular music before it could gain more widespread appreciation. Similarly, some composers working in the American popular and European art music traditions, who were motivated more by an interest in the musical aspects of jazz than in its marketing, worked to incorporate jazz ideas and styles into their music. While much of the tamer, more accessible music from the 1920s is of only marginal interest to the jazz purist, its interest to young jazz musicians, and American society at large, did much to bring about the Swing Era, the only period in which jazz and popular music were one and the same.

Paul Whiteman, the self-proclaimed "King of Jazz," led one of the most popular groups of the 1920s. Classically trained, physically authoritative (he weighed around three hundred pounds and wore a comb-over and moustache that were easily caricatured), and skilled at marketing, Whiteman made no secret of his intentions as a musician; he stated his goal as a musician to "make a lady out of jazz." The Orchestra recorded prodigiously throughout the 1920s and 1930s, and featured sophisticated arrangements for a salon orchestra, with a full string section, that ranged from fairly straightforward popular song arrangements to treatments of themes from popular classical composers, all colored to varying degrees with the banjo and syncopation that represented jazz to most audiences. His first hit was probably his biggest: his 1920 recording of "Whispering," complete with a chorus-long slide whistle solo, is genuinely insipid. It also became a standard quickly, recorded dozens of times throughout the 1920s and 1930s, and used as the harmonic basis for "Groovin' High" by Dizzy Gillespie in the 1940s. He also maintained a "Modern Music" series of compositions for his ensemble, and commissioned jazz-inflected works from many composers from the European art music tradition, including Stravinsky and, most famously today, Gershwin's *Rhapsody In Blue*. For all his efforts to maintain highbrow and pop credibility, he also made an effort to work with the best white jazz musicians available in his day, and at various times his orchestra included Bix Beiderbecke, Jack Teagarden, Eddie Lang, Miff Mole and the Dorsey brothers, among others. Tracks like "There Ain't No Sweet Man That's Worth the Salt of my Tears" rely as much on the playing of Beiderbecke and violinist Joe Venuti as they do on the kaleidoscopic arrangement typical of Whitman's readings. While the orchestra played beautifully, and his arrangements were skilled if a little flashy, Whiteman's success came greatly as a result of his sharp ability to identify and market the next trend in American popular music. With the advent of electrical recording in 1925, Whiteman was among the first to re-record earlier hits with an updated arrangement of "Whispering" (with the slide whistle still intact, although played with clearer articulation). At the end of his career, Whiteman was a disk jockey and hosted *Paul Whiteman's TV-Teen Club*, a program centered around dancing teenagers that launched the career of Dick Clark.

Jazz had an immediate and strong impact on musicians in Europe from the beginning. Extended tours of and stays in Europe by early jazz musicians like the ODJB and Sidney Bechet, who spent most of the 1920s in Paris and Berlin, made jazz readily accessible to audiences who were already familiar with recordings. European dance bands and singing groups practiced their own interpretations of jazz on a regional level—a 1997 film about the Berlin singing sextet The Comedian Harmonists has made that group's music from the early 1930s the most available regional example. Composers of art music, who had a greater transatlantic reach than popular musicians, also took a great interest in jazz and made their own attempts to integrate jazz approaches into classical performance. This was particularly true in France, where musical modernism took on a less formalist concept than it did in Germanic cultures. Erik Satie's remarkable, proto-minimalist ballet *Parade* (its production was an all-star affair, with choreography by Nijinsky and sets designed by Picasso) was centered around a quirky, repetitive ragtime, and Maurice Ravel's *Bolero*, a ubiquitous work even today, contains trombone glissandi and saxophone choruses that were a direct nod to jazz. Although less well known today, Darius Milhaud's *La Creation du Monde*, a Baroque styled dance suite, was composed in 1924, after Milhaud had traveled to New York, and is a remarkable work of stylistic fusion. And, in a blizzard of multiculturalism, George Gershwin, a popular songwriter from New York, became extremely well known for his art music, which fused French orchestration with the blue notes and syncopation of jazz and a Tin Pan Alley sense of melody. While Gershwin is mainly considered a popular music figure today, his art music works of the 1920s, including his *Piano Concerto In F, An American In Paris*, and *Rhapsody in Blue* were taken very seriously in the orchestral music world, and were considered landmarks of new music in their time.

6

THE SWING ERA, PART I
Big Bands

The Swing Era, usually defined as the period between around 1935–1945, was a high water mark in commercial terms for Jazz—a period in which it dominated American popular music and sensibilities. However, while big band swing is usually discussed in the context in which it dominated the hit parade, the music had been developing among large dance bands throughout the 1920s and early 1930s. Playing in hotels and ballrooms, bands tended to be known as either "sweet," meaning they played sentimental arrangements of popular songs (the most famous sweet band today is probably Guy Lombardo and His Royal Canadians, whose cloying arrangement of "Auld Lang Syne" still accompanies New Year's Eve parties), or "hot," essentially meaning jazz. However, most bands had both sweet and hot repertoire, and it is the combination of tight arrangements of popular tunes with swinging rhythm and solos that determines the big band style as it is commonly understood.

The social nature of dance band performances dictated that most big bands did not travel for record often.

Throughout the United States, so-called territory bands concentrated their gigs in local areas. In some of the more active regions, like Kansas and Texas, bands developed rivalries (sometimes fierce and not so friendly), and settled their disputes over predominance at well-attended battles of the bands. Much of what developed into the swing style began within the context of these territory bands. Of course, New York area musicians had the liberty of living at the broadcasting and recording center of America, and were influential beyond their geographical reach. Even outside of New York, a few "name bands" had the fame and financial support to tour nationwide on a nearly constant basis. Otherwise, the stylistic development of the territory bands, while not undocumented, is obscured by an abundance of bands with limited audiences.

As a result of the Great Depression, which kept audiences home and professional musicians looking for more stable work, the recording industry entered a major slump in the 1930s. At the same time, however, radios became affordable, and by the mid-1930s they became the main form of entertainment in the home. Broadcasts of big bands from hotels and ballrooms throughout the country were instrumental in bringing about a resurgence in record sales, and helped create a loyal and knowledgeable fan base.

INSTRUMENTATION

The typical swing big band consists of a rhythm section, with bass, drums, and piano or guitar (or both) at its core, with multiple trumpets, trombones, and reeds (saxophones, often doubling on clarinet) comprising a wind section. Throughout the Swing Era, most bands also had one or two vocalists (one male and one female, ideally), who were featured in a few numbers every set.

WINDS

The winds in big bands depend largely on the work of an arranger to determine what and how they play. This is a very different approach than in smaller groups, with different demands on the players. Rather than developing a bold, distinctive sound as an improvising soloist (although that is necessary as well, in solos, of course), the wind player must have at his disposal excellent reading skills and an ability to blend with his section.

For the most part, arrangers tend to see the winds as three sections, which is to say that the trumpets, trombones, and reeds tend to play three distinct, harmonized lines. Very often, the wind sections will engage in a call and response, and often, arrangements will be based on riffs—short repeated lines. The use of riffs is common enough that entire tunes might be based on riffing ("One O'Clock Jump" is a well known example), and such arrangements are often called "head" arrangements, not because of the head and solos form, but because the arrangement does not require notation and can be carried around in the musicians' heads.

RHYTHM

The general rhythmic feel of swing is a fast four-beat, easily distinguished from the march-like two beat feel of earlier styles of jazz. This new feel is basically effected by the drums and bass; guitarists tend to stick to the steady, one chord per beat chunk that was developed in the 1910s, and pianists play quite sparsely, often only punctuating accents with chords.

Much of the timekeeping duties are left for the bassist, who plays one note per beat, either playing the tonic and dominant of the chord repeatedly, or "walking." The technique of walking involves playing a different note on each beat, usually linking chord tones on strong beats of the measure by stepwise motion on the weak beats. Much more easily recognized than described, walking bass lines became the dominant style of bass playing in jazz from around 1935 on, and formulate a cliché by which many people identify jazz in general. And while it is commonly associated with the swing style, walking bass found its way into just about every style; a 1931 recording of "I'll Be Glad When You're Dead, You Rascal You" by Red McKenzie and His Mound City Blue Blowers, for instance, features a walking bass throughout, while remaining a good example of Chicago style hot playing.

Drummers in big bands tend to play lightly and fleetly in comparison with drummers in earlier styles. The steady pulse is still kept in the bass drum, but additionally and more prominently on either the ride cymbal (usually the largest cymbal on a drum set, the mass of the ride cymbal keeps its sound dry and crisp relative to a splashier crash cymbal), or on the hi hat. The hi hat is actually a pair of cymbals facing each other on a stand, which can be brought together with a pedal operated by the left foot (usually). When closed and struck with a stick, they produce a short, sharp, "chick" sound, and the traditional swing hi hat pattern involves closing the cymbals on beats two and four, and alternating between a quarter note on strong beats and eighth notes on weak beats. It is easily recognized on-omatopoeically: tss-tictic-tss-tictic, etc. Most good swing drummers varied the pattern considerably, of course, but as a foundation, this pattern drove most mid-tempo and fast swing performances.

It is impossible to provide an accurate picture of the variety and number of big bands that made significant recordings in a book of this scope. The four bands featured here represent extremes of Swing Era big bands: the prototype, the most sophisticated and intellectual, the hardest swinging, and the most popular (in a sense, although the title really belongs to Glenn Miller in terms of hits and record sales). Most other bands can be understood in relation to these four.

FLETCHER HENDERSON

The Fletcher Henderson Orchestra was the most commercially successful black band of the 1920s. Their slick arrangements, mostly the work of Don Redman and later Henderson himself, and strong soloists provided a blueprint for musicians to follow throughout the Swing Era.

Henderson (1897–1952) came from a middle-class background, and received a Bachelor's Degree in Chemistry from Atlanta University. He moved from Georgia to New York in 1920 to continue his research in Chemistry, but within the year he was making his living as a song plugger, playing popular songs on Tin Pan Alley to increase sheet music sales. By 1924, Henderson was leading his own band at the Club Alabam in New York, and that band was later hired by the Roseland Ballroom, where they would stay in residence for ten years.

The Henderson Orchestra featured some of the best African American musicians available, including, for a year, Louis Armstrong. They especially benefited from the presence of two giants of the Swing Era: tenor saxophonist Coleman Hawkins (who will be discussed later) and alto saxophonist and arranger Don Redman (1900–1964). Redman had been a child prodigy, and attended Boston Conservatory, which was among the first American conservatories to admit black musicians. Redman was not the most skilled soloist, but as an arranger, he brought a harmonic sophistication and clear scoring to his arrangements that quickly caught on with the public.

While some of Redman's arranging style bears resemblance to Paul Whiteman in its fondness for chromaticism and the occasional oddball percussion hit, most of Redman's ideas about big band arrangement became standard stylistic traits of the Swing Era. By the time he left Henderson's group in 1927 (to join McKinney's Cotton Pickers, which he similarly transformed into a modern swing band), Redman featured the antiphonal scoring (brass and reeds alternating phrases), solos accompanied by riffs from the horn section, and rhythmically altered themes that became the foundation of swing arrangement.

Henderson took over the arranging duties himself after around 1930 (Benny Carter, a fine saxophonist, trumpeter and arranger provided some arrangements in the interim), and mostly followed the lead of his predecessors, although with slightly leaner arrangements.

By the mid-1930s, Henderson found more success setting his arrangements to other bands than as a leader performing them himself. Financial, booking, and health troubles eventually led to a mass walkout; about half of Henderson's orchestra quit at once in November, 1934, and while he was

FLETCHER HENDERSON AND HIS ORCHESTRA, "HOTTER THAN 'ELL"

Ken Burns Jazz, Disc 1, Track 23

"Hotter Than 'Ell," recorded in 1934, is an arrangement by Horace Henderson, Fletcher's brother, who worked within the style established by Fletcher. Although it is not the best demonstration of the strength of Henderson's soloists, it contains all the hallmarks of the Swing Era big band arranging style. Harmonically, "Hotter Than 'Ell" is identical to George Gershwin's popular song "I Got Rhythm." Since Ethel Waters' recording of "I Got Rhythm" in 1930, the 32-bar, AABA composition has been so commonly recast by jazz musicians that so-called **rhythm changes** are as common and well understood as the 12-bar blues.

able to reform a group within a year, it was no longer Henderson's primary source of work. He was eventually hired by Benny Goodman as an arranger and pianist in 1939.

DUKE ELLINGTON

With Louis Armstrong and Charlie Parker, Edward Kennedy "Duke" Ellington completes the jazz trinity—the three musicians whose careers are most discussed, whose music is most influential to other musicians, and whose names are most familiar outside of jazz circles. His work as a composer alone earns his reputation. He brought a formal and harmonic sophistication to his music that was new for jazz, and made a concerted and explicit effort to elevate the music's status from popular music to the high art of African American culture. He also had the longest career of any big band leader, maintaining a steadily working orchestra from its beginnings in 1924 until his death in 1974.

Ellington was born April 29, 1899, into an affluent family by African American standards. His father was a butler to a wealthy family (or families—the details of his employment are not clear), and his mother doted on her only child. As and adult, Ellington marketed his comfortable background ably, adopting an eloquent and reserved speaking style and impeccable fashion sense throughout his life. He had learned piano as a teenager, taking the piano roll of James P. Johnson's "Carolina Shout" as a starting point. Before long, he was working with his first band, with New Jersey-born drummer Sonny Greer and trumpeter Arthur Whetsol. By 1924, Ellington was leading a band, called "The Washingtonians," in New York.

Ellington always seemed to hire forceful musical personalities whose own playing style helped form the sound of his band. In 1926, the year he made the first recordings that clearly demonstrated his style (and brilliantly so—"East

Saint Louis Toodle-Oo" from that year is one of Ellington's many recordings that are considered classics), the band featured Sidney Bechet, Greer (who was a distinctive colorist with a fondness for chimes, tympani, and other odd percussion), Tricky Sam Nanton and Bubber Miley. Miley became known as the chief progenitor of gutbucket trumpet style, marked by use of the plunger with a straight mute (which adds nasality to the basic timbre of the trumpet) and by literally growling while playing. Nanton applied a similar approach to the trombone, and the frequent use of raunchy answering phrases from one or the other player became a trademark of Ellington's arrangements. The impact of Miley's playing on Ellington's musical ideas was more or less permanent; when Miley left the orchestra, his replacement was Cootie Williams, whose gutbucket playing was every bit as remarkable as Miley's. Bechet's tenure in the band was a short one, but his replacement, Barney Bigard, was also a bold clarinetist from New Orleans, and Bigard would act as mentor for the growing reed section, which would soon include alto saxophonist Johnny Hodges, a Bechet protége.

In 1927, Ellington won an audition to lead the house band at Harlem's Cotton Club, a famous "black and tan" club (a club in which black entertainers performed for white audiences) with a nationwide radio broadcast. Ellington's regular exposure to a national audience made him famous, and by 1931, the Orchestra had expanded in size, introduced the first of several classic Ellington compositions like "Mood Indigo," and played at the White House.

In 1939, Ellington hired Billy Strayhorn as a lyricist. Together, Ellington and Strayhorn developed a professional relationship so close that it is often difficult to distinguish between the work of the two on first listen. It was a mutually beneficial arrangement; Ellington was supplied with classic compositions like "Take the A Train" (whose lyrics offer directions from midtown Manhattan to Ellington's home in Harlem) and "Chelsea Bridge," and Strayhorn was able to compose for the finest and most respected band around, while staying behind the scenes to avoid controversy surrounding his homosexuality.

As an arranger, Ellington consistently showed an interest in viewing form beyond the repeated chorus structure of other arrangers. As early as 1926, Ellington was working with numbers of themes in a suite-like arrangement, and by 1943's "Black, Brown & Beige," he was composing major works with complicated forms and some duration. One of the forms that has become identified with Ellington is the arch form, in which a series of sections are played successively, and then in reversed order after the midpoint. An early and famous example is "Sepia Panorama," in which three contrasting sections (each different from the other in phrase structure) lead up to two choruses of 12-bar blues, and then return afterwards in reverse.

While many swing musicians lost some influence and creativity after the beginning of bebop, Ellington continued to make significant works and have profound influence until his death in 1974. His later music will be discussed briefly later in this book.

COUNT BASIE

Although they came to prominence fairly late in the Swing Era, the Count Basie band epitomized swing, in both the stylistic sense and the broader, more subjective sense. In the late 1930s, Basie's band played high energy, blues based charts with strong emphasis on solos provided by some of the strongest players in jazz. The rhythm section was incomparable. With Basie at the piano, Freddie Green on guitar, Walter Page on bass and Jo Jones at the drums, Basie's rhythm section worked like a gentle giant, well aware of their strength and power, but preferring to express it with quiet restraint that only enhanced it. Basie himself was one of the sparest pianists in history, content to let his band speak for him. But the few notes he would play (mostly in a few short phrases during the introduction, with almost no left had work) were always impeccably placed, and on occasion, he could burn the house down with fierce, stride-influenced solos.

Bill Basie was born in Red Bank, New Jersey, in 1904, and grew up with the East Coast stride piano scene of James P. Johnson and Fats Waller. Like many others, he began his professional career touring with the Theatrical Owners Booking Association (TOBA), a vaudeville circuit that specialized in booking African American entertainers. TOBA was often said jokingly to be an acronym for "Tough On Black Asses" (or Artists), because pay was low, theaters were sub-par, and the tour was grueling. When an act with which he was touring disbanded on the road, Basie was stranded in Kansas City. The Kansas City territory band scene was a particularly active and fertile one, and Basie quickly found work with Walter Page's Blue Devils before he eventually joined pianist Bennie Moten's band as second pianist, taking Page and other Blue Devils with him. When Moten died in 1935, Basie formed his own group with many of the same musicians, and was shortly thereafter signed (after producer John Hammond heard a radio broadcast) to record for MCA records. Basie would continue to lead a big band for the next fifty years, until his death in 1984.

The Basie band existed in two incarnations. During the Swing Era, the band stayed close to their roots as a Kansas City territory band. Most of their repertoire consisted of head arrangements, with heavy riffing over rhythm changes or 12-bar blues structures, driven powerfully by the rhythm section and featuring long solos. One of his biggest hits, "Jumpin' at the Woodside," for instance, is a slight variation on rhythm changes with barely any discernable melody. Rather, the saxophones provide a simple riff for sixteen measures (answered by the brass), the bridge is played only as a background for soloing, and the riff returns for the final eight measures of the chorus. What drives this, and most Basie performances, is not any kind of compositional cleverness, but creative soloing (the strongest soloist in the band was always tenor saxophonist Lester Young, who will be discussed in the next chapter) and the infectious drive of Jo Jones' hi-hat.

In 1950, personnel changes and financial pressure caused Basie to disband his orchestra, and his return to big band leadership in 1953 was with a largely different group and an entirely different approach to playing. The Basie band of the 1950s relied on tight performances of more fleshed-out arrangements, and did not feature the lengthy solos of his previous band. While the second Basie band still swung mightily, riffs were replaced by rich harmonies, frequently provided by staff arranger Neil Hefti and then-young trumpeter Thad Jones. The new band excelled, in fact, in soft ballads, when they were able to show off the tight harmonies. This new approach was probably best put forth on the 1957 LP originally titled $E = MC^2$, now available as *The Complete Atomic Basie* on Blue Note records. While the album opens with a rare piano feature called "The Kid From Red Bank," most of the recording features the laid back, tight ensemble playing for which the band was famous, and closes with Hefti's "Li'l Darlin," one of the slowest and most atmospheric big band recordings ever made.

BENNY GOODMAN

With his accessible playing style, full, sweet sound, and the benefit of some of the best arrangements from the black big bands, clarinetist Benny Goodman (1909–1986) was a major celebrity, bringing swing to the top of the hit parade and earning the nick name "King of Swing." While he is often portrayed in jazz histories as an opportunist and taskmaster who made his living on Fletcher Henderson's work and browbeat his band, such a description does not reflect his relationship with Henderson, nor the quality of his band, whose bold sound, driven by the flashy but solid playing of Gene Krupa, was all its own.

The rags-to-riches biography of Goodman is the stuff of Hollywood, and, in fact, was the subject of a 1955 film for which the Goodman orchestra itself provided the soundtrack. Goodman was the son of poor Jewish immigrants in Chicago. He began playing clarinet in a band program at a local Jewish Community Center, and developed facile technique early from lessons with a strong classical clarinet teacher. He gigged professionally as a teenager, moved to New York in 1928, and was leading his own band on a regular radio broadcast by 1934. With a budget from his radio show and encouragement from friend and producer John Hammond, Goodman purchased arrangements from the leading African American arrangers of the day; many of his biggest hits had been performed note for note by the Fletcher Henderson Orchestra some years before.

The Goodman band made their biggest breakthrough in the summer of 1935, on a tour of the western United States. During a set in California, Goodman was surprised to learn that, largely due to the difference in time zone from the East Coast, his audience was more familiar with, and much more enthusiastic about, the hotter, up-tempo swing that he reserved for the end of his radio broadcasts—too late for a New York audience, but in prime time on the West Coast. After this discovery, and the success of his tour afterwards, Goodman became a celebrity of the highest order, and brought swing to the mainstream of American popular culture with him.

With his fame, Goodman had the power to accomplish a number of firsts in the jazz world. His was the first band to feature both white and black musicians as regular members, although due to the still segregated music union, black musicians such as pianist Teddy Wilson, vibraphonist Lionel Hampton, and guitarist Charlie Christian could only be hired as guest artists. Goodman simply hired them as guests for every performance. He also famously performed at Carnegie Hall on January 16, 1938—not the first time jazz was presented there, but the first time jazz was the only thing on the bill. The concert was recorded, and their performance that night of "Sing, Sing, Sing," an unusual, minor key, riff-based tune that strongly featured the drumming of Gene Krupa, is a classic, and the signature performance by which the Goodman orchestra is best known today.

Goodman's orchestra also featured the concept of a "band within a band." With Lionel Hampton, pianist Teddy Wilson, Gene Krupa, and, by 1939, a different group featureing guitarist Charlie Christian, Goodman performed and recorded significantly more music by small combos than most bandleaders. And every member of the small group was a frequently imitated pioneer on his instrument. Christian, in fact, would play an important role in the development of bebop in the 1940s, and due to his early death in 1942 his playing with Goodman on tracks like "Rose Room" are among the few recorded examples of his cutting-edge soloing style.

OTHER BANDS

Cab Calloway (1907–1994) was among the most popular African American vocalists and bandleaders. In addition to his trademark white suit and tailcoat and conked hair, Calloway had a rich, exuberant voice and a penchant for scat singing that earned him the nickname "the Hi-De-Ho Man." While Calloway's arrangements tended to feature his singing, his band was always tightly rehearsed and featured excellent musicians, including a young Dizzy Gillespie on trumpet (who would later be central to the development of bebop).

Calloway had perhaps the deepest sense of irony of the swing era; a clean liver in his private life, he performed a number of songs, like "Minnie the Moocher" and "Kicking the Gong Around," that celebrated drug use. And in a curious (but not often discussed) 1941 recording of the Hammerstein/Romberg song "Lordy," he lampoons the stereotypical black dialect of the lyrics with a sophisticated, operatic performance, complete with rolled r's in the word "Lordy."

The chief rival to Benny Goodman on clarinet during the swing era was *Artie Shaw* (1910–2005). Shaw first hit the charts in 1938 with a recording of "Begin the Beguine" and immediately developed a reputation as a sweet-styled interpreter of pop tunes. Shaw saw himself, however, as a more serious musician, and felt shackled by his popular success. He did compose and record some challenging music with complicated forms and harmonies, but, soured by his own career, Shaw dropped out of music altogether several times. In addition to his music career, Shaw was a published novelist of some talent.

Jimmy Lunceford (1902–1947) led another strongly admired band out of New York Which had moved there from Memphis, Tennessee. With hits like "For Dancers Only," Lunceford's band benefited from robust and sophisticated arrangements, mostly by Sy Oliver, and an exciting and creative drummer in Jimmy Crawford.

Although his career was notably short, *Glenn Miller* (1904–1944) may have eclipsed even Benny Goodman in popularity. Miller's band was stylistically much closer to sweet popular music than hot jazz, but hits like "In the Mood" are too stubbornly popular and too well written to be ignored. At the peak of his fame, Miller joined the Air Force in 1942, and led a band to entertain troops in Europe. A 1944 flight from London to Paris on which Miller was a passenger disappeared without a trace before landing, and the mystery of his demise may have contributed to his continuing popularity.

THE SWING ERA, PART II
Small Groups and Soloists

Big bands were by no means the only outlet for musicians in the swing era. In smaller clubs around the country, like the ones that had cropped up on a block of 52nd Street on the West Side of Manhattan in such abundance that the block was known as "Swing Street," small combos and jam sessions were the source of important music. Late night "cutting sessions," during which two or more well reputed soloists jammed in an effort to out-play each other, were common, and often reported in black newspapers as if they were boxing matches. Cutting sessions in Kansas City, particulary are between Lester Young and Coleman Hawkins in December of 1933, have become urban legend, and the subject of articles, fiction, and Robert Altman's notable 1996 film *Kansas City*.

While some of the great swing era soloists like Lester Young made their most public mark as part of a big band, others, like Art Tatum and Slam Stewart, spent most of their careers in small combos or solo performances.

COLEMAN HAWKINS AND LESTER YOUNG

In the way that the trumpet was the premiere lead instrument of New Orleans style jazz bands, the tenor saxophone enjoyed a privileged status and a glut of star soloists during the swing era. The number of great tenor saxophonists active during the 1930s and 1940s is tremendous, and otherwise brilliant players like Chu Berry, Ben Webster and Don Byas have been overshadowed by the towering legacy of rivals Coleman Hawkins and Lester Young. While Hawkins may have been more boldly virtuosic, Young's approach was more influential to younger musicians and served as more of a prototype for jazz saxophone from bebop forward.

The two could not have had more different playing styles. While Hawkins played with a heavy, dark and powerful sound with a rich vibrato, Young at his peak sounded lighter than air, with a bright (often called "alto-like") sound and almost no vibrato. Young could make the most of limited materials, expanding a three-note idea into a dramatic solo; Hawkins flew all over the map, and played florid sixteenth-note lines without effort.

Lester "Pres" Young (his nickname was provided by Billie Holiday, proclaiming him the President of the Tenor Saxophone) was born near New Orleans in 1909. His professional career started early, because he was born into a vaudevillian family band. Under his father's stern leadership, Young was soundly chastised at least once for lack of reading skills, so he taught himself music notation, and left the band at age eighteen. After several years freelancing (including stints with King Oliver), Young settled in Kansas City and joined Count Basie's band in 1935. His first recording, with a quintet culled from the personnel of the Basie band, had immediate and long lasting impact. Both "Shoe Shine Boy" and "Oh! Lady Be Good" featured Young prominently, and on both recordings, his solos are engaging, eminently singable, and necessary for young sax players to learn note for note.

Young's style is easily recognizable, and trademark licks and techniques are abundant on the first recording, and throughout later Basie recordings like "Lester Leaps In." Most of Young's solos start with a brief, two or three note phrase, which frequently is repeated as part of a longer second phrase. One of the ways Young achieves such remarkable coherence as a soloist is through this kind of repetition: the first or last three notes of one phrase become the first or only notes of the next phrase, so that the entire solo seems to grow organically, and with increasing drama. Two of Young's other signature techniques are really the same thing—the alternation between two notes, or the same note with different fingerings (creating a slight change in timbre), several times. Both of these licks are placed at the beginning of a chorus or at the return of the A section after a bridge with steadfast consistency throughout Young's career. But to emphasize his consistent and maybe limiting style is to miss out on the remarkable creativity behind working with such limited means and the energy and drama he could produce.

Young was inducted into the army at the end of 1944, where he had a terrible year, spending most of it confined to military barracks after being charged with drug possession (Young was always open about marijuana use, but his excessive one-year sentence was likely a result of racism). His return to a music career in December of 1945 is frequently portrayed as a tragic fall from grace, and a long, slow deterioration of his body and playing abilities. This is unfair—he had been developing a darker sound with a wider vibrato and lazy attack before he entered the service, and his late career is marked by inconsistency rather than decline. Regardless, the light, buoyant solos of the 1930s were mostly long gone, returning only in glimpses during some of his best late solos. And his worst recordings from the 1950s are truly awful, and rather depressing. His death in 1959 came after years of alcoholism and depressive behavior.

If for nothing else, Coleman Hawkins could have staked his claim to jazz history on a single recording. "Body and Soul" was recognized as a masterpiece almost immediately upon its release in 1939. For almost exactly three minutes, Hawkins solos in an almost constant stream of sixteenth notes (he dispenses with introduction and head and jumps right into his solo) with an effortless flow and rhythmic flexibility that belies the angularity and chromaticism of his lines. It was, and still is, required listening and memo-

COLEMAN HAWKINS, "BODY AND SOUL"

Ken Burns Jazz, CD 3, Track 1

While long, technical treatises could be, and often are written about the technical and harmonic complexity of this *tour de force* of solo tenor saxophone, it is perhaps best approached for the first time in a more relaxed fashion. On one level, the recording is a pure, distilled statement of the art of soloing in the swing style. After a four measure introduction on the piano, Hawkins takes over the lead role immediately and only alludes to the written melody for the first eight measures (even then, it is immediately altered rhythmically, and ornamented with Hawkins's own filigree within the first measure). His playing here shows all of his stylistic trademarks – most notably, the unusual combination of a light attack and quick fingers with a dark tone and almost ponderous vibrato. A few moments stand out as climactic points in Hawkins's two-chorus solo: the falling lines at 2:40, the rise in pitch and dynamic level at the beginning of the final bridge (2:15) and the last A section of this 32-bar AABA structure (2:35). But for the most part, the entire three minutes is a single, long, and varied stream of ideas with little repetition.

rization for all jazz saxophonists. Of course, by the time he recorded the tune, Hawkins was already a dominant figure. From his tenure with the Fletcher Henderson Orchestra, during which he transformed from a percussive "slap tongue" player into a lyrical and restless melodic one, Hawkins's playing served as a model for swing saxophone.

Hawkins is sometimes described as a harmonic, or "vertical" soloist. While many soloists before him (and Young after) might have focused on adding variations to the melody of the tune (or making a new one that fits the changes), Hawkins had an extensive understanding of harmonic theory, and used it to expand and ornament the harmonic structure of the tune he was playing. The concept of vertical and horizontal (melodic) soloing is often presented as a dichotomy, but this is a mistake. There are degrees of both approaches in every musician's style—Louis Armstrong was perfectly likely to arpeggiate chords during his solos, and Hawkins was equally capable of using rhythmic variety and direction in his. The degree to, and ease with which Hawkins could negotiate complicated harmonic tricks and arpeggios, however, have marked him as a primarily vertical soloist.

ROY ELDRIDGE

Part of playing the trumpet in the 1930s and 1940s was dealing with Louis Armstrong. Armstrong was still a dominant voice in the swing era, and for the most part, trumpeters played within the limits of what he could play. If anyone was able to extend the possibilities with faster, higher, more harmonically sophisticated playing, it was Roy Eldridge.

Eldridge was born into a musical family—his brother Joe was a saxophonist—in Pittsburgh in 1911. He was playing trumpet professionally by age sixteen, and moved to New

York in 1930. Early in his career, his playing was heavily influenced by New Orleans trumpeter Jabbo Smith, a remarkably fast player, and Eldridge himself claims that he played a lot of notes with little feeling or sense of form until he heard Armstrong in 1932. After his breakthrough, Eldridge maintained his ability for fleet-fingered playing, but had a security and direction to his solos, which he featured first with Fletcher Henderson, then as a bandleader himself, and still later and most successfully as the lead trumpet for Gene Krupa's band, which he joined in 1941. Eldridge at his peak was an almost shockingly flexible soloist; it is not uncommon to hear a single phrase span a range of two or more octaves. By the end of the 1940s, Eldridge had already peaked and his high notes were more novelty than energy. At that point, Dizzy Gillespie, who owes a great deal to Eldridge stylistically, had already taken over where Eldridge left off when the physical strains of his style began to show. He died in 1989.

ART TATUM

In a famous and often told anecdote, Fats Waller once stopped a set in a night club upon Art Tatum's arrival to announce, "God is in the house." Using Waller's stride as a starting point, Tatum expanded the music technically and harmonically to the point that he became his inspiration's idol.

Born in Toledo, Ohio in 1909, Tatum was nearly blind since birth. He received classical training and could read music by Braille. For the bulk of his career, he played solo piano and appeared in small combos (including a trio in the mid-1940s that he led with bassist Slam Stewart and four-stringed guitarist Tiny Grimes). Most of the time, his combo recordings show him to be an excellent solo pianist—his extended descending melodic flourishes, which can already be somewhat repetitive in solo performances, are obnoxious behind someone else's solo.

Unfettered by other musicians, however, the same flurries of notes and harmonic exploration that detract from small group recordings are stunning. His recorded repertoire consisted largely of light popular tunes such as "Three Little Words" or "Tea for Two," played in a relaxed feel and with a light touch, but freely reharmonized in often surprising ways. Tatum also had an experimental side, and could happily stretch a 12-bar blues to the brink of explosion with chord substitutions. His classic 1949 recording of W.C. Handy's "Aunt Hagar's Blues," for instance, frequently discussed in university classrooms, is full of chord extensions and substitutions that create a strikingly modern, but still soulful rendition of a traditional blues. Although Tatum died young in 1956, his music was well documented on record, and his influence on the bebop generation was tremendous.

DJANGO REINHARDT

While he was by no means the first jazz guitar virtuoso, Belgian-born Django Reinhardt played with such fluid skill that he brought a viability to the concept of the guitar solo that jazz had not previously seen. Born to a Rom (once known as gypsy, which is considered a derogatory term) family in 1910, Reinhardt spent his early life on the road and never learned to read or write. He played violin as a child, and then banjo and guitar, and his recorded style indicates that he probably learned in the flamboyant gypsy flamenco style that was common for his ethnicity. In 1927, his caravan caught fire while he slept, and the burn to his left hand caused the tendons in his ring and fifth finger to shrink, drawing them back into a stiff claw. In spite of this, he was the fastest single-note guitarist jazz would see for

nearly forty years (the nature of his injury is not fully understood and often exaggerated to imply that he lost the
use of all but two fingers, or even that he lost the fingers
himself. In about three minutes of film that is known to
show his hands while playing, it is clear that he could use
his ring and fifth finger together to fret notes in chords, but
they probably stayed pulled away from the fretboard during solos).

Reinhardt's best known playing was as leader of the
Quintet of the Hot Club of France, which he formed with
violinist Stephane Grappelli in Paris in 1934. The group was
all strings—in addition to Reinhardt and Grappelli, there
were two rhythm guitarists and a bass—and they became
the first European group to earn the respect of an American audience. After the Quintet split in 1939 (over personal
differences between the prim and proper Grappelli and the
irresponsible Reinhardt over where to reside during World
War II), Reinhardt continued to perform and record until
his death in 1953.

BILLIE HOLIDAY

Although she might be better remembered today for her
brief, drug-addled and difficult biography—and the way
her ballad singing and repertoire choices reflected her hard
life—Billie Holiday nevertheless brought a new lightness
and rhythmic flexibility to jazz singing, showing Louis
Armstrong to be as big an influence as Bessie Smith. Born
in 1915 in Philadelphia and raised in Baltimore, little is
known about Holiday's early life beyond what she claims in
her own autobiography. Regardless, by 1928 she was living
in New York, and by the mid-1930s she was making classic
recordings as a singer. Most of her recordings at her peak
were made with small bands, and the very best showed the
remarkable musical connection she had with Lester Young,

BILLIE HOLIDAY WITH EDDIE HEYWOOD AND HIS ORCHESTRA, "SOLITUDE"

Ken Burns Jazz, CD 3, Track 7

This 1941 recording of the Duke Ellington composition certainly shows the repertoire typically associated with Holiday: a quiet ballad sung from the perspective of a jilted lover, complete with the threat of insanity and a call for divine intervention. It also aptly demonstrates the irony in Holiday's light voice and subtle phrasing. Much of the drama in Holiday's singing is effected rhythmically. Every phrase in this performance begins late relative to the rest of the band, with a single exception reserved for the last line. The sudden shift from behind-the-beat phrasing to a square, on time entrance adds a sense of urgency to the line "give me back my man," and adds a sense of desperation to the plea.

who remained a close friend and professional associate until her death.

ELLA FITZGERALD

If Billie Holiday was the singer that found a place outside of the big band, Ella Fitzgerald was the one who epitomized the possibilities within one. Born in 1917, she was discovered at the age of sixteen after winning Amateur Night at the Apollo Theater, a legendary test of young performers' skills—the Apollo audience could make someone famous, but just as easily boo someone off stage and out of a career. She made her first recordings with the Chick Webb Orchestra, whose omission from discussion in this book is due only to the fact that Webb's fame and status as the greatest drummer of the swing era was rarely well documented on record. As can be heard in one of her biggest hits with Webb,

"A-Tisket A-Tasket," Fitzgerald had a powerful, bright and clear voice, capable of great precision. While a few critics of her singing sometimes point to a lack of depth in her performances, her technical skill, and ability to scat lines closer to what a saxophone might play than what the human voice should be able to do, can not be ignored.

8

BEBOP AND
THE MOLDY FIGS

The effects of World War II on culture were global, and jazz was not immune to the changes. With compulsory military service, rations on food, rubber and petroleum (all of which are central to touring as a performer), and dwindling leisure time among Americans who stayed in the country to work (as well as a dearth of dance partners for the female majority at home), it became financially and practically too difficult to maintain the personnel and schedule of most working big bands. Meanwhile, the recording industry felt the effect of the war as well; a shortage of shellac drove the price of records up and the availability down.

Of course, popular taste changed in the 1940s as quickly as is does today. As the 1940s progressed, hard swing like Basie's became less popular in favor of sweeter, straighter bands like Glenn Miller's, and popular singing was reaching a golden age of sorts, with singers like Frank Sinatra, Bing Crosby and Dinah Shore topping the charts with jazz-influenced, but decidedly straighter recordings.

Some big bands, like Duke Ellington's, were able to continue working, if not thriving, after the war. For the most part, however, the jazz audience was smaller than it had been, and clubs and ensembles followed suit.

For some jazz enthusiasts, the decline in popularity of swing called for a return to New Orleans roots; for others, the appropriate response was a new music that reflected the hypermodernism of post-war America. In articles and letters in jazz magazines like *Downbeat* and *Metronome* that had started to appear in the late 1930s, critics chose sides as either beboppers or Moldy Figs, defending or decrying the work of young musicians in New York, and sometimes entering heated exchanges.

While critics squabbled, older musicians enjoyed increased attention and reinvigorated careers. Louis Armstrong returned to small, New Orleans style combos in 1947, and made some of his best recordings in fifteen years, often featuring trombonist Jack Teagarden. Sidney Bechet also made a comeback, albeit on a slightly smaller scale. He had been performing throughout the 1930s, and even released some early experiments in overdubbing in 1941, but he had not been able to maintain the level of success that Armstrong had until the late 1940s. In 1945, Bechet formed a working group with trumpeter Bunk Johnson which did not last long but began a resurgence of interest in both players. Johnson, who was born in New Orleans in 1889, became a sort of fetish for jazz purists. Because of his age (he had claimed to be ten years older than he was), and the false claim that he had taught Louis Armstrong, Johnson was lauded by many as the authentic voice of jazz. No mind was paid to the fact that his playing did not really resemble recordings of New Orleans musicians from the 1920s. On the contrary, his quiet, simple approach to playing (and his choice of repertoire, since he did not shy away from popular tunes of the 1940s) indicates that Johnson was part of a scene of New Orleans musicians who had developed their own tradition of music apart from the mainstream of jazz.

The attention of the modernist faction of jazz fans

turned, as it always does, to New York, where young African American musicians (including Charlie Christian, who was famous for his work with Benny Goodman) were developing a new approach to jazz, with an even newer approach to its cultural position. The musicians who developed their music in Harlem at late night jam sessions and had taken over the scene on Manhattan's 52nd Street showed little concern for developing a mainstream audience; they rejected the clean image and uniform look of big bands for more individual and varied fashion, and played undanceable music with barebones arrangements and long, chromatic solos. In interviews, musicians in the new generation like Dizzy Gillespie and Max Roach demonstrated a new approach to racial politics that was a part of the nascent civil rights movement in black America. They even showed disdain for the word "jazz" itself, preferring to distinguish their music from past genres with the name "rebop," "bebop," or just "bop."

As revolutionary as the bebop scene was culturally, though, their music in many ways was a simple extrapolation from the trends that swing era jam sessions had already established. Bebop never really strayed from the head-and-chorus structures, 4/4 time with swung eighth notes, or popularity of 12-bar blues and rhythm changes that were already common in jazz. In fact, many swing musicians who already excelled at small-group playing, such as bassist Slam Stewart and saxophonist Don Byas, easily incorporated ideas from bebop into their own playing and comfortably performed with the bebop generation (while some others like Cab Calloway publicly condemned the new music as noise).

For all the impact the bebop generation had on jazz stylistically, technically and culturally, it is easy to lose sight of just how small the scene was. Musicians around the country were thinking along similar lines during jam sessions in cities like Detroit and Pittsburgh, but at its core, bebop is

music that was developed by a handful of musicians, mostly at two clubs in Harlem (Minton's Playhouse on West
118th Street and Monroe's, a short   cab ride uptown on
West 134th), during the 1940s. Their impact may have been
greater because it seemed to have come out of nowhere. In
August of 1942, in an effort to secure royalty payments
for radio broadcasts, the Musician's Union went on strike,
banning all recording except for so-called "V-discs" for dis-
tribution to the armed forces. By the time the recording ban
reached its end a year later, bebop was a well developed but
undocumented style, and small, independent record labels
formed that were able to take advantage of the strike's effect on the three major labels of the time, creating a new
market and a new means for recording music that might
not appeal to the broad popular audience.

ELEMENTS OF BEBOP STYLE

At its essence, bebop is chamber music, played almost exclusively by small groups with only one or two horns and
rhythm. The typical bebop quintet consists of trumpet, alto
or tenor saxophone, piano, bass, and drums. Trombone and
guitar are a notable exception, but not the rule; the light,
sparse textures of most bebop groups excluded the deep, loud
playing of all but a handful of trombonists and guitarists.

Bebop performances focus on solos, almost to the exclu-
sion of other elements. Arrangements are always sparse
and lean, with none of the riffing and trading of the swing
tradition—the head (when present, which is not always the
case) is played almost always in unison with only a few harmonized notes, and the solos begin right away. The rhythm
section is also comparatively constrained—bass players
walk the changes, and pianists play one chord per measure
in most performances.

Bebop drummers made the most obvious changes from

swing style in the rhythm section. While swing maintains a steady, emphatic stomp on four beats of the bar, articulated with a bass drum on every beat, bebop drummers keep time almost exclusively on the ride cymbal, often varying the quarter-note/two eighth-note pattern considerably, and reserving the bass drum for "dropping bombs," or adding loud, irregular accents in unexpected places.

While structurally and harmonically, bebop heads were still based on standard forms and changes from popular music, the melodies themselves were new compositions that resembled the solos to follow. On more than one occasion (especially in the case of Charlie Parker), the process of composing a bebop melody on standard changes was retroactive. For example, a recording of rhythm changes with no composed head would be given a new title, and the first improvised chorus of the recording would become a new head, learned by other musicians and established as a standard. Most often, however, recomposed heads were new compositions in their own right, recasting the harmonic structure of an older tune into a hipper context. One particularly dramatic example of recomposition is Miles Davis's 1947 composition "Donna Lee." Using the chord changes from "(Back Home Again In) Indiana," a corny popular song of local pride from 1917 that had already been transformed into a vehicle for swing jam sessions, Davis composed a dizzying, chromatic run of eighth-notes played at breakneck speed, putting the harmony into an entirely new context (years later, Lester Young would quote the bebop tune during a recorded solo on "Indiana"). In addition to providing context and stylistic unity to a performance by using a new head, recomposition provided the distinct advantage of allowing musicians and record companies to avoid royalty payments on copyrighted material.

The harmonic structure of bebop heads may have come directly from swing repertoire, but the approach to playing chords was, in Dizzy Gillespie's opinion at least, the

TRITONE SUBSTITUTION

One of the most common chord substitutions in bebop is known as the tritone substitution (or just "tritone sub"). Most dominant chords can be substituted on the triad a tritone (also called a diminished fifth or augmented fourth) away. Because the third and seventh of the two chords are the same (for example, C dominant contains C, E, G, and B-flat, while G-flat dominant contains G-flat, B-flat, D-flat and F-flat, which is the same pitch as E), they can serve the same function in a given harmonic progression. So the common progression of ii-V-I that ends a very large number of phrases in jazz would be played as ii-flat II-I (in the key of C, d minor – G7 – C would be d minor – D-flat7 – C). Things can get extremely complicated quickly with this kind of harmonic trickery, and soloists pride themselves on their ability to negotiate harmonic twists and turns.

fundamental difference between bebop and earlier styles. Bebop harmony differentiates itself in two basic ways, both frequently argued to be under the direct influence of Art Tatum. While previously, jazz relied almost entirely on triads and seventh chords, bebop pianists preferred to emphasize extensions of the chord—the ninths, elevenths and thirteenths, creating colors that were relatively dissonant and even bizarre. To complicate things even further, bebop musicians were fond of reharmonization—substituting chords, and playing two or three (or more) chords in a measure that previously held only one.

DIZZY GILLESPIE

John Birks "Dizzy" Gillespie was responsible for much of bebop's extra-musical image, sporting a goatee and fake glasses, speaking humorously but with a political charge, and frequently singing scat with the kind of syllables from which the name "bebop" was derived. He was also an exceptional trumpet player, and probably bebop's most prolific and accomplished composer (Thelonious Monk notwithstanding—his unusual relationship to the rest of his generation will be discussed in Chapter 10). While his public image was that of a clown (he is probably better known to people under forty years old for appearances with Kermit the Frog than with Charlie Parker), Gillespie took a serious, intellectual approach to music, studying harmony carefully and constantly, and making a concerted effort to find a place for Afro-Cuban rhythmic ideas in his music.

Gillespie was born on October 21, 1917, in Cheraw, South Carolina. He moved with his family to Philadelphia, where he started playing trumpet professionally, and moved to New York in 1937. His first steady employment and recording came that year as a replacement for Roy Eldridge in Teddy Hill's big band. Gillespie had modeled his playing after Eldridge, and while he was more technically confident and flexible before long, he continued to play with the rapid and angular lines, sudden leaps into the high register, and strong tone that Eldridge inspired for the rest of his career.

In 1939, Gillespie was hired by Cab Calloway, who ran one of the finest big bands of the time. In his two years with Calloway, Gillespie developed his playing style, distancing himself from Eldridge somewhat with a mellower sound and eccentric pauses to dwell on dissonant notes. He also met trumpeter Mario Bauza, who introduced Gillespie to the music of Bauza's native Afro-Cuban culture. Afro-Cuban music and rhythms would become an integral part of many of Gillespie's compositions, such as "A Night In Tunisia," and he introduced congas to mainstream jazz, hiring Chano Pozo in 1947. Gillespie was fired from the Calloway band in 1941 after being falsely accused of throwing a spitball during a performance; it was later discovered to be the work of another prankster, but the notoriously strict and demanding Calloway was tired of the pranks and goofy behavior that earned Gillespie his nickname.

Gillespie had been a regular participant in the almost daily jam sessions at Minton's, where the house rhythm section usually included pianist Thelonious Monk and drummer Kenny Clarke, and where young innovators like Charlie Parker and Bud Powell and older musicians with an interest in new music, like Lester Young and Slam Stewart, joined in regularly. By 1945, he was leading a band at the Onyx club on 52nd Street, and in February of 1945, he made the first of a long series of recordings with Charlie Parker that brought both players to the center of attention for the jazz world.

"SALT PEANUTS," DIZZY GILLESPIE AND HIS ALL STAR QUINTET

Ken Burns Jazz, CD 3, Track 9

"Salt Peanuts," recorded on May 11, 1945, exemplifies Gillespie's composition style, and his fondness for complicating and obfuscating forms and harmonies held over from the swing style. The tune itself is a simple, memorable bebop melody over rhythm changes. However, over twenty-five per cent of the performance consists of breaks, introductions, and tag endings that do not fit the chorus structure. If the recording were not otherwise joyful and light, it would be confusing and unbalanced. Unusual for bebop performance practice, the first solo chorus does not occur until nearly halfway through the recording; instead, Gillespie exposits the very simple melody through a very complicated formal structure. After an eight-measure introduction from drummer Sid Catlett, the ensemble joins in with another eight-measure introduction of its own. The head, with its simple and immediately recognizable call and response, has become a jazz cliché; it is first played by Gillespie and Parker in unison, then, after another eight-measure break, it is repeated on alto saxophone alone, with Gillespie singing the title as the response, and Parker improvising a brief solo on the bridge. With over a third of the three-minute performance complete, the first solo chorus is further delayed by two more eight-measure breaks featuring the rhythm section and a chromatic descent by the entire group respectively. Solos by pianist Al Haig and Parker follow (Haig, a graduate of Oberlin Conservatory of Music, was seminal in the development of bebop accompaniment, and one of the few white musicians at the center of the scene). The stop-time break following these solos is expanded to ten measures to allow for Gillespie's bold introduction to his own solo chorus. Gillespie's solo is exuberant, and contains all the trademarks of his style—long flurries of eighth-notes throughout the range of the instrument with unexpected long tones, and tendency towards ending phrases with non-chord tones. Catlett takes the final chorus, rhythmically quoting the head to bring in the rest of the quintet for a repetition of the ensemble introduction, this time used as a tag ending.

After a split with Parker in 1946, Gillespie went on to lead his own big band, which successfully incorporated bebop ideas into its performances, as well as increasing use of Afro-Cuban rhythms and percussion. Unlike many bebop musicians, Gillespie lamented the transformation of jazz from popular dance music to concert music. He continued to consider himself more entertainer than artist, and made frequent appearances as an actor and comedian as well as a musician, and eventually became a public ambassador for the Bahá'í Faith, while still leading a large ensemble, before his death in 1993.

BUD POWELL

Lifelong New Yorker Earl "Bud" Powell is generally and appropriately considered the father of bebop piano. With fantastic technique and the influence of Art Tatum, Powell recast the role of piano as a solo instrument to conform to the busy but spare aesthetic of Gillespie and Parker. By reducing left hand playing from the steady, stride influenced chunk that was still prevalent in the swing style to occasional stabs to punctuate long, speedy melodic phrases in the right hand, he redefined the concept of jazz pianism not just for bop, but for most pianists after him.

Powell was born in 1924, and as a teenager he was already a regular in the audience at Minton's, and sat in with the band occasionally to spell house pianist Thelonious Monk. By 1944, he saw Monk as a mentor, and made his first recordings as a member of Cootie Williams's band. In 1947, Powell made the first of a long series of recordings as the leader of a trio—the first with drummer Max Roach and bassist Curley Russell, although the personnel changed frequently. In the trio recordings, Powell shows himself to be a more versatile musician than his reputation indicates. He was an accomplished composer of complex and difficult works like "Tempus Fugit," and while his left hand is still usually quite spare, he frequently demonstrates a remarkable gift for countermelody that reflects his strong interest in the music of Bach.

In the mid-1950s, Powell's poor mental and physical health affected his playing, and his output became far more unpredictable. He was withdrawn and behaved erratically. He was institutionalized several times between 1945 and 1955, and died, having already contracted tuberculosis, in 1966. It is possible that his psychological condition was exacerbated by head trauma he had suffered at the hands and batons of racist police officers while he was with Cootie Williams; it is almost certain that it was exacerbated by electroshock therapy he received during his first stay in a hospital. Regardless, he was able to perform remarkably well on occasion, such as a legendary performance at Massey Hall in Toronto in 1953 with Charlie Parker, Dizzy Gillespie, bassist Charles Mingus and Max Roach.

OTHER BEBOP MUSICIANS

Trumpeter *Theodore "Fats" Navarro* (1923–1950) had a brief but important career, playing simpler lines with a sweeter tone than Dizzy Gillespie, but with a clarity and force in his playing, and a gift for melody, that would be deeply influential to younger musicians. His most significant work was in a quintet led by *Tadd Dameron* (1917–1965), a pianist and composer who shied away from the limelight and preferred not to take solos, but contributed a number of standards to the bebop repertoire, including "Hot House."

Dexter Gordon (1923–1990) was the major tenor saxophonist of bebop. Like Gillespie and Navarro, Gordon spent part of his early career in Billy Eckstine's band. He derived his sense of swing and lack of vibrato from Lester Young, and had a bold, powerful sound and a penchant for quoting popular tunes in his solos.

The speed and flexibility required of bebop soloists are not properties to which the trombone is well suited. But instead of finding a way to adapt the new style to the capabilities of the instrument, *J.J. Johnson* (1924–2001) adapted the capabilities of the instrument, developing formidable technique that enabled him to play solos as quickly and articulately as a musician that had the luxury of keys or valves.

CHARLIE PARKER

Of all the musicians hailed as geniuses and definitive figures in jazz history, none has been able to generate full-blown obsession like alto saxophonist Charles Christopher Parker, nicknamed "Yardbird," or simply "Bird." So strong was the impact of his brief career that a generation of jazz musicians emulated not just his playing, but his behavior and drug habits. A young fan named Dean Benedetti, who was already collecting Parker's complete recordings as soon as they were released, was so enamored of Parker's music that he followed Parker from Los Angeles to New York, carrying cumbersome portable recording devices to countless gigs. His tapes, discovered recently and released as a boxed set by Mosaic Records in 1990, reveal that he usually paused the recording whenever Parker was not playing. Even in the twenty-first century, jazz scholar Phil Schaap has hosted a daily radio broadcast on WKCR, the radio station of Columbia University, entitled "Bird Flight," for the last twenty-five years. Each show is entirely devoted to Parker's music, and Schaap frequently spends much of his hour to playing the same recording (or even a portion thereof) multiple times. Far from a lone voice in the wilderness, Schaap and his devotion to Parker are well known

to just about every New Yorker with even a passing interest in jazz.

Parker's brief and hard life, marked by abuse of alcohol
and heroin, as well as a stay in Camarillo State Hospital's
psychiatric ward (California), has been romanticized and
transformed into the cliché of the troubled genius that
defines the post-war jazz musician for many. In turn, the
cliché has distorted his place in jazz history and his impact
on jazz and American culture at large. Facts get in the way
of attempts to downplay his biography in favor of his music. Parker dropped out of high school, married at sixteen
years old, moved to Los Angeles for a time, selling his plane
ticket back to New York apparently because he had found
a good connection for heroin, and died at age thirty-four
in 1955—the physician filling out Parker's death certificate
mistakenly believed him to be twenty years older from the
condition of his body. However, as much as Parker may
have lived a script for a television movie of the week, he
was not distracted from making some of the most consistently creative and exciting music of his generation in clubs
and recording studios, and his many recordings deserve approach from a similarly focused perspective.

The appeal of Parker's music is not immediately apparent to many listeners. He played with a hard, bright
tone that frequently breaks into reed squeaks; it seems to
be antithetical to Johnny Hodges' sweet, round tone that
had previously served as the model of alto saxophone.
His rhythmic approach is similarly unforgiving, and he
seems to spin out endless lines of eighth notes, littered
with a few stock phrases and musical quotes that he uses
in the same way from tune to tune. But what would seem
monotonous and annoying in many other musicians becomes forceful and creative in Parker. Repeated listening
reveals the intricacy of his lines and the incredible variety
of ways Parker could work within the strict limits of his
style.

EARLY CAREER

Parker was born in Kansas City, Kansas, on August 29, 1920, and moved with his family across the river to Kansas City, Missouri, in 1927. He began playing baritone and alto horn (brass instruments closely related to the tuba, but higher in pitch)in the school band before switching to alto saxophone in 1933. Within two years, he dropped out of school to take a full time job in the saxophone section of a local swing band led by pianist Lawrence "88" Keyes. For Parker, beginning his professional career at such an early age was not an indication of prodigious talent as much as determination. By his own admission, he could only improvise in one key on a few basic sets of changes, and was laughed off the bandstand after attempting a solo beyond his reach on at least one occasion.

The years before Parker's first recordings in 1940 were marked by intense study. By 1938, Parker was playing in Jay McShann's band, still based in Kansas City, but more popular than Keyes. It was during this time that Parker earned his nickname. According to the most popular explanation, McShann ran over a chicken in his car on the way to a gig, and Parker demanded that he pull over to collect and later eat the "yardbird." In 1939, Parker moved to New York for the first time. For nearly a year, Parker gained experience at jam sessions at Monroe's, and regularly heard Art Tatum perform at Jimmy's Chicken Shack, where he worked as a dishwasher.

Whether Parker was transformed by his time in New York, or simply learned his craft over years of hard work, by the time he returned to Kansas City and McShann, he was knowledgeable and responsible enough to lead the saxophone section, and was a featured soloist on a performance of "Body and Soul" on his first recording session. The McShann band was a hard swinging, blues based band in the Kansas City mold, but even on his first recordings, Parker plays with the double-time runs and emphasis on chord extensions that were the cornerstone of his mature style, and he even briefly quotes Coleman Hawkins' famous 1939 recording. The first recordings were made at a radio station for broadcast rather than commercial sale, but later McShann recordings for public release received positive attention from other musicians for Parker's creative, Lester Young influenced playing (or at least what Young might play after taking Benzedrine). When the band traveled to Manhattan in 1942, Parker parted ways with McShann and stayed in New York.

NEW YORK AND DIZZY GILLESPIE

Parker's move to New York proved successful. After a year or two playing steadily, Parker had honed his skills and developed a reputation as a rising star. He was beginning to outclass his employers by the time he was recording again in 1944, and by April of 1945, Parker was playing in a quintet led by Dizzy Gillespie that played regularly at the Three Deuces on 52nd Street.

Parker's 1945 recordings, first under Gillespie's leadership, and then, on November 26, Parker's first as a leader, stand as the premier recordings of the bebop era. The Gillespie dates included compositions and arrangements like "Salt Peanuts" and "Groovin' High" that became bebop standards almost immediately.

In contrast to Gillespie's tightly arranged recordings, Parker seems to be a much more relaxed leader; only three of the five recordings from November 1945 even use composed heads, and the scheduled pianist never made it to the recording session in the first place. The session itself was chaotic—two pianists, Argonne Thornton (who shortly took the Muslim name Sadik Hakim) and Dizzy Gillespie (an adequate pianist) were in the studio. It is still not entirely certain who played piano on which takes from the session, although Gillespie's dense chords in low registers are fairly easily distinguished from Thornton's more traditional approach. The record label avoided all ambiguity and contractual obligations by listing the pianist as "Hen Gates." Parker had difficulties with his horn that day and broke from the session to find a better instrument. Miles Davis, the trumpeter for the date, fell asleep on the floor of the recording studio, and all manner of musicians and other hangers on were reported to come and go throughout the day. The first tune to be recorded that day, "Billie's Bounce," was a 12-bar blues in a comfortable tempo, which is now frequently performed by high school students; it took the group five attempts until they had a performance worthy of release. At the end of the day, however, the group had completed the definitive statement of Parker's version of bebop, and the record most fans recommend as the one with which to start one's obsession over Parker.

"KO-KO," CHARLIE PARKER'S RE-BOPPERS

Ken Burns Jazz, CD 3, Track 11

The last tune recorded that day, "KoKo," contains what many consider the best example of Parker's up-tempo playing committed to record. The performance begins with a harmonically ambiguous introduction played in unison by Gillespie on trumpet and Parker with no bass or piano. Gillespie only played trumpet on the introduction and coda of "KoKo" on this session. Davis, who had recently left the Juilliard School of Music, apparently could not manage the complex and speedy introduction, although he soloed nicely on other tunes that day. It is possible that he was going through a phase typical of brass players training for orchestral performance: in approaching written music, concentration on producing a solid tone can supersede flexibility until a student is comfortable with traditional technique. Regardless, Gillespie moved to the piano after the introduction, to accompany Parker for two choruses of soloing over the chord changes for "Cherokee," a 32-bar, AABA tune written and first recorded by Ray Noble. These changes had become a staple of Parker's repertoire, and a test piece for young musicians because of a complicated bridge that moves through a number of distantly related keys. Incorporating some phrases that he had developed for these changes over previous years, Parker unleashes an intense barrage of ideas at a frightening pace. At the same time, there is cohesion to his two-chorus solo that makes it memorable, and, with a little practice, even singable. Following Parker's choruses, Max Roach takes an entire chorus to himself using materials as spare as Parker's were bountiful. Almost the entire thirty-two measures consists of eighth-notes played on the snare drum with accents from the bass drum, but Roach's solo has the converse effect of Parker's. Through the use of dynamics alone, Roach creates a clear articulation of the four phrases of the chorus without boring the listener. The recording ends as it began, with Gillespie again on the trumpet, playing the same ambiguous introduction, but truncated by four measures.

LOS ANGELES AND BACK

Almost immediately after his first recording session as a leader, Parker traveled with Gillespie to an unsuccessful stint at a club in Los Angeles. While there, Parker's heroin addiction, which he had developed as a teenager, caught up with him professionally. When he did not take the return flight to New York after the gig, Gillespie made a permanent split with Parker. In the meantime, Parker seems to have had a long, slow mental and physical breakdown. Eight months into his stay in Los Angeles, on July 29, 1946, a late, haggard, and obviously ill Parker took part in a shocking recording session which was later released against his wishes. The four tunes recorded that day show Parker at his very worst, often unable to finish phrases. Three of the four performances are better off forgotten altogether, but Parker's performance of "Lover Man" that day is controversial and interesting. Parker considered it his worst recording, and disavowed it altogether, and many fans agree with his assessment. For some, however, "Lover Man" is beautiful in a ghastly, tragic way. Parker misses his entrance at the beginning of the performance, and falters through the first A section, but by the end of the recording seems to be able to construct a solo around the limitations he had that day. It is a deeply disturbing recording, not to be listened to lightly, but sadly attractive to some. Upon returning to his hotel after the session, Parker set fire to his room (whether it was an accident is unclear), and he was arrested and committed to Camarillo for six months.

The time in Camarillo was well spent. A reinvigorated Parker returned to the recording studio just three weeks after his release, and recorded an unusual set with Errol Garner on piano and Earl Coleman singing. Parker at this point had a darker, mellower tone than he had used previously, but still played the baroque, blues inflected lines for which he was known. He was relaxed, creative, and very productive for the two months he remained in California (even penning a pleasant blues entitled "Relaxin' at Camarillo).

Upon his return to New York in April 1947, Parker reformed his quintet with Miles Davis, pianist Duke Jordan, bassist Tommy Potter and Max Roach, and kept the group together and steadily working and recording for a year and a half. This was the most stable and tightest group Parker would work with. It was during these years that bebop had finally gained a steady national audience, and many of his recordings from the period, including "Scrapple from the Apple" and a fantastic rendition of "Embraceable You," became classics.

NORMAN GRANZ, JAZZ AT
THE PHILHARMONIC, AND VERVE RECORDS

Starting in 1948, Parker recorded exclusively for Norman Granz's Verve recording label. Granz had started his career in jazz as a political activist, organizing jazz performances at Philharmonic Hall in Los Angeles, first to benefit Mexican and Mexican American young people who were involved in racially motivated riots known as the "Zoot Suite Riots," and later to draw attention to racial segregation by insisting on allowing racial integration among his audiences. By 1948, Granz had successfully grown his shows into large tours featuring dozens of musicians, including Louis Armstrong and younger musicians like pianist Oscar Peterson.

Part of Granz's mission in signing Parker was to bring his style to a larger audience, and Parker's recordings for Verve include unusual contexts, such as Latin jazz ensembles and with strings. Granz was also able to reunite Parker with Gillespie for a recording in June, 1950 with Thelonious Monk at the piano for the first and only time in the studio with Parker.

The 1950s saw an increasing unevenness in Parker's output. His work was sometimes in great form, such as the Massey Hall performance of 1953. At other times, his work was uninspired in front of a "pickup" group, (a backing band of musicians local to where a traveling soloist plays that are able to throw together a performance with no rehearsal). By the end of 1954, Parker's career was essentially over; he was beset with health problems from alternating periods of heroin abuse with periods of alcohol abuse, and a few gigs in the beginning of 1955 were unremarkable, if not regrettable. On March 9 of that year, not healthy enough to travel to a gig he had scheduled in Boston, he went to the apartment of jazz patroness Baroness Nica de Koenigswater to rest, and died there four days later.

10

THELONIOUS MONK

There is probably not a single published passage about pianist and composer Thelonious Monk that does not contain at least one of the words "unique," "unusual," or "original" in the first sentence. His music is generally presented in introductory books on jazz in the bebop chapter, and for good reason. As the house pianist at Minton's Playhouse, Monk was at the center of the development of bebop from the very beginning. But most of the time, his music is antithetical to the movement he helped to found. While the emphasis on chord extensions and dissonance in bebop, which he often receives credit for introducing, lend a flexibility and energy to the music of Gillespie, Parker, and others, Monk's use of them often adds to the sense of deliberate awkwardness in his playing that contrasts greatly with his colleagues. In the time Bud Powell might play sixty-four notes, Monk might stab out two or three with a sharp, pounding attack.

Monk was far enough afield from bebop and hard bop that his first recordings as a leader for Blue Note records in 1947 were controversial among critics and did not sell well. Many of his compositions were admired, and in some cases, like "'Round Midnight" and "Ruby, My Dear" were already becoming standards, but as a pianist he was admired mostly by other musicians and cultish initiates. But Monk's influence as a pianist as well as composer can not be over-estimated. Drawing direct inspiration from stride pianists like James P. Johnson and Willie "The Lion" Smith, Monk in turn directly inspired the first generation of avant-garde musicians, especially Cecil Taylor. From this perspective, Monk's career can be placed at the beginning of a split in the jazz tradition between what has been conventionally viewed as the mainstream and avant-garde traditions in jazz.

Monk's life was so focused on music from such an early age that the details of his biography are fairly uninteresting. Born on October 10, 1917, in Rocky Mount, North Carolina, Monk moved to New York with his mother and two siblings to an apartment on West 68th Street when he was four years old, and maintained his residence in that neighborhood for more or less the rest of his life. Raised mostly by his mother alone (his father spent only two years in New York, returning to the warmer climate of North Carolina for health reasons), Monk began studying piano formally at age nine, began playing professionally in his teens, and dropped out of Stuyvesant High School (the city's best high school for math, science, and music, although Monk was not involved in the music program there) to join a touring gospel act in 1935.

By the time Monk was hired as the house pianist in 1941 (a post he would hold for a year, but he continued to join in sessions through the mid-1940s), his style as a pianist and composer was already largely mature, and his early compositions already featured the extended voicings and chromatic motion that became the core of bebop harmony, especially Dizzy Gillespie's version. Rhythmically, however, most of the Minton's scene was more inclined to follow the light, speedy innovations of drummer Max Roach and Kenny Clarke than Monk's own, deliberately off-putting rhythmic sense. Monk plays in fits and starts, and uses silence and unexpected emphases to play against the solid groove of jazz drumming (or, alone, against the striding plod of his left hand)—a frequent trick of Monk's is to enter each measure a half-beat later than he did in the previous one, and to make up for his four-and-a-half beat phrasing with extended silence at the end of the phrase, more or less obliterating the bar line altogether. This kind of rhythmic sleight-of-hand must be distracting for a soloist trying to make the most of a stream of eighth notes over complicated harmonies, and Charlie Parker, for instance, may have spoken highly of Monk's influence and ability as a teacher of harmony, but he only entered a recording studio with him once, in an enlightening 1950 set with Dizzy Gillespie that contains some of the squarest playing of Monk's career.

Despite the respect paid him by other musicians, Monk struggled at the fringes of the New York jazz scene throughout the 1940s and much of the 1950s. His difficulties were exacerbated in 1951 when, taking the rap for his friend Bud Powell, Monk was arrested for drug possession. At the time, unfortunate local laws punished performers with any drug charges by revoking the "cabaret license" necessary to perform in nightclubs in Manhattan, and Monk spent six years unable to legally play much in his hometown. Real, public success and admiration eluded Monk until the late 1950s, largely on the strength of his recordings for Riverside records, with whom he signed a contract and began recording in 1955. In 1957, his cabaret card was reinstated, and he was able to make more public appearances in New York, including a number of highly publicized concerts at Town Hall in the late 1950s, and a long stand at the Five Spot Café in 1957, where his Quartet, with John Coltrane on tenor saxophone, brought the attention and respect of jazz enthusiasts to himself, the Five Spot, and the young Coltrane.

That is not to say that Monk's early career left no recorded legacy. Between 1947 and 1955, Monk entered the recording studio around fifteen times, leading sessions first

"EPISTROPHY," THELONIUS MONK

Ken Burns Jazz, CD 3, Track 15

"Epistrophy," which Monk first recorded in 1948 in a quartet that featured Milt Jackson on vibraphone, is an excellent example of how the appeal of Monk's music may have been lost on the bebop generation, but found its audience among the young early avant-gardists of the 1950s. In the 1948 recording, Monk opens the tune with a loping triplet figure that barely keeps up with the rest of the group throughout the head. It takes a keen sense of rhythm to elicit a sense of having no rhythm, and similarly, Monk's ear for chord voicing, and a touch much more subtle than it seems, gives him the ability to make any piano he plays sound like an out of tune upright, and it seems as if he is able to play bent notes that are physically impossible on a piano. The form of "Epistrophy" is also unusual and complicated, but built with simple, economic materials that only make things more difficult to follow. Technically, the tune is a 32-bar AA'BA structure, but with such a high degree of repetition harmonically and melodically that both initial A sections come across as a single, massive chromatic smear. The first eight measure A section of the composition consists of a repeated melodic line over two chords related by half step, and repeated a whole step higher for the second four bars. The process is repeated in reverse for the second eight measures. With such a high degree of repetition, and harmonic structure that does not clearly indicate tonal direction, Monk anticipated by a good ten years or more the modal jazz of Miles Davis and the formal obscurantism of Cecil Taylor. Monk continues his trickery during his solo in 1948 version, playing isolated phrases, often closely related to the simple melody, but often in unexpected ways. At one point, Monk plays a phrase, and repeats it as if he had lost the beat and come in early, but a single repeated note at the end of the phrase makes his awareness of time apparent.

for Blue Note, and later for the Prestige label (which, with its New Jersey location and pay-per-session policy, gained a reputation as a "junkie label," for musicians with drug habits and no cabaret card to pick up some quick cash—regardless, the label was also responsible for many great albums from musicians like Miles Davis and John Coltrane during periods of stylistic development).

Between 1954 and 1971 (at which point Monk was performing less and less—he retired from recording in 1972 and made his last public appearance in 1976, as poor mental and physical health took his energy until his death after a stroke in 1982), Monk made about six LPs' worth of solo recordings. Alone, Monk's approach to playing is different than with a band, which is still rhythmically and harmonically awkward (but like a boxer, his awkwardness makes his work at once difficult and successful), but with a clear stride in the left hand. His repertoire for solo performance follows suit: while certain original compositions, like "'Round Midnight," received solo treatments on several occasions, Monk was more likely to concentrate on early popular and swing melodies, like "Just A Gigolo," or "Sweet and Lovely." Monk's sound at the piano is still unmistakably his, and heavier than someone like Fats Waller, with far denser harmonies, but his solo recordings show Monk sidestepping bebop altogether and taking an essentially older approach to playing His sparse, tricky playing in combos set the stage for Cecil Taylor and other pianists of the late 1950s and 1960s.

THE 1950S
The Beginning of Jazz Postmodernism

The shadow cast by the first generation of bebop musicians was long, and the changes they made to previous ideas about jazz, both musically and culturally, were permanent. In removing their music from dance halls and recasting jazz as concert music, the bebop scene created the pure jazz artist, who was free to follow his interests without the limits of an easily understood genre, or even a strong, danceable beat. The 1950s, largely as a reaction to the challenges made by Charlie Parker, saw the formal entry of jazz into postmodernism. While previous to the 1950s, it was fairly easy to apply a teleological model of jazz history without being too far off the mark (New Orleans begat Chicago, which begat Fletcher Henderson, which begat swing, which begat bebop), by around 1955, it is nearly impossible to describe a single trend among jazz musicians.

Traditionally, jazz introductions have pointed out three major movements in jazz in the 1950s: hard bop, essentially an extension of bebop ideas; cool jazz, a group of mostly white musicians, and Miles Davis, who had a more reserved, quieter aesthetic than the hard bop scene; and

Postmodernism is a word with a multitude of definitions and connotations. Most frequently, it is used to describe artistic and critical movements of the late 1970s and 1980s, during which time many artists strove to break down barriers between genres, styles, and even between art and nature. Arguments have been made in the past, however, that postmodern ideas can be traced back to as early as the 15th century, and critics have tended to use the word in their own way to make their own points.

In the context of this book, "postmodernism" is used to contrast modernist ideas of history, in which each generation progresses to the next logical step, improving what their parents had done. After bebop, obvious trends among the increasingly varied substyles of jazz began to break down. And postmodern jazz musicians were less interested in taking the ideas of earlier musicians to the next level. Rather, they were primarily interested in developing their own voice without regard for any perceived direction that jazz as a whole might be taking.

"Third Stream," a concept coined by jazz scholar and composer Gunther Schuller and epitomized by the Modern Jazz Quartet, that combined concepts from bebop with structures and harmonies from European art music. While this book follows suit in order to avoid confusion, it should be pointed out that these three divisions are somewhat arbitrary and do not reflect the kind of stylistic splintering that happened after bebop. While it is sometimes difficult to understand how Count Basie and Benny Goodman can both fit under the stylistic umbrella of "swing," it is nearly impossible to understand common trends and ideas between Jimmy Giuffre and Dave Brubeck—the "cool" umbrella must be immense to cover that much ground. Additionally, there is plenty of music from the 1950s that does not fit the commonly acknowledged subgenres of early post-bop jazz.

The second incarnation of Count Basie's band, for instance, was fully contemporary and current by 1950s standards, and could only have developed its style after the swing era proper had closed. And while the avant-garde designation is generally reserved in jazz texts for radical musicians of the 1960s, the fact of the matter is that three of the central figures of avant-garde jazz—Cecil Taylor, Sun Ra and Ornette Coleman—had all produced major works and had active careers before 1960.

While musicians were contending with their new, post-bop status as artists, they also dealt with new possibilities in recording due to advances in technology. Columbia began releasing LPs in 1948. By switching materials for phonograph discs from brittle shellac to strong, flexible polyvinylchloride, it was possible to fit the grooves on a record much closer together, and the grooves themselves could hold greater detail, allowing the record to be spun more slowly. LPs ("Long Playing" records) could contain about twenty-five minutes of continuous music before it became necessary to flip them over, about five times as much as older recordings could contain. Furthermore, magnetic tape, which had been available experimentally for sound recording since around the mid-1930s, was finally stable enough to become the preferred method for professional recording. With tape, it was not only possible to record longer segments of sound than the metal disks they had replaced, but all kinds of trickery was possible. Tape allowed for editing and splicing, so mistakes could be removed, and a single recorded work could be compiled from the best moments of separate takes. Additionally, overdubbing and speed change created new ways to make music in the studio, and as early as the late 1940s, adventurous musicians pop guitarist Les Paul experimented with multi-track performances, sometimes accompanying themselves at altered pitch and speed. On one level, new recording technology allowed jazz recordings to come closer to live performance without time limits, while on another, it allowed a new approach to music making completely divorced from the live experience.

HARD BOP AND SOUL JAZZ

For many musicians, some of whom had been active in the bebop scene from its beginning, the solution to the problems set forth by Dizzy Gillespie and Charlie Parker was simply to continue making music in their style. The death of Parker in 1955 was seen by most critics and musicians as a turning point in jazz history, however, and in an effort to demonstrate the formal end of the bebop generation, they began to call their music hard bop.

There is little, if anything, about hard bop that can be easily seen as harder than bebop. Hard bop musicians still stuck to the small combos, 32-bar AABA and 12-bar blues structures, and virtuosic solos that their predecessors established as the norm. If anything, the name critics gave to this music drew a contrast to the concurrent subgenre of cool jazz. What was new about hard bop was mostly on more subtle levels: the range of tempo is a little wider, with fast numbers faster and ballads slower; and drummers tend to play a bit more aggressively. But most of the stylistic changes happened in the constructions of the heads, which generally sound less like the unison melodies composed by Parker or Gillespie.

MAX ROACH AND CLIFFORD BROWN

In 1954, Max Roach started a cooperative quintet with a young but astonishing trumpeter from Wilmington, Delaware named Clifford Brown. Brown, whose assertive, flamboyant style was derived from the playing of Fats Navarro, Dizzy Gillespie, and Miles Davis, had a tragically short career, dying in a car accident in 1956 at the age of twenty-five. In the two years of his association with Roach, fortunately, he recorded about twenty LPs' worth of music, and he had already established himself as the top hard bop trumpeter through his work in Europe, where he traveled with Lionel Hampton in 1953.

In their general approach to performance, the Brown-Roach Quintet stayed close to the bebop that Roach was instrumental in developing. They recorded several standards, and most of the new compositions stayed close to the 32-bar AABA structure. Roach had developed his style since his years with Parker and Gillespie, playing with even more independence between hands and feet, and taking long solos that often had a melodic quality, alluding rhythmically and timbrally to the head. Brown's style as a soloist, instantly recognizable and a model for many players after his death (most notably Freddie Hubbard), featured long sequences of eighth notes, with a warmer sound than Gillespie's, and often more rhythmically square and less syncopated.

It was the compositional and arranging style that was new, however. Brown was a gifted composer and arranger who filled his heads with unusual tricks. His composition "Joy Spring," for instance is unusual in modulating up a half step between the first and second A sections of the 32-bar AABA tune (better represented as AA'BA). And his unique arrangement of Cole Porter's "I Get a Kick Out of You" is so rhythmically complicated that critics and musicians still disagree about how to notate it. While the arrangement contains the same number of beats, and the same sixteen beats per phrase as the original tune, the group kicks off in clear measures of three beats each, and continues to alternate between triple and duple meters unpredictably while still maintaining accessibility. It is telling that, in the original recording, even a group of this caliber played the head slightly slower than the rest of the recording.

SONNY ROLLINS

Starting in 1955, the tenor saxophonist for the Brown-Roach Quintet was Sonny Rollins (b. 1930). He was already well known and fresh from the first of several sabbaticals from public performance he still periodically takes to concentrate on his playing. From the beginning, Rollins played with a dark, gruff tone more akin to Coleman Hawkins (but with much less vibrato) than Lester Young. His first recordings (he had worked with Bud Powell, Thelonious Monk and Miles Davis in the early 1920s) show a tendency towards the same long phrases of eighth-notes that most bebop musicians used. But as he developed his style he infused his playing with more rhythmic variety, and with a sense of wit and humor that he shares with Monk and few others.

In the period between his first and second sabbaticals (his second was 1959–1961), Rollins was in demand as a sideman and led his own groups in a number of recordings. His choice of repertoire was unusual—part of his humor was displayed in his ability to use silly, unconventional pop songs like "I'm an Old Cowhand" as the basis for long, engaging performances. In choosing unconventional repertoire, often with simple, catchy melodies, Rollins provided himself with direct inspiration for his solos. His habit of referring to the head during his solo in often surprising contexts remains part of his style, and can be heard clearly, for instance, in his picking apart of the opening notes of "St. Thomas," perhaps his best known composition.

While Rollins never completely abandons bebop harmony or melody conventions, he has always been interested in applying them in daring ways. In the 1950s, Rollins was among the first to lead a trio with no piano, in the 1960s he wrestled with the music (and musicians) of Ornette Coleman and John Coltrane, and he embraced rhythm and blues and electric instruments after yet another sabbatical in the early 1970s.

ART BLAKEY AND HORACE SILVER

Pittsburgh-born drummer Art Blakey, who coined the term "hard bop" as the title of a 1956 LP, played powerfully and aggressively, and with a pronounced backbeat that brought elements of gospel, rhythm and blues, and early rock and roll to his music. In contrast to the sophisticated, tricky compositions and arrangements of the Brown-Roach Quintet, Blakey's Jazz Messengers focus on simple, relatively sparse, and strongly blues inflected music. With obvious nods to the newly popular soul music of Ray Charles, Blakey's music, and the music of his disciples, came to be known as funky jazz or soul jazz.

Blakey began his career with Kansas City pianist Mary Lou Williams, and he worked with many of bebop's brightest stars in Billy Eckstine's band, but he gained his fame with a quintet formed in 1955 with pianist Horace Silver. It was the first lineup of a band he would continue to lead for the next thirty-five years—the Jazz Messengers became known as a training ground for young post-bop musicians. The constantly shifting lineup included, in various incarnations, trumpeters Kenny Dorham, Lee Morgan, Donald Byrd and Wynton Marsalis; saxophonists Jackie McLean, John Gilmore and Wayne Shorter; and pianists Horace Silver, Cedar Walton and Keith Jarrett.

Silver left the Jazz Messengers in 1956 to lead his own combo, and still performs his original compositions today. Silver's playing is as sparse, simple and bluesy as Bud Powell's was busy, complicated and harmonically sophisticated. Many of his compositions have become standards, such as "Song For My Father" and "Filthy McNasty."

COOL JAZZ AND THE WEST COAST SCENE

Other musicians, less enthralled by the Latin and R&B rhythms and extroverted solos of bebop than by the

HORACE SILVER AND THE JAZZ MESSENGERS, "DOODLIN'"

Ken Burns Jazz, CD 4, Track 1

Recorded in 1954, this performance of an early incarnation of the Jazz Messengers clocks in at over six minutes, comfortably taking advantage of the increased capacity of LPs over four-minute singles. Throughout the performance, this 12 bar blues shows the deep influence of the simplicity and repetition of gospel, soul, and rhythm & blues, as well as the sparse textures and pounding touch of Thelonious Monk. The head itself is un-usually long – three choruses of composed music take up the first 70 seconds of the recording, and the head follows the same AAB structure over 36 bars that blues lyrics have traditionally followed over 12.

Aside from the unusual structure of the head, the perfor-mance could easily have taken place in Harlem in 1945 by older musicians – tenor saxophonist Hank Mobley, especially, has a similar, if slightly more rhythmically varied, approach to Charlie Parker.

increasingly complicated harmonic approach, contrasted themselves from Parker and Gillespie with relaxed tempos, restrained dynamics, and increased subtlety. Musicians from various backgrounds and cities, with dozens of differ-ent styles and approaches to music making, but who shared this restraint and interest in gentle, introspective music (as well as white skin more often than not), have been grouped by convention as purveyors of cool jazz, and associated with the West Coast.

The jazz scene in Los Angeles in the 1950s was domi-nated by white musicians with the traditional technique and music reading skills necessary for a career in studio work and film soundtracks. Many of the best Californian musicians, such as saxophonists Art Pepper and Bud Shank, had spent time in an unusual (and unusually large) big band led by Stan Kenton. The Kenton Orchestra—which at times employed a full string section and classical wind instruments unusual for jazz, like oboe, horn and tuba—was at once popular and very experimental. Kenton was receptive to bebop, and hired arrangers like Pete Rugolo and Bob Graettinger who were interested in contemporary European art music composers like Paul Hindemith and Edgar Varese. Many of the Kenton band's stranger arrangements are still quite popular among avant-garde jazz fans, and Kenton's harmonic and textural daring certainly rubbed off on the West Coast scene.

However, many of the musicians associated with cool jazz have also been falsely grouped with the West Coast by lackadaisical critics. One of the seminal groups of cool jazz, the Miles Davis Nonet, consisted largely of New York-based musicians, and pianist Lennie Tristano and his students were mostly East Coast players. New York even had its own progressive swing band as a source of the music. Claude Thornhill's big band, while never at the top of the record sales charts, played a few unusual arrangements throughout the 1940s that showed a strong bebop influence and foreshadowed Davis's *Birth of the Cool* sessions.

THE TRISTANO SCHOOL

Born in Chicago in 1919, blind pianist Lennie Tristano spent most of his career in New York, and played with a somewhat austere, harmonically sophisticated style that emphasized melody and counterpoint. While he did not record as frequently as others, his work had a strong impact on many musicians and critics, and his recordings include very early examples of tape manipulation, editing and even free improvisation.

Tristano was also a focused and dedicated educator, and many of his students (and band mates) followed his lessons and practice routines with a nearly cultish dedication. As a teacher, Tristano focused largely on ear training, and had his students learn solos from classic recordings by Louis Armstrong, Lester Young, Bud Powell, and others, regardless of their instruments. Among his students, saxophonists Warne Marsh and Lee Konitz and guitarist Billy Bauer had the most public careers.

Tristano's complicated and precise playing style often featured long streams of eighth notes phrased with unusual cross accents. The aptly titled "Cross Current," from his 1949 LP *Intuition*, for instance, was a 32-bar AA'BA composition (related loosely to rhythm changes), in which the theme began with five-beat phrases played against solid 4/4 time. This kind of precision and emphasis on melodic movement, reminiscent of Bach, does not lend itself well to a strong, aggressive rhythm section. Tristano himself is usually quite subdued under the solos of his students, and the Tristano school had difficulty finding appropriate drummers. While some experiments with different drummers worked well, such as a surprising 1961 LP by Lee Konitz featuring Elvin Jones (who normally out-banged even Art Blakey), for the most part, Tristano school recordings feature fairly anonymous time keeping with wire brushes, or no drums at all.

DAVE BRUBECK

One of the most commercially successful jazz musicians of the 1950s and 1960s was pianist Dave Brubeck, the son of a classically trained pianist mother and a one time composition student of Darius Milhaud. Brubeck applied techniques and forms from European art music to his accessible, breezy jazz quartet to such acclaim that he appeared on the cover of *Time* magazine in 1954.

Brubeck's first group was an octet that worked with many of the same ideas in California that the Miles Davis Nonet would use in New York. In 1951, Brubeck hired alto saxophonist Paul Desmond to complete a new quartet. Desmond was a brilliant, if low key, player. His solos tended towards the lyrical, and he featured a soft attack and a smooth tone with a hint of air.

Brubeck was able to capitalize on the new concept of jazz as art. With compositions that used forms reminiscent of eighteenth-century European art music, a classical pedigree, and a large audience of college students, Brubeck was among the first jazz musicians to tour concert halls of universities and colleges, during a time when the academy saw jazz as party music. His most successful LP, *Time Out* from 1959, consisted entirely of original compositions by Brubeck and Desmond, and was largely focused on music written in time signatures other than 4/4 (still very unusual at the time). At once experimental and easily grasped, tunes like "Take Five" and "Blue Rondo A La Turk" (the title is a play on a work by Mozart, and copies its form, but applies an asymmetrical meter of 2+2+2+3 common in Tur-

THE DAVE BRUBECK QUARTET, "TAKE FIVE"

Ken Burns Jazz, CD 4, Track 5

Based entirely in the unusual time signature of 5/4 (five beats to the measure instead of the traditional 4), "Take Five" begins with a loping vamp that became, and remained, so popular that what must have seemed at one point disconcerting has now become cliché. Appropriately, this rhythmically unusual performance is centered around an extended drum solo by Joe Morello, who plays over the repeated vamp of the A section (the bridge of this 64 bar AABA structure is heard only during the head).

key) firmly ensconced Brubeck and his music in American middlebrow culture.

GERRY MULLIGAN AND CHET BAKER

Baritone saxophonist Gerry Mulligan had already partici-pated in the prototypical cool jazz ensemble, as a performer and arranger for the Miles Davis Nonet (discussed in the next chapter) before he formed the piano-less quartet with trumpeter Chet Baker that gained him the most attention of his career.

The quartet, formed in 1952, was surprisingly sparse, with the subdued, simple drumming of Chico Hamilton (who could be wildly adventurous in other projects), and comping under solos provided by the other wind. Their per-formances depended on the lyricism of the two horn play-ers. Mulligan, one of the only baritone sax players to make a serious name for himself as a soloist, had a surprising flexibility and concentrated his playing on the upper reg-ister of his horn. The effect was not unlike Lester Young's playing in the 1930s, although the context was quite differ-ent. Baker was destined for legendary status, with movie star good looks, an extremely quiet, lyrical playing style, a smooth, almost girlish singing voice, and a heroin addiction that probably ended his life.

THIRD STREAM

In response to a trend among cool jazz musicians to use forms, harmonies and instruments more commonly heard in European art music, orchestral hornist/composer/jazz scholar Gunther Schuller began to speak and write about a "third stream" of American music, found halfway between jazz and classical traditions. He worked as a composer, producer and educator to further its development as an independent genre of music. The idea that jazz musicians could be interested in classical music, and vice versa, was nothing new by the late 1950s, as already exemplified by Duke Ellington, George Gershwin, Paul Whiteman, Darius Milhaud, and dozens of other musicians of "both" strains. But both classical music and jazz had undergone radical changes since World War II, and this kind of conscious effort to shape culture exemplified the spirit of the times, and brought about many major works of both European influenced jazz and jazz influenced European art music.

12

MILES DAVIS

If a single musician had to be chosen to summarize jazz since World War II, it would surely be trumpeter Miles Davis. From his first recordings with Charlie Parker in the 1940s to his final experiment in hip-hop jazz in 1991, Davis consistently found himself as the focal point of a new jazz substyle. Whether he was recording the first definitive works of cool jazz, modal jazz, fusion or smooth jazz, Davis had a distinctive, instantly recognizable approach to his instrument. His fondness for the Harmon mute, an unusual aluminum mute that he played close to a microphone for a deep yet pinched sound, has become a trope in American music; used in any context, the mute implies coolness and sophistication. His simple lines and frequent cracked notes belied a technical sureness to his playing to such a degree that debate over his ability still rages, despite the evidence of rapid, difficult phrases pulled off with ease until the last few years of his career (still much later in life than many trumpet players who begin to show the decline of their abilities).

Beyond his constant musical innovation, Miles Davis's impeccable clothing, irascible temper and apparent (although not real) disregard for his audience made him the apotheosis of cool. Davis approached his career with a sense of detached stylistic amnesia, often willing to play repertoire from his past, but never in the same way he had before. He developed a relationship with producer Teo Macero that allowed Davis to leave his recording projects incomplete, assembled the studio editing desk while Davis went on to new ideas. His friendship with Jean-Paul Sartre, marriages to celebrities like actress Cicely Tyson, and interest in offbeat art, such as the music of offhandedly nihilistic proto-punks the Stooges, all added to his reputation as jazz's existentialist superstar.

Davis has been discussed in print more than perhaps any other jazz musician. The number of book-length works

THREE BIOGRAPHICAL TREATMENTS OF MILES DAVIS

Among the dozen or so book-length studies of Miles Davis currently in print, three stand out as particularly valuable biographical works. J.K. Chambers' *Milestones: The Music and Times of Miles Davis* (DaCapo Press, 1998) remains the longest and most detailed study of Davis's life and music. While Chambers's lack of sympathy for Davis's later work distorts his descriptions, the first half of the over 800-page book is thorough and expertly researched and written. Davis's own autobiography (ghostwritten by Quincy Troupe), *Miles* (Simon & Schuster, 1990) is a very entertaining read – one of the highlights of jazz writing as literature. While littered with the coarse language that Davis used in his daily speech, the book also provides a fascinating insight into the way one of the most image conscious figures in jazz chose to present himself. Ian Carr's *Miles Davis: The Definitive Biography* (Thunder's Mouth Press, 2006) depends largely on the former two books as source material, but serves as a much needed unbiased and detailed survey of Davis's life and music after 1967, including the most articulate defense of Davis's controversial music of the 1980s.

on his life, career, and cultural impact is quite large, with multiple biographies of over five hundred pages in print. In order to avoid similar length, this chapter concentrates on providing a grasp of the various stylistic periods of Davis's career. Any number of biographies provide ample supplemental information about Davis's middle-class background, brief training at Juilliard Conservatory, multiple wives, encounters with the law, and other personal details.

BEBOP WITH PARKER

The musical partnership between Charlie Parker and Dizzy Gillespie may have been legendary, but Parker's association with the young Miles Davis was longer and more productive. Davis was nineteen years old and in a recording studio for only the second time in his life when he played on the November 26, 1945, session that resulted in Parker's first real classic recordings. Davis continued his relationship with Parker, sometimes as sideman, and sometimes as leader, through 1948, and then sporadically through the 1950s.

The 1945 session with Parker was an inauspicious debut, but by 1947, Davis had developed into a confident soloist and composer, with a style and sound that owed nearly nothing to the influence of Dizzy Gillespie or of his peer Fats Navarro. As a trumpeter, Davis played with a full, dark tone that reflected classical training (as well as a mushy articulation that reflected bad playing habits), and he concentrated largely on the middle register of the instrument, shunning the flashy high notes that had been part and parcel of jazz trumpet since Louis Armstrong. He also tended to swing his eighth notes heavily, and emphasize the ninth of chords frequently.

Davis has sometimes had the habit of crediting the compositions of his performances incorrectly, stealing the work of others and, puzzlingly, offering his own work as that of family members and friends instead of himself. Often, it is difficult to determine which of his compositions are his and which are by others, and there is a similarity of approach among first generation of bebop composers that complicates things. It is likely, though, that his first recordings as a leader, which feature rare performances of Parker on tenor saxophone, contain original music by Davis. In works like "Donna Lee" and "Sippin' at Bells," Davis takes a similar approach to Charlie Parker as a composer, working fast moving melodies around standard chord changes. If there is a clear distinction to Davis's work, it is his frequent use of repeated step-wise figures.

BIRTH OF THE COOL

In 1948, Davis began showing up at informal gatherings in the basement studio apartment of Gil Evans on 55th Street in Manhattan. Evans had been the chief arranger for Claude Thornhill throughout the 1940s, and the self-taught white arranger with an interest in classical music was a fast friend and mentor to the classically trained black jazz musician. Evans's apartment had become a salon of sorts for musicians like Lee Konitz, George Russell and Davis, where all manner of discussion took place about composition, arranging, and how to capture the heavily orchestrated sound of the Thornhill band without the financial strain of a large orchestra. From the ideas formed at these discussions (mostly by Evans and Gerry Mulligan), Davis formed a nine-piece band with the unusual instrumentation of trumpet, alto saxophone, trombone, french horn, baritone saxophone, tuba and rhythm—all of the colors available in the Thornhill band with none of the expense of multiple-horn sections. Armed with arrangements by Evans, Mulligan, and pianist John Lewis, the group performed a few dates in the summer of 1948 at the Royal Roost, a chicken restaurant on Broadway that booked big jazz acts, between sets by the Count Basie Orchestra. As a few radio broadcasts that have been recorded and released have indicated, the band was not a hit by any stretch, receiving only a smattering of applause and audibly ignored by the talkative crowd during ballads. The following year, Capitol records, restocking their roster of jazz musicians after another year-long recording ban, signed Davis to a contract and recorded the group, which had been reformed for the sessions, for a series of 78s. The recordings were compiled on an LP in 1957, entitled *Birth of the Cool*, and have been collectively known by that name since.

Even with such a brief existence, the *Birth of the Cool* band had tremendous impact, and the recordings are landmarks of post-bop jazz. With its unusual instrumentation and gifted arrangers, the nonet made a major break from solo-oriented bebop and focused on tight, complex arrangements. On tracks like Evans's arrangement of "Moon Dreams," for instance, barely a single note is improvised, and individual voices only appear for a moment or two for color before dropping back into the ensemble sound ("Moon Dreams" is also fascinating structurally: the coda is nearly as long as the single chorus the group plays, and the effect is that of the somewhat sentimental melody melting into a dissonant swirl before fading away). Even in up-tempo numbers, like Mulligan's arrangement of Davis's composition "Deception," the emphasis is on ensemble color and unusual harmonic voices—while the unusual theme is followed by a chorus and a half of solos, it is the comping by the rest of the band that leaves an impression.

THE PRESTIGE ALBUMS

After the success of the *Birth of the Cool* sessions, Davis immediately distanced himself from cool jazz and explored the fast tempos and driving tempos of bebop once again. In 1951, he signed a contract with the Prestige label, and made a number of LPs for them for the next five years. Unfortunately, he also spent much of that time battling a drug problem, and the ill health and inconsistent playing that accompanies it. The resurgence in Davis' playing and creativity happened in 1954, with a trio of successful recording sessions. That April, he recorded "Walkin'" and "Blue 'n' Boogie" in a sextet that featured Lucky Thompson on tenor saxophone, J.J. Johnson on trombone, and a rhythm section consisting of pianist Horace Silver, bassist Percy Heath and drummer Kenny Clarke. The two performances took full advantage of LP technology, clocking in at over thirteen and eight minutes respectively, and comprised the first classic recordings of hard bop. Two months later, with Sonny Rollins replacing Thompson, he recorded four Rollins originals, and with a Christmas Eve session featuring Milt Jackson on vibraphones and Thelonious Monk on piano, the collective recordings, released as *Bag's Groove*, formed the masterpiece of his work as a hard bop trumpet player.

THE FIRST GREAT QUINTET

Following the successes of 1954 and a well received performance at the Newport Jazz Festival the next year, Davis, typically, burned all his bridges to head in a new direction. He formed a quintet with young, promising musicians, signed a contract with Columbia (before fulfilling his contract with Prestige, which led to some delayed releases and half-serious recording sessions), and began to change his sound once again. The new group was a carefully constructed exercise in balance. Tenor saxophonist John Coltrane, who was developing his "sheets of sound" style that will be discussed in Chapter 14, played busy, double time runs that contrasted greatly with Davis's own lyrical, spacious phrasing. The fiery drumming of Philly Joe Jones (whose near-telepathic sensitivity to Davis's own playing made him the core around which the group was constructed) was set against the light touch of pianist Red Garland. And bassist Paul Chambers was his own balance—a solid walker with a powerful sound, he was also capable of horn-like, melodic soloing reminiscent of Slam Stewart in its phrasing.

The First Quintet (obviously so-named only after the formation of a Second Quintet in the 1960s) became one of the most popular small groups of the 1950s, but not without controversy. As a leader, Davis was more focused on the music performed than the niceties of public performance, and he developed a reputation for having disdain for his audience. He regularly turned his back to the crowd (not as a rude gesture, but in order to focus on the band), refused to announce his show (by 1956, he had no voice to do so anyway—he permanently damaged his vocal chords during a shouting match entered too soon after an operation, and spoke in a whisper for the rest of his life), and demanded a maximum three sets per night during a time when most bands were expected to do double that work.

Davis's first album for Columbia, *Round About Midnight*, was recorded in 1955, while Davis was still under contract with Prestige. The album has some transitional qualities; Davis introduces his new sound with some old tunes, performing Monk's "Round Midnight" and Parker's "Ah-Leu-Cha," which he had performed since the 1940s. Davis' playing on the album is more lyrical, sparser, and more assured than it had been previously. His Harmon-muted solo on "Round Midnight" sounds appropriately half-asleep. Where other jazz musicians traditionally ornament a melody with extra notes, Davis simplifies things, by playing whole notes or longer, steadily descending in pitch with every phrase. Coltrane's solo on the next chorus is a double-time release of all the harmonic and rhythmic tensions established by Davis.

GIL EVANS

Throughout the late 1950s and early 1960s, Davis maintained a close relationship with Gil Evans, and while the quintet format was continuing to enjoy success both live and on record, Davis and Evans made a series of recordings with large ensembles that explored a different approach to music.

The large group recordings of Evans's arrangements, starting with *Miles Ahead* in 1957, are perhaps the first great jazz recordings wholly dependent on studio techniques. In *Miles Ahead*, Davis's producers began using the technique of tape splicing, editing together the best parts of several takes to create a version that only exists in the recorded form. And Evans's consistently colorful arrangements took full advantage of multi-tracking (the use of a separate area of tape for each instrument to allow separate processing) and mixing. In *Sketches of Spain*, a 1960 LP that features Davis in a flamenco-influenced setting, there are frequent moments in which two or three clarinets are mixed significantly louder than the entire brass section, creating textures and sonorities that are extremely difficult to achieve in a live setting.

Harmonically, the Gil Evans collaborations present the beginning of a striking departure from bebop. Working from a strong interest in early twentieth century French composers, who frequently explore single chords and scales for minutes at a time, Evans had begun slowing the harmonic rhythm of his arrangements radically, and on his arrangement of "I Loves You Porgy" from 1958's *Porgy and Bess*, he provided Davis with a scale on which to improvise instead of a composed melody. Clarinetist Jimmy Giuffre had been working with a similarly reduced harmonic language derived from American folk music by that time, and the rising popularity of rock during the late 1950s also indicates a general trend in American musical taste towards harmonically simple and static playing. But for Davis, Evans's approach, in combination with conversations with pianist and composer George Russell, were beginning to permanently affect his style and approach to playing.

KIND OF BLUE

John Coltrane was fired from the quintet in 1956, largely because Coltrane's heroin habit was getting the best of him. After two years spent conquering his addiction, rebuilding his playing, and developing his style as a member of the Thelonious Monk Quartet, Coltrane rejoined Davis. Now the group had grown to a sextet with the addition of the blues- and funk-inflected hard bopper Cannonball Adderley on alto saxophone, and briefly in 1958 with pianist Bill Evans—a more overtly romantic player than Garland, with a subtle touch that echoed Gil Evans's (the two men were not related) orchestrations as well as any single instrument can. Evans was replaced by Wynton Kelly by 1959, but returned for one recording session that March.

Kind of Blue, which consists almost entirely of first complete takes ("Flamenco Sketches" required two), and which was recorded with almost no rehearsal over two days in 1959, became the best selling jazz recording ever made, and still sells around 5,000 copies every week. Equal parts jazz landmark and make-out album, it rewards the listener on every level, and established modal jazz as a sub-genre that is still being explored today.

The opening track, "So What," is probably the most popular from the album, and the solos, especially Davis', became necessary memorization material for young musicians exploring modal jazz. Like many other terms commonly used in jazz, "modal jazz" is a partially true misnomer; what distinguishes the performances on *Kind Of Blue* from previous albums is not strict adherence to specific modes (types of scales), but a radically slowed harmonic rhythm. "So What," for instance, is a 32-bar AABA tune (the head is a simple call and response between the bass and the rest of the group, whose two-note reply rhythmically echoes the title), but the two sections contain only one chord each. After the first two phrases are played in D Dorian (also called "jazz minor," the Dorian mode is similar to the natural minor scale, but with a raised sixth degree), the bridge is nothing but the A section raised a half step, to E-flat Dorian. With the inevitable return of the A section, a two chorus solo contains twenty-four consecutive measures without a single chord change.

It is the final track on *Kind Of Blue*, however, that contains the most radical approach to performance, and would have made a better example of modal jazz had its unusual structure caught on among other musicians. "Flamenco Sketches," which is based roughly on the introduction to Bill Evans's "Peace Piece," contains no head and no fixed rhythmic structure whatsoever, beyond the steady, quiet pulse of bass and drums throughout. Nothing is provided to the musicians beyond a set series of scales on which to build an improvised solo of any duration. On the two re-corded versions of the work, the four soloists each take a different approach to their playing, with different amounts of time spent on each mode and different ways of signaling the change of modes to the rest of the band. Evans's solo on both takes is particularly stunning.

THE SECOND GREAT QUINTET

The success of *Kind Of Blue* had the effect, unfortunately for Davis, of bringing sufficient attention to John Coltrane and Cannonball Adderley that they felt compelled to leave the sextet to start their own bands. Partly due to the lack of a wind section, but also due to Davis's pattern of ennui after success, Davis spent much of the early 1960s searching for a way to rebuild his group and regain his status as the center of attention after Ornette Coleman's radical music stole the spotlight in 1959.

The rebuild took some time. After some more conservative recordings with new, and sometimes old musicians (both John Coltrane and Philly Joe Jones appeared on the best of his transitional albums from this period, 1961's *Someday My Prince Will Come*), Davis finally had settled on a rhythm section, at least. By the middle of 1963, Davis was working with three young, virtuosic, and daring musicians: Ron Carter, a fleet-fingered bassist with a background in cello; Herbie Hancock, a pianist who combined Bud Powell's fast and inventive lines with Bill Evans's touch and harmony; and, perhaps most remarkably, seventeen-year-old Tony Williams on drums. Williams was a shocking prodigy— the year before, he made his recording debut with Jackie McLean and was already a driving drummer with an extreme dynamic range and a raging sense of tempo, able to play polyrhythms that seasoned veterans had trouble following.

Finding a saxophone player to complete the quintet proved difficult. It was a chore to keep up with such a virtuosic and daring rhythm section. George Coleman was the initial choice, and he appears on the first recordings of the new quintet, which make up half of the album *Seven Steps To Heaven* (the other half is the last recording of a previous quintet, who sound tired and boring in the context of the later recordings). Coleman's playing may have been too similar to John Coltrane's. Regardless, he was out of the group after a year, and after a brief experiment with Sam Rivers on tenor (here, the contrast was too great, and while Rivers is a fantastically creative player, he sounds more at home in free jazz contexts), Davis hired Wayne Shorter away from Art Blakey's Jazz Messengers to complete the group. Shorter is another Coltrane disciple (in 1964, it was nearly impossible to find a young tenor player who was not), but also a gifted composer of rhythmically and harmonically tricky tunes that fit the newly conceived group perfectly.

In the Second Quintet, Davis largely took the lead from his young group. The lightning reflexes of the rhythm section, and the harmonic complexity of Shorter's writing and playing gave the group a rhythmic drive that was new to Davis's music, especially after years with a reputation as a ballad specialist. And the risks the group took at times tore at the conventional structural framework—the performances at the Plugged Nickel in Chicago in 1965, recorded and finally released in 1987, feature twenty minute performances of tunes with only a passing glance at the head, before the group bursts forth into complicated improvisation that borders on totally free. On record, the group was more tightly arranged, though no less adventurous. The title track of the 1967 LP *Nefertiti*, a typically complex Shorter composition, contains not a single from winds or piano solo; instead, the band plays the head repeatedly while Tony Williams chatters away on the drums with astonishing creativity. More typically, the recorded work of the Second Quintet featured the same kind of heated group exchanges that they played live, but with stricter adherence to the already complicated heads.

EARLY ELECTRICITY

By the late 1960s, the American popular music scene had made the transition from jazz and vocals to rock and R&B, and Davis, always seeking to break new ground, could not help but react. He had seen Cannonball Adderley's 1960s group, which featured Josef Zawinul on electric piano. In late 1967, he acquired one, and replaced the acoustic piano with it—Hancock learned about the change by arriving at a rehearsal and finding no piano to play. Over the course of the next year, Davis expanded his interest in electronic instruments and in the rhythms and sonorities of rock and R&B, particularly the sculpted noise of Jimi Hendrix and the driving funk rhythms of James Brown and Sly & the Family Stone. Over the course of three or four years, Davis shocked many jazz purists by releasing increasingly rock-influenced albums with the increasing use of electronics, which climaxed on record with the best selling 1968 album *Bitches Brew*, and in live performances with the transformation into what has sometimes been called the Third Quintet.

The Third Quintet forms the core of the larger ensemble that performs on *Bitches Brew*. As young as Davis's rhythm section had been, they were not quite capable of, or willing to, provide the powerful rock feel Davis was approaching (a year later, all three would be playing their own versions of jazz/rock fusion, with Williams's band Lifetime coming closest to total abandonment of jazz). The new group featured Chick Corea on electric piano(he was more comfortable with the instrument than Hancock was at the time), drummer Jack DeJohnette, who was Williams's equal in terms of technique and creativity, but who drove the group even harder; and English bassist Dave Holland. *Bitches Brew* expanded the ensemble greatly, adding second (and sometimes third) piano, electric bass, percussion, bass clarinet, and perhaps most notably, the electric guitar of John McLaughlin, who will be discussed later in the book.

Assembled in the studio with editing by producer Teo Macero (as would be Davis's modus operandi until he left Columbia in 1986), *Bitches Brew* is a muddy, indistinct, rambling mess of exquisite beauty. There is little in the way of formal structure. Composed heads are followed by long, rambling jams, and solos have been all but completely replaced by group interaction. For jazz purists unwilling to take the step away from acoustic instruments, *Bitches Brew* sounded like a rude gesture. For the rest of the country, though, it was a necessary part of every rock fan's record collection.

FUSION

As Davis became more interested in busy, driving rhythm sections and the sustained sounds of electric instruments, he became much sparer as a player himself, spitting out short phrases with long spaces between them. By the 1970s, Davis had learned to apply electronics to his own playing, using a wah pedal (ironically, invented to allow electric guitarists to imitate plunger mute effects of trumpet players) to manipulate his heavily amplified trumpet playing. He also played dense chords on an electronic organ to signal structural changes to the rest of his band. As much as the music sounded like a cluttered mess to many audiences, Davis kept extremely tight control of his performances, conducting and cueing the band constantly when he was not playing. And the short phrases that Davis used more as interjections than solos often contained some of the most virtuosic playing of his career—five or six notes in the upper and lower registers of the trumpet in an odd, angular run.

The personnel changes Davis periodically made had become a regular part of his work by 1970. His group after *Bitches Brew* and until he temporarily retired from music in 1975 had become a continually shifting lineup, sometimes with multiple pianists, sometimes with none at all. Michael Henderson, an electric bassist with an R&B resume, had become a semi-permanent fixture in the band by 1972, but some musicians, like pianist Keith Jarrett, came and went seemingly at random. Often, the fusion group at their most effective featured the electric guitar duo of Pete Cosey and Reggie Lucas. Lucas was a solid and reliable rhythm guitarist, while Cosey, always in sunglasses, and physically massive, provided strange, consistently creative, and occasionally noisy solos.

WARNER BROTHERS AND PROTO-SMOOTH JAZZ

After retiring in 1975, and with his health and playing ability in question, Davis returned to performing again in 1981. His approach in the 1980s was much the same as it had been before his retirement, but pop music in the 1980s had changed considerably. Models for Davis's pop elements now were Prince and Michael Jackson, instead of Jimi Hendrix and Sly & the Family Stone. His biggest hits from the last decade of his career were covers of recent pop songs: Michael Jackson's "Human Nature" and Cyndi Lauper's "Time After Time."

As his hits suggest, the rejuvenated Davis was more willing to return to the ballad style that had brought him his greatest fame. His playing, however, remained sparse, and the groups behind him were often synthesizer-drenched pop bands, heavily influenced by the music of the 1980s pop charts and MTV.

In terms of personnel, Davis continued to seek out younger, gifted musicians who could carry out his new ideas. In two instances, his choices were controversial. On the 1986 album *Tutu*, Davis chose to forgo a band altogether, instead playing over backing tracks provided in their entirety by multi-instrumentalist Marcus Miller. Miller is a gifted electric bassist, and the best tracks on Tutu are bass heavy grooves, like the reggae inflected "Don't Lose Your Mind." But on other tracks, overdependence on state-of-the-art music technology has dated the album horribly, and yet other moments depend too much on Davis's skills at lyrical playing; when he is not soloing, it could be elevator music. And by 1989, Davis began to showcase a "piccolo bassist" who went by the single name Foley. Foley, whose bass is tuned like a guitar with the top two strings missing, played in a style heavily influenced by Eddie Van Halen, whose virtuosic guitar solos worked brilliantly in his own rock band, but heard in Davis's context, sounded like inappropriate grandstanding. Foley's reputation as a spotlight hogging megalomaniac was not helped by his arrogant attitude in interviews, and his career seems to have begun and ended with his tenure with Davis.

In his last two projects, Miles Davis took a look back at his career, and leaped forward into new territory at the same time. His last album, *Doo Bop*, was an experiment in fusion once again, this time attempting to place his playing in the context of rap music, which was just finding its feet as a steady genre of music. His choice of rappers and producers for this project was unfortunate. Easy Mo Bee was not at the cutting edge of his field, the way Davis's sidemen had traditionally been, and the album was a preventable failure. His final performance, on the other hand, was a triumph, and the only career retrospective in which he participated. At the 1991 Montreux Jazz Festival, Davis participated in a concert of his music, featuring the first public performances of many of the large ensemble works he recorded with Gil Evans. Although Davis was ill and had mostly lost his chops at this point, he still had presence on the stage, as well as the capable playing of Wallace Roney, a Davis protégé who handled much of the soloing while Davis rested between statements of the melody. The concert and its subsequent release on record was a reconciliation between Davis and the jazz enthusiasts who felt abandoned by him since the late 1960s.

13

AVANT-GARDE JAZZ
OF THE 1950S
AND EARLY 1960S

By the second half of the 1950s, bebop and its offshoots had been the predominant music of the jazz world for a good ten years. Dependence on complicated harmonies and on negotiating chord changes at higher and higher rates was beginning to limit the possibilities for improvising soloists. Like knitting, creating a bebop solo had become a repetitive and structured affair—when there is only time to fit two or three notes over a chord, there are only a few ways to structure a thirty-two measure solo while maintaining a personal style and sound.

A similar trend had been occurring among academic composers who were working in the European art music tradition, where the dominant style of composition in the 1950s was total serialization. Most composers' work consisted of setting up strict orders of pitches, dynamics, attacks, timbres, etc., and working through permutations of these series to create the final piece. The trend began to break down after word spread of American composer John Cage's

1951 composition *Music of Changes*, a solo piano piece that rivaled the best works of total serialists like Pierre Boulez and Karlheinz Stockhausen, but written entirely through the process of flipping coins. When it became apparent that the control of serialism resulted in music that could just as easily be written completely at random, most composers felt compelled to find other ways to work.

In jazz, there were a handful of musicians, some influenced by the crisis of classical music, others willfully ignorant of it, who felt that the limits imposed by bebop were insurmountable. These musicians worked at restructuring the rules of the jazz tradition entirely. For some, like pianist Cecil Taylor and soprano saxophonist Steve Lacy, the solution to the problems of bebop were found in the sidestepping of bebop established by Thelonious Monk. Tradition-minded avant-gardists like Charles Mingus and Sun Ra looked backwards, developing ideas established by Fletcher Henderson and Duke Ellington in new ways. And a third group, led by alto saxophonist Ornette Coleman, kept the surface appearance of bebop, with small groups and blues inflected solos, but rejected the fundamental rules of chorus structures and pre-arranged harmonies.

Within a few years, the avant-gardists discussed in this chapter would be in good company, as an entire generation of musicians established a new sub-genre of jazz guided by their work. But in the late 1950s, these musicians developed their new approaches to music in near isolation, and much of the new music was guaranteed to reach the public as a source of controversy at best, and apathy at worst. In the case of Ornette Coleman, controversy worked to his benefit; as the center of just about every heated discussion about jazz in 1959, Coleman rose to prominence quickly, and is still more often appreciated for his early albums than for his music since 1970. Sun Ra's groups, on the other hand, fought for attention and lived in poverty for decades.

CHARLES MINGUS

Bassist and composer Charles Mingus might have bristled at the news that he was included in the avant-garde chapter of a book on jazz; he bristled at most news, anyway—his short and violent temper are legendary. If the case can be made that he rightfully belongs in the soul jazz tradition (established by Horace Silver), the new formal concepts and collective improvisation in his music, plus his efforts to re-form jazz on almost every musical and extra-musical level certainly merit his inclusion here.

Born in Nogales, Arizona, in 1922 and raised in Los Angeles, Mingus started playing the bass in his high school jazz band after unsuccessful experiences he had while studying the trumpet and cello. After a few years of study with a classical bassist and with jazz bass and tuba player Red Callender, Mingus spent the 1940s backing several well-known acts, including Louis Armstrong and Lionel Hampton. He first came to national prominence as a member of a trio with vibraphonist Red Norvo and guitarist Tal Farlow. With the Norvo Trio, Mingus used the space allowed him in the drummer-less group to establish himself as a virtuosic soloist with a powerful sound, the heir apparent to Duke Ellington bassist Jimmy Blanton. Mingus left Norvo in 1950, after he was prevented from making a television appearance as the only African American member of the racially integrated trio He settled in New York, where he played frequently with Charlie Parker and Bud Powell and became a member of the Jazz Composers' Workshop, a semi-formal organization of musicians and composers that included Teo Macero.

The kind of cooperative self-governing espoused by the Jazz Composers' Workshop became a guiding factor in many of Mingus's business decisions. In 1952, he started his own record label, Debut, with Max Roach, and by 1955 he ran his own workshop ensemble. In 1960, to considerable attention, he put on a rebel jazz festival, across the island from the Newport Jazz Festival, in protest of Newport's apparent curatorial policy of ticket sales over artistic vision. The Rebel Festival was run in all aspects by the musicians who took part, and was, by most reports, much more musically successful than the Newport festival, which booked several folk and pop acts. By then, Mingus was also forgoing notation, preferring to dictate parts to his musicians orally, which resulted in a more cooperative and social approach to group performance.

Mingus' music, on the surface, owes a great deal to the rich orchestration of Duke Ellington and the energy and simplicity of the music of Southern black churches. Structurally, his devotion to Ellington is apparent in the increasing use of large scale forms such as 1956's complicated suite *Pithecanthropus Erectus*. Mingus, however, went further with formal complexity than Ellington, and often arranged parts in a more linear fashion, avoiding the balanced repetition of sections that Ellington employed. A common technique of Mingus, and a very effective one, is to build a piece slowly over several repetitions of a riff, adding soloists until the performance is built into chaos. He used this very effectively on "Haitian Fight Song," recorded in 1955 and again in 1957. At other times, he disrupts his own forms with radical shifts in tempo and odd phrasing—"Fables of Faubus," recorded in 1960 with what was probably his best quartet, features a seventy-one measure theme and several tempo changes, as well as vocals that reflect his usual combination of moral indignation and general anger.

By 1963, Mingus was performing as a pianist as well as a bassist. His piano playing was capable if not virtuosic, but he approached his performances with the same energy and chaos that infused his earlier work. He also recorded *Black Saint and the Sinner Lady*, an ambitious, multi-movement work for large ensemble, which was constructed in the recording studio. With the available technique of editing and overdubbing, the moments of collective, free playing and

"ORIGINAL FAUBUS FABLES," CHARLES MINGUS

Ken Burns Jazz, CD 4, Track 10

This first recording of "Fables of Faubus" is saturated with the kind of anger and demand for respect at the core of Mingus's approach to music and the music business. Recorded live at a club appearance, Mingus's spoken introduction begins with an admonition to the audience and employees to remain silent throughout the performance, and a dedication to the "all American heel." What follows is a deeply complicated head, full of feel changes and odd phrase lengths, as well as biting lyrics about the Arkansas governor (and other white politicians) and his racist policies, although the anger spills over into a general condemnation of racism, the Ku Klux Klan, and fascism. In their respective solos, both Eric Dolphy on alto saxophone and Mingus reference "When Johnny Comes Marching Home" (Dolphy more explicitly), drawing the apt comparison between the then current civil rights struggles and the Civil War.

shifts of tempo became even more complicated. Shortly after that recording, however, he went through an extended period of low activity. His preference for long stands at one club over touring (he felt it was best to develop an audience and his music at the same time in residency settings), and his cantankerous personality and uncanny ability to consistently alienate record company executives were contributing factors to this lull.

Mingus suffered from Lou Gehrig's Disease (properly known as Amyotrophic Lateral Sclerosis or ALS, the disease is likely genetic in nature, its onset is unpredictable, and its progression is rapid and eventually fatal), and by the late 1970s he was wheelchair-bound and unable to perform. However, the score for an incomplete work from 1961, *Epitaph*, a kind of career retrospective in the form of a suite for thirty musicians was discovered after his death in 1979, completed by Gunther Schuller, and premiered and recorded in 1982.

SUN RA

Sun Ra was born Herman "Sonny" Blount in Birmingham, Alabama, in 1914, but that is beside the point. As Sun Ra, the name he had adopted on a permanent basis by the mid-1950s, he created a mythology and philosophy that rendered his early life moot. Even as a bandleader, he recorded an unknown number of singles and albums (often estimated to be in the hundreds), and released them seventy-five copies at a time, often without catalog numbers or even cover art. As an active arranger and producer in the doo-wop community in Chicago in the 1950s, it can sometimes even be difficult to determine whether some of his work can even be classified as a part of the jazz tradition. But without question, Sun Ra's particular bizarre version of jazz, with its exoticism and science fiction trappings, free improvisation, and burning swing (even without benefit of tempo) were a topic of conversation among just about everyone interested in jazz by the 1960s, and a deep influence on many of the free jazz, funk, and rock musicians that heard him.

A performance by the Sun Ra Arkestra (or the Myth Science Arkestra, or the Intergalactic Arkestra, or any of the several names under which the band performed) was a multimedia affair long before "performance art" was so named. Concerts regularly featured fanciful costumes, dancers, chanting, and parades, and they frequently ended in parking lots. The music could range from Fletcher Henderson arrangements to tunes from Disney movies to torrents of electronic noise, and a semi-coherent amalgam of Egyptology, outer space travel, and racial politics was always present in lyrics and commentary.

All this pomp and circumstance, as well as Sun Ra's deliberately absurd version of his own biography (he claimed to be an angel from Saturn, and by 1981 he regularly announced himself with the greeting, "Some call me Mister Ra, others call me Mister Ree. You can call me Mister Mystery.") belied an experienced and thoughtful pianist and arranger; he spent time in both capacities with the Fletcher Henderson Orchestra, and a fine ear for harmony.

After his tenure with Henderson in 1946, Sun Ra settled in Chicago, where he began leading a band and producing local vocal groups. By 1953, he was already Sun Ra, and the Arkestra featured the formidable reed section of Marshall Allen, John Gilmore, and Pat Patrick. Gilmore in particular was a stunning and innovative soloist—he had played with Earl Hines the year before he joined Ra, was a member of the Jazz Messengers in 1964, and was admired by John Coltrane. Regrettably, much of the critical attention given to him has been spent lamenting his choice to remain with Sun Ra for forty years. While there is no doubt that Gilmore could have been an important leader on his own, he was still an important part of the Arkestra, and Ra's arrangements, which were much more carefully worked out than they often appeared, seemed to have been a sufficient challenge for him.

The Arkestra probably had a more local than national impact in Chicago, but their loose, exotic performances and recordings left a much stronger mark through their inspiration of funk pioneers Earth, Wind and Fire, and on the next generation of Chicago avant-gardists (discussed in Chapter 17). Sun Ra focused his disorganized recording projects at the time on his own compositions, which show the inspiration of the popular Polynesian-style lounge acts of the time, as well as Dizzy Gillespie's Latin influenced big band; his generically exotic percussion and harmonies were accentuated with song titles that reflected an interest in ancient Egypt, like "Ankhnaton." A tape of a 1960 performance, first released some forty years later on the Atavistic label with the title *Music from Tomorrow's World*, however, reveals that the band also played standards like Gershwin's "'S Wonderful." Sun Ra was also already using electric piano by then, and continued his interest in electronic instruments throughout his long career.

Sun Ra and his Arkestra relocated to New York in 1960, living communally to save costs and to allow for Sun Ra's habit of calling rehearsals suddenly at any hour (they eventually relocated to Philadelphia to escape the considerable cost of living in New York). In 1961, Sun Ra recorded an album for the Savoy label that had promoted Charlie Parker. *The Futuristic Sound of Sun Ra* contains the most accessible Sun Ra on record, with a reduced ensemble that features the three reed players as well as bassist Ronnie Boykins. Sun Ra's pianism is in the foreground on this record—with a light touch and a busy left hand, he shows himself to be an accomplished hard bop player.

It was one of the last times his abilities as a player would go unquestioned. In New York, where he worked tightly with his group in near isolation, but also with the support of a nascent free jazz scene, Sun Ra began to expand the free improvisation that had always been an element in his music, and he explored pure noise for its own sake. Every member of the Arkestra had percussion instruments at their disposal, and frequently, the entire group participated in a shower of tempo-less percussive sound, alternating with simple chants about outer space from vocalist June Tyson that are taken up by the rest of the band. As a soloist, Ra was still playing in a hard bop style at times, but often preferred a more gestural approach on loud synthesizers. One of the best examples of his electronic playing at its wildest, or one of the most unbearable if the listener is not prepared for it, can be found on 1973's *Concert for the Comet Kohoutek* (not released until the early 1990s). Close to half the concert is devoted to Sun Ra's nearly violent torrents of electronic sound, and the effect is almost visceral. But ever the traditionalist, even at his freest his concerts are well balanced with simple, swinging riffs and chants. As he aged, Sun Ra made his experience with Fletcher Henderson more apparent, often playing Henderson's charts at blistering speeds, and playing fairly faithful arrangements of songs from Disney movies. After his death (or his return to Saturn) in 1993, the Arkestra continued to perform, first under the direction of Gilmore, and then after Gilmore's death, under Marshall Allen, who still performs in his early eighties.

CECIL TAYLOR

Few musicians have been as discussed, argued over, and misunderstood as pianist Cecil Taylor. Often portrayed as a free improviser, an atonal composer, and a pitchless keyboard banger, he can be all three on occasion but on the whole is none of them. Critics often spend more time arguing about his uneasy relationship with the press and intimidating musical density than they do approaching his music. He has become an international symbol for music that is good for you, but not good to listen to.

That reputation is a shame—his music is not nearly as ugly as many writers might indicate. But any confusion about Cecil Taylor is also partly Cecil Taylor's fault by design. Since his first LP in 1955, Taylor has made a career of obfuscating his own, often traditional ideas in his music and his public portrayal. He is prickly and suspicious in interviews, and protective of both his biography and his musical means.

Taylor was born on March 25, 1929, in Corona, Queens, New York, the only child of a middle-class family in a racially mixed neighborhood. His mother, who had grown up in New Jersey, around the corner from Duke Ellington's drummer Sonny Greer, was a dancer, and she encouraged

Cecil in music from an early age. He began piano lessons at age six, and may have studied percussion with his uncle, William Ragland, who was a professional in New York. He certainly attended performances with Ragland, and was a fan of Chick Webb, Cab Calloway, and especially Duke Ellington, whom he still cites as a primary influence.

Taylor is among the first significant musicians to have undergone formal training in jazz, as a composition and arranging major at New England Conservatory in Boston, where he received a Diploma in Popular Music with a concentration on arranging in 1951 (his education is frequently misrepresented as one in classical music). At NEC, Taylor became acquainted with contemporary European art music to a greater degree than many jazz musicians, and the influence of Bartok and Stockhausen on his playing has often unfairly given his music the reputation of belonging in the classical bin more than the jazz bin at record stores. He also worked with and listened to musicians living in or passing through the thriving Boston jazz scene, and he developed a strong fondness for Dizzy Gillespie, Miles Davis, and especially Thelonious Monk.

After a few years on the Boston jazz scene, Taylor moved to New York in 1955, where he formed a quartet with soprano saxophonist Steve Lacy (whom he knew in Boston), bassist Buell Neidlinger and drummer Dennis Charles. The quartet was an unusual mix of backgrounds—Neidlinger was a classically trained, orchestral bass player, while Charles was a self-taught drummer who often used ideas from the folk music of his original home in St. Croix—and reflected the cross-influences of Taylor's music at the time. The Taylor quartet (or trio, since Lacy was a part-time member at best, and left the group first over Taylor's reluctance to perform and his insistence on constant rehearsal) made their first recording (and held their first long-term stand, at the Five Spot Café in Greenwich Village) to considerable attention and acclaim in 1955. But the best example of Taylor's early work is the 1959 LP *Looking Ahead!*, with Earl Griffith on vibraphone instead of Lacy. In many respects, the Cecil Taylor Quartet followed the lead of hard bop bands like Art Blakey's, with strong, powerful, and swinging drumming, standard changes and clear blues elements. Three traits of Taylor's playing, however, set him apart from the jazz mainstream, and continue to be distinguishing characteristics of his music today: his virtuosic technique (genre aside, few pianists are capable of Taylor's velocity or his control of attack and dynamics), the obfuscation of traditional elements, and sudden shifts in style from phrase to phrase. "Excursions On a Wobbly Rail," the closing track of *Looking Ahead!*, is a good example. The tune features solos on the changes of Duke Ellington's "Take the A Train," but the performance begins with a brief introduction in a remote key and free of tempo, and the first sixteen measures of the head are dissonant and sparsely scored, so that the net effect is confusion for the listener until the second chorus, when Neidlinger's walking bass outlines the harmonic structure more clearly. As a soloist, Taylor switches among three distinct styles, often within a single phrase. At times, he plays disjunct, staccato lines that almost seem accidental; suddenly he might play a rapid line reminiscent of Bud Powell, or a harmonically rich alternation of chords between the left and right hands. During Griffith's two solos on the performance, Taylor is a busy accompanist, often blurring the line between solo and group improvisation. He relies on riffs, a light touch, and clear harmony, with an obvious nod to Ellington. However, where Ellington is simple and relaxed, Taylor is restless—the year before he recorded *Looking Ahead!*, Taylor had driven trumpeter Kenny Dorham out of the recording studio with his busy comping—but for musicians who were more willing to explore ensemble textures, it was an exciting approach to hard bop.

Within a year or so of recording *Looking Ahead!*, Taylor was working with entirely different musicians, and he was beginning to take a more radical approach to composition and performance. After several years with Dennis Charles, Taylor hired Sunny Murray on drums. Murray was among the first drummers to be genuinely comfortable in tempo-less music for long stretches of time, and Taylor began to work largely in such a context, experimenting with totally free improvisation, and composing melodies with indeterminate rhythms.

Over the course of the 1970s and 1980s, Taylor continued to explore large scale, tempo free compositions with the Unit, in larger groups, and solo. With his dissonant and often percussive playing and the dense textures of his group

"CONQUISTADOR," CECIL TAYLOR UNIT

Conquistador!, Blue Note B2-84260, Track 1

By 1966, when he recorded two major works for Blue Note, Taylor concentrated solely on original music, often with little guidance given to the musicians in his ensembles (he had stopped using notation in 1961, following the lead of Charles Mingus). Of the two Blue Note LPs, *Unit Structures* is the better known – a difficult, dissonant and intimidating work for large ensemble that frequently serves as an introduction and immediate turnoff to Taylor's music. *Conquistador!* is more musically successful. Scored for an expanded group (Taylor had been calling his group the Cecil Taylor Unit by the 1960s, and based it around a core quartet with bassist Henry Grimes, drummer Andrew Cyrille, and alto saxophonist Jimmy Lyons) and taking up one side of an LP, "Conquistador" begins with Taylor's usual disconcerting and barely related introduction, but settles into a long, multi-themed modal exploration centered around the Dorian mode in D (like "So What" before it). Throughout the work, Taylor constantly changes the texture and style of his performance, and plays a dizzyingly intense and virtuosic solo.

performances, Taylor can often appear to be the center of a barely controlled train wreck—and he often is, although it is usually a beautiful train wreck, and there is usually melody and traditional harmony at its heart. His frequent solo performances, such as 1976's *Indent*, benefit from the clarity of one performer's ideas, and are often easier to take. Taylor is an engaging and intense soloist who can stun listeners into concentrated silence with a single chord. Since 1990, Taylor, still a prickly and energetic performer and composer, has mellowed somewhat, or at least made the Duke Ellington and blues influences in his music more immediately apparent. He has also incorporated his poetry and dance into performances more, and he frequently begins concerts with unusual explorations of his own scratchy voice and somewhat affected accent. His poetry, in a sense, is a new way to distract the audience from the more traditional core of his musical approach. Now approaching his eightieth year, Taylor continues to push his own limits, and occasionally the limits of his audience, in unexpected ways.

ORNETTE COLEMAN

When Cecil Taylor began his career in New York in 1955, he was, for many critics, the center of attention and the beginning of a new future for jazz. By 1959, Taylor was completely overshadowed by the almost absurdly public New York arrival of Texan Ornette Coleman, an alto saxophone player with a much more recognizably jazz sound, but a more fundamentally radical approach to performance than Taylor.

At the core of Coleman's music throughout his career has been a stubborn refusal to accept the standard chorus structure of the jazz tradition as law. As a composer of hundreds of memorable melodies, some full of lament, but most jovial and witty, Coleman consistently avoids repeating what he has already written on just about every level. Solos in Coleman's jazz work follow the spirit of the melody, but not the harmonic or rhythmic structure. Everyone in his groups is encouraged to take the music in whatever direction they see fit without regard to the meter or harmonic plan of the head. Even traditional concepts of pitch have been questioned by Coleman from the very beginning of his career. He frequently plays bent notes, and non-bent notes that simply aren't in traditional pitch; fans call it "expressive intonation," and detractors call it "out of tune."

Coleman, born March 19, 1930, in Fort Worth, Texas, and raised in poverty, started playing alto saxophone at the age of fourteen before he switched to tenor and ultimately back to alto. Within a year of taking up music, he was already attending high school by day and helping to support his family by playing in rhythm and blues bands at night. He was also already getting into trouble for playing bebop at small town dances. He settled in Los Angeles in 1954, after arriving with a touring rhythm & blues act, and took a job as an elevator operator to support himself. As he worked, he developed his own ideas about music and found musicians who were willing to work with him (and others who ridiculed his approach). After two LPs recorded in Los Angeles in 1958 and early 1959, his cause was championed by pianist John Lewis, who arranged for Coleman and trumpeter Don Cherry to attend Lewis's new Lenox Jazz School in Massachusetts. Here, Coleman had a profound effect on some older musicians, notably clarinetist Jimmy Giuffre. After his summer in Lenox, Coleman settled in New York and in November of 1959 began a celebrated tenure at the Five Spot, already known as the club at the cutting edge of the jazz avant-garde since Cecil Taylor's 1955 stand.

At the Five Spot, Coleman became a cause celebre and the center of a media circus. Coleman was a perfect topic of conversation when he first arrived in New York. He was handsome and affable, but often wryly cryptic when he spoke. He played an unusual instrument; his alto saxophone was constructed from white plastic, and while it was often dismissed as a toy by his detractors, it was actually an excellent horn—Charlie Parker played one for a time. His music was radical for jazz purists, but its warm appeal was obvious to others—the ideal starter for a heated discussion over a drink or two. For fans, appreciation of Coleman's music became a status symbol; he was literally publicly embraced by classical composer and conductor Leonard Bernstein, for instance, who jumped on the stage after a performance to give Coleman a hug. Others considered his radical approach a fraud, asserting instead that he could not follow chord changes, and that he propagated a false rationalization to cover up the fact that he could not understand music at all. Whether a listener found the music brilliant or awful, it was compelling, and Coleman made a series of LPs for Atlantic records between 1959 and 1962 that rank as classics—now available as an eight-CD boxed set that uniquely serves as an excellent introduction to one man's music and remains worth every penny for the experience.

Listening to the Atlantic recordings fifty years later, it can be difficult to understand what all the fuss was about. The radical aspects of Coleman's music have been subsumed and surpassed by radical musicians from the 1960s onwards, and the only shocking sounds are the off-center pitches in Coleman's solos. Instead of stubborn radicalism, contemporary listeners hear the remarkable interaction of the piano-less quartet, the ebullient creativity of Coleman's and Cherry's solos, and the singable if quirky compositions. On some tracks, like "Ramblin'" or "Chronology" (which is based on rhythm changes), the harmonic structure and phrasing are held more or less in tact by the powerful and warm sound of Charlie Haden's walking bass. On other tracks, like "Congeniality," Coleman takes advantage of the freedom from structure and writes multi-sectioned themes with changing tempos and meters.

"CHRONOLOGY,"
ORNETTE COLEMAN QUARTET

Ken Burns Jazz, CD 4, Track 9

Coleman's quirky take on rhythm changes reduces the A section of the head by one measure, resulting in a 29-bar AABA structure. Once the head has been played, however, all bets are off.

For the most part, Haden and Blackwell are content to approach the solo accompaniment as if this were a more traditional performance on rhythm changes – however, Haden in particular shows the lightning quick reflexes necessary to follow Cherry and Coleman down occasional harmonic twists and turns, using chromatic lines to blur harmonic direction in is his playing.

One session from the Atlantic recordings stands out as unusual even by Coleman's standards, and was a particularly influential work for the free jazz musicians of the 1960s. *Free Jazz* (the title came before the musical movement was named) is scored for a double quartet. The Ornette Coleman Quartet (Coleman, Cherry, Haden and drummer Ed Blackwell) is joined by a quartet of the same instrumentation: Eric Dolphy on alto saxophone, trumpeter Freddie Hubbard, Scott LaFaro on bass and Billy Higgins on drums. For thirty-seven minutes, both quartets play at once in a multi-sectioned piece that superficially sounds like total chaos. In fact, *Free Jazz* is a very carefully organized recording, with specific roles placed on each instrument, on the instruments in pairs, and on the two quartets as separate but cooperative groups. Throughout much of the recording, Haden and Higgins (in the right channel of the stereo recording) keep steady time, while LaFaro and Blackwell (in the left) play with the time somewhat more freely, although mostly at double time. *Free Jazz* was recorded immediately after Coleman had spent two days in the studio with Gunther Schuller, and the tightly controlled form, combined with freewheeling improvisation, reflect the influence of the Third Stream experiments in which Coleman had just participated.

The Atlantic recordings were a strong enough legacy that Coleman is often still pigeonholed by their style. It became too much even for Coleman, who retired briefly in 1963, partly out of fear of offending if he developed too much musically. When he returned to performance and recording after two years away, Coleman had developed quite a bit. His sound and approach to soloing had changed. He developed an edgier tone, and concentrated on shorter, more angular phrases than he had before, and he began performing on trumpet and violin, which he had taught himself to play during his sabbatical. Characteristically, Coleman took a unique approach to each of his new instruments, which have accounted for at least a few minutes of every concert since he started playing them. On the violin, which he holds left-handed, Coleman plays across all four strings frenetically, adding more texture than pitch to usually energetic, uptempo settings. His trumpet playing is a bit more traditional, but not much, with a concentration on the upper register and long, chromatic lines.

Coleman was also overflowing with creative ideas. He seemed to always have at least two or three major projects going at once, and he accomplished this feat by charging exorbitant fees for occasional performances instead of touring with one act for little pay. For his 1971 LP *Science Fiction*, Coleman recorded with a number of different projects, sometimes performing the same works in different styles with different bands. He even recorded a throwback to his origins in rhythm & blues. Coleman also began an interest in composition for classical ensembles, which climaxed with his 1972 work for orchestra, *Skies of America*. Since the early 1970s, he main focus as a performer has been Prime

Time, a large group of electric instruments (often a double trio of guitar, bass and drums with Coleman rounding out a septet) that combines his unique approach to form and harmony with a funk sensibility. On 1973's *Dancing in Your Head*, Prime Time performs two versions of Coleman's "Theme From A Symphony"—it is the group at their best.

14

JOHN COLTRANE

Many of the best known figures in jazz are discussed in reverential tones, and their recorded solos are often learned note for note, repeated, and paraphrased as if they were sacred texts. Only tenor saxophonist John Coltrane has been properly sanctified, by a small Christian church in San Francisco that literally worship him along with apostles and prophets.

To a large degree, Coltrane's legacy is one of combining the musical and the spiritual. By the middle of the 1960s, when he was a bona fide superstar, Coltrane was titling his music with references to religion on a habitual basis—"A Love Supreme," "Ascension," "Meditations," etc.—and in interviews he spoke openly about his religious beliefs, which involved a kind of pantheistic devotion to self-betterment. Before he had any kind of spiritual awakening, however, Coltrane was guided by his own drive to improve. He was not a natural musician, but one who practiced with dedication and diligence. He was still changing and refining his ideas and playing style in the final months of his life.

His career was remarkably short when weighed against his impact on jazz and the extraordinary degree of change in his music. Like his early mentor, Miles Davis, Coltrane seemed to reconstruct his concept of music with every couple albums. Unlike Davis, Coltrane did so in only twelve years as a recording artist. Starting with his first national exposure as a little known but competent and already controversial side man for Davis in 1955, Coltrane became a lightning-quick, note heavy hard bop soloist, then the best known and most thorough exponent of modal jazz, and then the public face of New York style free jazz, all before Davis bought his first electric piano.

THE EARLY YEARS

John William Coltrane was born in Hamlet, North Carolina, in 1926 and raised in the slightly less tiny city of High Point. He was a fair student, and started playing clarinet and alto horn (a kind of high-pitched tuba common in marching bands) in the school band before he settled on the alto saxophone. He moved to Philadelphia after high school, where his mother had already settled to find work when Coltrane's father died. In Philadelphia, Coltrane studied music at the Ornstein School of Music It was here that he discovered the music of Charlie Parker, who would become an inspiration. Drafted into the Navy in 1945, Coltrane was stationed in a military band in Hawaii. Informal recordings from the following year show that he was immersed in bebop, but not yet able to negotiate changes with confidence.

Returning to Philadelphia in 1946, Coltrane found a jazz culture that had embraced bebop as much as he had in Hawaii, and he became close to musicians there, including the Heath brothers, Percy and Jimmy, and drummer Philly Joe Jones. In the late 1940s and early 1950s, Coltrane worked as a saxophonist in a wide variety of contexts. He initially found a good deal of work in rhythm & blues acts like that of King Kolax. The showy, groove oriented style of the group required Coltrane to develop a vocabulary of high register squeals and low squawks, both of which would find their way into his own music in a different context. In 1948, Coltrane bought his first tenor saxophone in order to take another with alto saxophonist Eddie "Cleanhead" Vinson. For Coltrane, the switch was revelatory, and he made it permanent. He would later tour with a small Dizzy Gillespie band, where he could properly work on his bebop playing, and in 1954, he worked with his childhood idol, alto saxophonist Johnny Hodges (incidentally, he also met Cecil Taylor at that time, who sat in with the band for at least a night or two in central Pennsylvania).

By 1955, Coltrane was a well-seasoned soloist and when Miles Davis formed a quintet with Philadelphia musicians Red Garland and Philly Joe Jones, Coltrane was the logical second choice to complete the group following Sonny Rollins' departure to Chicago.

WITH MILES DAVIS

For many critics, Davis' decision to hire Coltrane was a dubious one. Davis, who was at the top of his career as a ballad player with a laid back delivery and a dark tone, seemed to undermine his own agenda with Coltrane, whose technical ability was beyond question, but whose busy solos struck many as overly aggressive. Furthermore, Coltrane's sound on tenor, which later became the model of post-bop tenor saxophone, was a shock in the mid-1950s. Instead of the lightness of Lester Young or the dark, heavy vibrato of Coleman Hawkins, Coltrane played with a bright, steely sound and little vibrato.

In fact, it was the contrast between Davis's and Coltrane's styles that kept the quintet interesting. On the 1955 recording of "'Round Midnight" that was discussed in Chapter 12, Coltrane not only demonstrates a remarkable versatility with his dark, breathy harmonizing in the opening chorus, but he follows Davis's long tones and suspended phrasing with a double time chorus that is as rhythmically varied and angular as Davis had been slow and focused. On faster tracks from the same session, like "Tadd's Delight," Coltrane shows the first signs of his interest in chord-on-chord playing, or arpeggiating a related, but different chord than the one the rhythm section provides.

In 1957, Coltrane was fired by Davis—Coltrane had been addicted to heroin since he started using it around 1948, and he was out of control, falling asleep on the bandstand and beginning to lose control of his instrument. Losing his job, which at the time was the best saxophone position available in jazz, served as a wake-up call. Coltrane quit drugs cold turkey and began to rebuild his career with a new commitment to building his technique and applying his own ideas of jazz harmony. That year, he recorded a few LPs for Prestige, including his first as a leader, as well as an ill-fated project led by a seventeen year old tuba player named Ray Draper (better discussed than heard). Most notably, he spent the summer and autumn of 1957 in the Thelonious Monk Quartet—Coltrane credited Monk for both teaching him about music and for leaving him the space to make his own discoveries. The best document of the 1957 Monk Quartet, a Carnegie Hall concert for which a tape was discovered, remastered and released in 2005, bears out the latter assertion—on "Epistrophy," for instance, Coltrane plays a blistering chord-on-chord solo for two choruses with barely any piano accompaniment at all. Coltrane's habit of running arpeggios at terrifying velocity throughout the range of his instrument would be called "sheets of sound" by critic Ira Gitler, and the phrase would become the common name of this period of Coltrane's career.

In 1959, Coltrane, who was now reunited with Davis, made two pivotal recordings. The first, *Giant Steps*, contained the biggest achievement of Coltrane's "sheets of sound" style; the second, Davis's *Kind Of Blue*, was the impetus for Coltrane's first major stylistic shift. The title track of *Giant Steps* is, almost literally, Coltrane's last word on the harmonic complexity of bebop. With two chords per measure and the superhuman tempo of 290 beats per minute, "Giant Steps" proved too much for the scheduled pianist, Cedar Walton (who thought it was a ballad when he received the sheet music), and Tommy Flanagan was called in for the recording. The chord progression of the tune is unique in western music. Using a series of chords related by major thirds, it uses traditional sounds and means, but is not oriented towards a single tonic Instead, it settles on the keys of E-flat, G and B only momentarily, and all within about fourteen seconds.

For Coltrane, *Kind Of Blue* could not have come at a better time. With "Giant Steps," Coltrane had reached a limit—it was about as far as any musician could go with rapidly changing, complex harmonies. The modal jazz of *Kind Of Blue*, and especially "So What" offered a new direction that Coltrane would pursue for the rest of his career.

THE CLASSIC QUARTET

Coltrane left the Davis Sextet in 1960 to form his own group, and when Coltrane's new quartet was fully assembled, it was apparent that he was headed in a different musical direction than Davis.

Coltrane took over a year to solidify the personnel of his quartet. He already had the reputation of taking longer than average solos—in a famous exchange with Miles Davis, Coltrane responded to a complaint about the duration of his solos, saying, "I don't know how to stop." The now legendary reply from Davis: "Take the horn out of your mouth." With his new interest in modal jazz, he needed a group that could maintain energy and interest while Coltrane explored only one or two chords for half an hour or more. The musicians he finally chose provided that interest and much more.

Pianist McCoy Tyner (b. 1938), who had previously been employed in the Art Farmer/Benny Golson Jazztet, plays in a style very much in tune with Coltrane's interests. As Bill Evans had on "So What," Tyner based much of his sound on chords voiced in fourths rather than the traditional thirds. This open and slightly dissonant chord voicing allowed for more space for the soloist, and the sound is less tonally goal-oriented than a traditional triad. These qualities are helpful when a single chord's duration might be measured in minutes instead of beats. But where Evans has a light touch, Tyner is driving and percussive. He frequently returns to a pounded open fifth in the low register of the piano, which serves in one sense as a drone (Coltrane took a strong interest in Indian classical music, which is generally played over a steady drone), and in another sense as a punctuation for the hammered sixteenth notes of Tyner's solos.

If Tyner was an unusually muscular pianist, drummer Elvin Jones (1927-2004) was a behemoth. Jones was born into a jazz family; his brother Hank is a successful hard bop pianist, and his brother Thad was an accomplished trumpeter and arranger for big bands who will be discussed in the next chapter. Although Jones was capable of great subtlety and a light touch, occasionally heard on ballads, he rarely bothered with it. Jones had developed uncommon independence among his hands and feet, and is often called a polyrhythmic drummer. Polymetric is more apt, which is to say through subdivision of the beat, he frequently implies multiple meters at the same time. More importantly, he does so with intense energy and stunning power. Live, the Coltrane Quartet often sounded like a duo, with Coltrane soloing over Jones, who drummed loudly enough to drown out the rest of the quartet.

Jimmy Garrison (1934–1976) provided the bass to complete the quartet, and he often receives short shrift. Largely out of necessity, Garrison did not join in with the virtuosic flamboyance of the rest of the quartet, but played often simply, maintaining lines based on the tonic and fifth of the chord for minutes on end with a strong, solid sound. As a soloist, he could go on as long as Coltrane, playing double and triple stops and simple melodies in a style largely influenced by Charlie Haden.

With each passing record, the Coltrane Quartet seems to reach a new level of intensity. Coltrane had been strongly interested in Eastern cultures since he had kicked heroin (in a sense, he seemed to be replacing heroin with spirituality as his non-musical addiction), and the drones of Indian classical music fit in nicely with the harmonic stasis of his modal jazz. He also began playing soprano saxophone, partly inspired by Steve Lacy, but also, as his style on the instrument indicates, because of the high, clear and nasal timbre that starts where the tenor leaves off, and the instrument's similarity to double reed instruments common in Indian and Arabic music. On "My Favorite Things," recorded in 1961, Coltrane found a way to reduce the Richard Rodgers song to essentially a single chord, moving only from e minor to E Major and back.

The major work of the Classic Quartet is 1964's *A Love Supreme*. It is an ambitious work: a four movement suite in which Coltrane attempts to summarize his spiritual beliefs. The title track is based entirely on a four-note motive, which is repeated by the bass after a short introduction, and later chanted by Coltrane. As is typical for Coltrane in this period, he picks at the motive obsessively for most of the eight minutes of the performance. With harmony reduced to a single chord with no changes, Coltrane is freed to explore every dissonance and consonance available—at one point he plays the main motive starting on each of the twelve notes of the chromatic scale. But his soloing is far from monotonous. Coltrane's greatest talent was his ability to build intensity over a very long period of time, increasing his range into the far reaches of the instrument, and finding a way to increase volume, pitch and power of his playing far beyond what seems possible.

Live, he could stretch things even further. Often, the audience can hear Coltrane thinking, as he works out every possible way to deal with a single pitch, sequence or motive. And he could go on, it seemed, for hours—a half-hour of choruses on a single mode was never out of the question for Coltrane, and as the many versions of such captured on tape indicate, he could keep it from being boring as well.

THE AVANT-GARDE

By around 1965, the explorations in Coltrane's solos were pulling apart the modal contexts of his tunes to a degree that tonality and meter began to become irrelevant. Soon he was asking for the same kind of freedom from the rest of the quartet.

In 1965, Coltrane recorded *Ascension* with the classic quartet augmented by a second bass player, two trumpeters and four more saxophones. In many ways, it was a typical Coltrane performance for the mid-1960s: an LP- long modal exploration featuring Coltrane's multiphonics (the production of more than one note at once, accomplished through fingering techniques and the voice), squeals and honks, and Elvin Jones's fiery drumming. But with as many as seven horns soloing at once, the net effect is initially overwhelming. When Coltrane released *Ascension* in 1965, it came as a shock to the public at large who did not have the benefit of hearing Coltrane in concert. Atlantic records had hours of Coltrane performances from the late 1950s in their archives, and were still releasing "new" albums of Coltrane's sheets of sound in 1964, and the most extreme Coltrane album before *Ascension* had been *A Love Supreme*. The kinds of sounds on *Ascension* were still quite new to Coltrane's audience, and it seemed like Coltrane had become a follower of a handful of controversial New York musicians instead of the mainstream cultural leader that he had been.

In fact, Coltrane had had a strong interest in the jazz avant-garde from the beginning of his career. He recorded as a side man to Cecil Taylor in 1958, and as a co-leader with Don Cherry and the other members of the Ornette Coleman Quartet (except for Coleman) in 1960. He had even taken (and paid for) lessons with John Gilmore and Coleman. He had also been expanding the group with a second bass as early as 1961 (which provided a repeating drone, like the tamboura in Indian classical music), as well as other horn players, like alto saxophonist Eric Dolphy.

By the end of 1965, Coltrane had permanently added two new members to his group. At fifteen and ten years younger than Coltrane respectively, tenor saxophonist Pharaoh Sanders and drummer Rashied Ali were young members of the generation of musicians inspired by Coltrane's modal flights and Taylor's rhythmic freedom. Sanders' musical vocabulary included a terrifyingly human-sounding shriek and warbling multiphonics; with Coltrane, these non-pitched colors and textures were the focus of Sanders playing (in other contexts he plays much more melodically, and it is likely that Coltrane asked for Sanders's textural playing specifically). In the same way that Sanders balanced Coltrane's still harmonically complex playing with pure color, Ali was hired to complement Elvin Jones's drumming with accents and textures out- of- time. Unlike Sunny Murray, who sustained long periods of busy playing with no sense of tempo whatsoever, Ali kept a general pulse, regularly increasing and decreasing his activity and volume like a series of crashing waves, but on a beat-to-beat level, he played gestures rather than rhythmic figures. Jones felt pushed aside by the young and cocky Ali and left Coltrane shortly afterwards, but he continued to perform until his death by heart failure in 2004.

Coltrane's new, freer approach to playing proved to be

too much for the conservative Tyner, as well. After leaving Coltrane at the end of 1965, Tyner continued to perform as a leader, maintaining his style but in less cluttered contexts, to considerable success that he still enjoys. It may have even been too free for Coltrane himself. After two 1965 recordings, *Kulu Se Mama* and *Om*, both of which are largely freely improvised with moments of beauty but just as many moments of self-indulgence, Coltrane began to concentrate on a more lyrical approach to his still wild and dissonant music. Coltrane replaced Tyner with his wife Alice, who was a talented hard bop pianist. Like Sanders, Alice Coltrane changed her playing style to match John's musical vision, playing long arpeggiated runs, apparently inspired by John's interest in the harp.

Most of the new, lyrical but dissonant music of the Coltrane Quintet went unheard on record until after Coltrane's death. His sound in 1967 had changed. He now played with a darker sound, and a rich vibrato somewhat like that of Albert Ayler (discussed in Chapter 16), and his lines were often longer. On *Stellar Regions* (recorded in 1967, but not released until 1995), Coltrane concentrates on slower, shorter performances than he had been playing, usually stating a simple, repetitive and chant-like head before soloing. The band remains largely subdued throughout, and Ali's rustling is in direct contrast to Jones's pounding on earlier recordings.

Coltrane died of liver cancer on July 17, 1967, leaving a legacy in the form of thousands of copycats, some inspired and some slavish.

15

THE 1960S, PART I
Inside

The stylistic fragmentation in jazz that began in the 1950s brought a wealth of distinct styles and manners of music in the 1960s; by the middle of the 1970s it would become a crisis. While hard bop and cool jazz still maintained a firm grip on the tradition of tonal, partially improvised music based on choruses, new approaches inspired by Cecil Taylor, Ornette Coleman and John Coltrane tore away many of the fundamental aspects of music-making that made "jazz" a clearly definable concept. With such a large variety of styles all laying claim as jazz, descriptors like "mainstream" and "fringe" become irrelevant. In 1964, a jazz fan could hypothetically have to choose a jazz performance from among several greats such as Louis Armstrong, Duke Ellington, Cecil Taylor and Lee Konitz, but she would have no problem agreeing that all of these musicians are an important and current part of the jazz tradition.

Rather than sift through dozens of different styles in an effort to find the one that most clearly defines mainstream jazz after 1960, one can get a grasp on post-1960 jazz at first by using a distinction that many musicians use themselves, between "inside" and "outside" musicians. Whether a

musician is "out" because he works outside traditional harmonies, forms or concepts of his instrument, or because he
must survive outside the standard means of financial support because his music is too weird for club owners, the difference between outside and inside is usually apparent, and
given the financial success of outside artists like Ornette
Coleman and the Art Ensemble of Chicago, more accurate
than the frequently used descriptions of "mainstream" and
"avant-garde."

This chapter discusses some of the trends and music of
the 1960s that might be properly called inside, in the sense
that traditional harmonies and chorus structure are primary elements of their construction.

BIG BANDS AND ARRANGERS
OF THE 1960S

While swing as pop music was over by the end of World
War II, a few bands were able to maintain their careers in
the 1950s. They were spurred on by the one-two combination of a resurgent Count Basie band and the quality and
popularity of Gil Evans's arrangements for Miles Davis;
big bands had entered a second golden age of sorts in the
1960s.

Television was a contributing factor, as well. Variety
shows and sitcoms regularly featured jazz and big band
arrangements as both featured acts and background music throughout the 1950s and 1960s. Notably, Nat "King"
Cole, a gifted singer and underrated pianist, became the first
African American host of a nationally broadcast television
program in 1956 on NBC. His program featured music by
his own trio as well as a big band under the direction of
Nelson Riddle. Riddle and Basie arranger Neil Hefti both
provided theme songs and background music for several
television programs. Both musicians wrote and arranged in

a style that combined the swing of the Basie band with the careful orchestration of Gil Evans, and both served as musical director for multiple projects by Frank Sinatra.

For many musicians, the expanding opportunities for commercial music provided by television made it possible to pursue a comfortable, lucrative music career without the pressures of maintaining a large ensemble on tour. Others, like J.J. Johnson, were able to keep working creatively after their audience had dried up. Johnson made a career of writing unobtrusive background music for television and film until a return to public performance in the late 1980s, effectively waiting out the taste of the American public until bebop became popular again.

For Quincy Jones and Oliver Nelson, the studio-based system of recording commercial music served as both an opportunity for work and a model of creative work. Nelson was a gifted saxophonist who began his career playing in several big bands, including Louie Bellson's band, and, for a short time, Duke Ellington's. But he gained most of his success as an arranger for big band projects. He contributed arrangements to big band projects by Wes Montgomery and Jimmy Smith among others, and provided the soundtrack to the late 1960s television program *Ironside*. His best known work is one of a series of albums featuring his playing and his arrangements for a seven-piece band, somewhat in the tradition of the *Birth of the Cool* nonet. *Blues and the Abstract Truth* is a masterful combination of early-Davis influence and modal-Davis influence (down to the inclusion of pianist Bill Evans). The album includes two tunes that became standards: the unusual, 16-bar minor blues "Stolen Moments" and the Miles-Davis-goes-to-the-rodeo Americana of "Hoe-Down."

Quincy Jones was one of the top big band arrangers of the late 1950s and 1960s. He began his career as a trumpet player, but he was soon arranging for a wide variety of projects, from Dizzy Gillespie to pop idol Lesley Gore ("It's My

Party" was Jones' first major commercial success) to rhythm
and blues singer Ray Charles. As a leader himself, Jones had
time to manage a project only occasionally. But LPs such as
1961's *The Quintessence*, while showing that commercial
accessibility was still at the core of his thoughts, are excellent jazz in their own right. "Robot Portrait," for instance,
bears the mark of Count Basie's influence in its swing and
the heavily riff-based arranging, but it is combined with a
distinct hard bop bluesiness in its melodies and Ellington-
style lush harmony. Jones's ability to negotiate the music
business behind the scenes, however, became his main focus
by 1970, and he was a remarkably successful music execu-
tive, who ran a media empire of sorts with a hand in the
production of music, film and television.

Duke Ellington even dipped his toes into the incidental music waters in the 1960s, providing the score for the
films *Anatomy of a Murder* and *Assault on a Queen* But
for the most part, the commercial music industry was centered in Los Angeles, and big band arrangements were still
approached as concert music on the East Coast. Ellington
had saved his band from extinction after a number of poor
reviews and unfilled concert halls almost entirely on the
merit of a single saxophone solo. At the 1956 Newport Festival during a performance of "Diminuendo in Blue and
Crescendo in Blue," tenor soloist Paul Gonsalves opened
up for a solo that ended up lasting twenty-seven choruses.
At the twenty-second chorus, the audience exploded, cheer-
ing and dancing in the aisles. The press reported on the
event, the recording was issued, and Ellington was elevated
from has-been to Grand Master of Jazz. In the 1960s, Ellington took advantage of his status and concentrated on
composing hour long, ambitious suites (often in collaboration with Billy Strayhorn), carefully arranging his set lists
for dramatic purposes. At times, he was too ambitious. In
the 1971's *Afro-Eurasian Eclipse*, he spent a good deal of
time experimenting with rock rhythms, but replacing wild

abandon with Ellington's subtlety and sophistication which resulted in flaccid music. But in their prime, such as the *Far East Suite* from 1966, Ellington and Strayhorn composed some of the best music of their careers.

The modern voice of East Coast big bands belonged to the Thad Jones-Mel Lewis Orchestra. Jones (1923–1986), the brother of Elvin, was a gifted cornetist and skilled arranger with nine years' experience in the Count Basie Orchestra and a confidant, blues informal solo style. With drummer Mel Lewis, Jones formed the group in 1965, and took the opportunity to apply post-bop harmonic ideas that had been suppressed with Basie He proceeded to rehearse the band into razor-sharp precision. Many of the Jones-Lewis recordings feature dizzying tempos and rhythms that would stymie many small combos.

BOSSA NOVA

In the 1950s, the Brazilian popular music scene went through some radical changes, bound up, as Brazilian pop music has always been, in political and economic changes that were also happening. A group of musicians, led by Joao Gilberto and Antonio Carlos Jobim and smitten with American cool jazz, began applying complex, bebop-derived harmonies, a light, almost detached style, and sparse instrumentation (often just Spanish guitar and voice) to samba. The new music reflected the leisure of the Brazilian upper class, with lyrics about pretty girls and sunny days, and was named bossa nova, meaning "new style" or "new thing."

In 1961, jazz guitarist Charlie Byrd toured Brazil, learned bossa nova, and brought the style back to play for tenor saxophonist Stan Getz. The album the two recorded together, *Jazz Samba*, was really more bossa nova than samba, and the appropriately laid back version of Jobim's "Desafinado" was a smash hit. For Getz, already one of the top cool jazz saxophonists, the lightly swaying feel fit his deliberate phrasing perfectly, and he would record a number of bossa nova albums, and usually at least one track per LP, for the rest of his career. The lightened, detached samba rhythms of bossa nova quickly became a standard rhythmic feel for jazz, and nearly as quickly a cliché in the hands of less inspired musicians than Getz.

THE ORGAN TRIO

In black working class bars and lounges across the northeastern United States, the Hammond B-3 organ was as common and necessary as a jukebox and bar stools. Playing the kind of soulful rhythm and blues pioneered by Louis Jordan in the 1940s and mastered by Ray Charles in the 1950s, organ trios, usually with tenor saxophone and drums (bass is easily handled by the organist with the left hand or with the feet on a pedal board) became the standard working class combo in the late 1950s.

Jimmy Smith (1928–2005) brought the organ trio into the jazz mainstream with his 1958 LP The Sermon. With his subtle touch (Smith was a master of the swell pedal—a foot-operated volume control that allows him to swell his phrases like a horn player and recede into the background when comping) and soft but insistent groove, Smith played music that was custom built for toe tapping and parties.

Smith's success in the late 1950s ushered in a host of organ trios, many of whom integrated ideas from modal jazz and bebop into their still funky music. Philadelphian Charles Earland (1941–1999) was among the funkiest. Earland played with a heavier hand than Smith, and his rhythmic language owed more to James Brown than Ray Charles. At the same time, though, he was capable of Coltrane-esque flights of fancy, sometimes pulling at the harmonic framework for minutes at a time. With an equal interest in bebop, blues, and the jazz avant-garde, Larry Young (1940–1978) took the kind of risks on the organ that Cecil Taylor had been taking on the piano ten years earlier. His 1966 LP *Unity* is a tour de force of modal jazz, featuring Elvin Jones on drums and top notch second generation modal players like trumpeter Woody Shaw and tenor saxaphonist Joe Henderson as guest soloists. Young also took an early leap into fusion, and will be discussed again in Chapter 19.

BLUE NOTE AND MODAL JAZZ

When Blue Note Records was founded by Alfred Lion in 1939, its primary focus was on releasing recordings by older boogie woogie pianists and Dixieland revival bands—with the glaring and prophetic exception of Thelonious Monk's first recordings in 1947. Around 1951, the label executives shifted their attention towards hard bop, and with recording contracts signed by Horace Silver, Art Blakey, Clifford Brown and Jimmy Smith, Blue Note established themselves as the central record label in the hard bop and soul jazz subgenres.

Over the course of the 1960s, Blue Note had guaranteed profits in the form of their hard bop and soul jazz catalog, and developed a roster of young, talented musicians who had come of age when Miles Davis was performing with the First Quintet. Like Davis's Second Quintet, these musicians saw the work of Cecil Taylor and Ornette Coleman as an established part of the jazz tradition, and comfortably abandoned changes and form without fear. In fact, Davis's Second Quintet was among them all recorded for Blue Note in the 1960s. Frequently appearing on each other's recordings as side men, the Blue Note roster, including Andrew Hill, Eric Dolphy, Sam Rivers, Freddie Hubbard, Tony Williams, and others, played in a stylistic middle ground—too many excursions into freedom and odd sounds to be hard bop, and too reliant on choruses of tonally or modally composed changes to be free jazz.

Eric Dolphy was closer in age to John Coltrane than to Tony Williams, but by the end of the 1950s, he had developed a style of playing so unusual and inimitable that he was in a class by himself without regard to generation. Dolphy was a proper multi-instrumentalist, equally virtuosic on alto saxophone, flute and bass clarinet. His early inspiration was Charlie Parker, and like many, his early solos are somewhat derivative of Parker's style. By the end of the 1950s, though, Dolphy had developed a vocabulary of angular, disjunct lines and a fluid lyricism, as well as a wicked sense of humor. Often, Dolphy begins solos with a sort of fanfare, beginning on a high, wrong-sounding note and descending through a rapid series of arpeggios that seem entirely out of context until he resolves the entire phrase on the last note.

Born and raised in Los Angeles, California in 1928, Dolphy moved to New York in 1959 and began a working relationship with Charles Mingus. He made several recordings under his own leadership in 1959 and 1960. In 1961, he became a semi-permanent member of the John Coltrane Quintet, just as Coltrane was beginning to expand his solos to marathon length and stretching at harmony. Dolphy balanced Coltrane's long, dissonant solos with long, dissonant solos of his own, albeit in a much lighter (and more openly bizarre) style.

Dolphy was a popular choice as a side man for adventurous jazz musicians—he appears on recordings by Coltrane, Andrew Hill, Oliver Nelson, George Russell, and most notably on Ornette Coleman's *Free Jazz*. As a leader, he made only one album for Blue Note (the label also released a live performance in 1999). *Out To Lunch* features Dolphy playing all three of his instruments and in his top form. On each track, adherence to the form established in the head is tenuous at best—more often it is absent altogether, or only alluded to in Richard Davis's bass playing. Unfortunately, the giddy creativity of the band on *Out To Lunch* could not be matched in later recordings and performances—shortly after the recording session, Dolphy left for Europe with Mingus, and had just quit the band to stay in Europe and establish himself more securely as a leader when he died at thirty years old.

As a leader, trumpeter Freddie Hubbard (b. 1938) was most comfortable in a hard bop context, playing in an extension of the style of Clifford Brown, but he was also comfortable playing in almost any context, including Ornette Coleman's *Free Jazz* (for which he frequently receives undue criticism for not being outside enough) and John Coltrane's *Ascension*. While Hubbard occasionally lapsed into bebop clichés during his solos, he always did so with a pure tone and virtuosic technique.

Tenor saxophonist Joe Henderson (1937–2001), along with Miles Davis alumni Sam Rivers and Wayne Shorter (both whom also led recordings on Blue Note), was among the first generation of post-Coltrane tenor saxophonists. It would be easy to dismiss Henderson as a laid back version of Coltrane, and unfair as well. While he focused on playing modal jazz in the style of the Coltrane Quartet, and similarly explored both rapid arpeggios and multiphonics, Henderson did so with a detachment and reserve that Coltrane never showed. While Coltrane can sometimes be accused of practicing on the band stand and working one or two notes repeatedly for minutes on end, Henderson played efficiently, and sometimes it can sound like he planned a pitchless squeak weeks in advance.

16

THE 1960S, PART II
Free Jazz

A musician developing a style of playing outside jazz in the 1960s had essentially a blank slate with which to work. By 1961, Charles Mingus had brought collective improvisation back as a viable texture, thereby emancipating jazz from solos. Similarly, Ornette Coleman ended chorus structure, and Cecil Taylor (or more appropriately his drummer Sunny Murray) ended steady tempo. John Coltrane had already developed a tolerance for extended dissonance and non-traditional sounds with the mainstream jazz audience (at least live), and Sun Ra's overt weirdness was beginning to have an impact outside Chicago, even if it was a small one.

Musicians in the 1960s actively sought out ways to emancipate themselves from tradition in both music and society, regardless of genre. Of course, the revolutionary elements in 1960s culture and politics are well known and frequently discussed, and musicians took part as much as anyone else. The same cultural forces that compelled jazz musicians to break from the entrenchment of bebop had previously been at work when the bebop generation adopted new fashion and language, and had partly stemmed from the reaction to totalitarianism and fascism that had compelled the United States to enter World War II and the Cold War.

It might seem incongruous, then, that a group of musicians so interested in revolution and individuality developed strict, easily identifiable and described genres of music as quickly as they did. Taken as a whole, as it often is, outside music (or free jazz, or the avant-garde, or energy music—no two people are happy with the same name for it) does encompass countless approaches and aesthetics. But playing music in a group is a social act as much as it is an artistic one, and musicians working together towards the same goals must, by necessity, use the same means. The similarities among outside musicians become more apparent than the differences when social circles are considered. Sun Ra, working in relative isolation with the Arkestra, who lived, ate, practiced, and played together, never strayed far from the combination of Henderson-style swing and exotic percussion that informed his earliest music, no matter how far he stretched the chaotic elements. Similarly, the tight-knit community of African American musicians in Chicago developed a formal school of music, and a fundamentally different approach to creative music than the less formal social circles in New York, where Ornette Coleman and Cecil Taylor were active as well as influential, and the Chicago musical and social conventions stayed closer to jazz tradition in many respects.

Geographic boundaries in outside jazz can be indistinct, as well. In creating music that refuses to be pinned down, and draws only small audiences even in the biggest cities, outside musicians take their opportunities and allies where they can find them, and musicians from New York, Chicago, across Europe and the rest of the world collaborate without arguments. But when the first rule of a tradition is to ignore tradition, every example has a counter-example. Differences in style among different geographic scenes are as good a place to begin discussion as any other.

Free jazz in New York, so called after the Ornette Coleman LP that shares some of its aesthetics, carries over much
more from hard bop and modal jazz than it often sounds at
first listen. Groups are generally based on standard small
combos of winds with rhythm section, although piano is
rarely present. While the bass and drums no longer have a
steady tempo to articulate, their roles are similar in free jazz
to what they are in hard bop. With the exception of timekeeping, the style remains more or less the same: bass players play steadily in the background, often strumming three
or four notes at once fairly steadily; and drums maintain
a steady wash of ride cymbal frequently, and the constant
click of closed hi-hat remains, although instead of a steady
backbeat, it is more likely to be a quick, spasmodic chatter of
the left foot. Free jazz performances also often begin with a
head, played in unison or simple harmony by winds. In free
jazz, however, no harmonic plan is established, and heads
are often simple and repetitive, and sometimes might only
contain two or three different notes.

After the head, though, all bets are off. While different
musicians have different styles, and free jazz prizes individuality above all else. A few general statements about
the style can be safely made. The emphasis on freedom
and break from tradition implies that anything goes, but
the deliberate avoidance of traditional rules and styles of
playing jazz establishes rules of its own. Free jazz performances are often called "atonal"; non-tonal is probably a
better word. Before the 1960s, many classical (and a handful of jazz) musicians and composers since the beginning
of the twentieth century had developed atonal methods
of composing by carefully arranging the 12 pitches of the
chromatic scale in ways that did not imply a hierarchy of
pitches. In free jazz, pitch more frequently does not come
up as an issue at all. Soloists often focus on color, creating gestures of unusual sounds with unusual techniques,
or they shape a line roughly with indistinct and sliding

pitches. Often, the shapes of free jazz lines are reminiscent of bebop with speedy flurries of notes, but individual pitches are no longer considered in relation to a chord, and it is the overall shape of the line that receives emphasis.

The similarities to hard bop, rather than the differences, are often what make free jazz hard to digest upon first hearing. If a gorilla is given a guitar, no one is shocked when it does not play a flamenco solo, but when an LP sleeve shows a photograph of well-dressed people with serious facial expressions holding saxophones and drum sticks, the chaos and seeming lack of cohesion on the record itself can be an unpleasant surprise. It is important to remember, then, that when music sounds strange, it is generally the result of a lot of strange sounds. Hunting for chord changes and discernable melodies in free jazz is a frequent but futile habit for many listeners, and the artistry of the best free jazz musicians becomes more apparent when the listener is willing to meet it on its own terms.

ALBERT AYLER

The initial shock of hearing Albert Ayler's larger-than-life tone on the tenor saxophone for the first time is so great that many listeners never get over it. Behind Ayler's massive, dark tone, with a wide vibrato that harkens back to Sidney Bechet, is a life spent devoted to music and a solid resume of professional work in blues, jazz, and marching bands (in his home town of Cleveland, Ohio, Ayler earned the nick name "Little Bird" as the area's most accomplished bebop saxophonist). But his music, which often starts with simple, martial melodies, followed by energetic screams that attack the listener like a swift kick to the head, probably puzzled more audiences than it enthralled during Ayler's lifetime. It continues to be an acquired taste that hides its most appealing aspects.

Ayler was born in 1936 to a musical family—his father played saxophone in local jazz groups, and taught both Ayler and his younger brother Donald alto. After a year of college, the family's finances forced him to drop out, and he entered the Army where he developed a fascination with military music, especially American marches and the French national anthem, which he would later paraphrase in his composition "Spirits Rejoice."

Like many other outside musicians, Ayler began his career in Europe, where he moved in 1961, and where audiences were more accepting of unorthodox music. Cecil Taylor had an extended tour in Europe that year (and met and played with Ayler), and Eric Dolphy found the same acceptance three years later, and would settle in Europe before his early death.

The most productive year of Ayler's brief career was 1964. Back in the United States, and with a fairly consistent quartet of drummer Sunny Murray, trumpeter Don Cherry (Donald Ayler, having switched to the trumpet, eventually replaced Cherry), and bassist Gary Peacock, Ayler made a number of LPs with groups ranging from a trio to a sextet. The LP *Spiritual Unity* from that year features Ayler in a trio setting with Peacock and Murray, and benefits from the clarity of the small group of the three musicians at their very best.

Ayler's method of creating a performance is fairly consistent, and evident from the opening track of *Spiritual Unity*, "Ghosts (First Variation)." Ayler rarely opens with the head. In this performance, he opens with a brief solo statement, but in other performances, the head might not arrive until ten minutes or more into the performance. "Ghosts" (there are two different performances of the tune on *Spiritual Unity*), like many of Ayler's melodies, is a simple, folk-like tune, and again this performance errs on the side of brevity, playing the tune directly, and only once, while other Ayler performances might repeat part of the head several times, and it might even become background for solos. Typically, after playing the head, the trio is free to explore in any way they want, and Ayler bursts into a tirade of complex chromatic lines, multiphonics, and high screeching. But he stays remarkably close to the melody, maintains the phrase structure and the general shape of each phrase, while throwing out pitch and meter altogether.

Ayler arrived at his unique style and sound when John Coltrane was expanding his sonic vocabulary into multiphonics and non-pitched sounds, and he shared a spiritual focus with Coltrane. The two became friends, and Ayler was a direct influence on Coltrane, as evidenced by the latter's vibrato and darker tone adopted after hearing the former.

In later years, Ayler often made the contrast between composed and improvised materials even greater than they are on *Spiritual Unity*. At John Coltrane's behest, he signed a contract with Impulse, Coltrane's label, and released a series of impressive recordings that contain both the most conservative and simple music of the 1960s and the most extreme—often at the same time.

In 1969, Ayler released the puzzling LP *New Grass*, marking a return to blues, and even singing himself, but still with Ayler's inimitable style. It may have been a fluke. At a later concert given in France, Ayler was in top form at his usual free jazz, and the opening track of *New Grass* contains a cryptic extended monologue from Ayler that seems to apologize to the audience for what they are about to hear, and at the same time for the selfish inaccessibility of his earlier music. Sadly, the issue can never be completely resolved—after going missing for at least a week, Ayler's corpse was discovered in the East River, and the cause of his death (drowning according to his death certificate, but an autopsy was never performed), whether by accident, suicide, or murder, was never determined.

ARCHIE SHEPP

Tenor saxophonist Archie Shepp, trained as a playwright, was the most outspoken, politically active and confrontational member of the 1960s free jazz scene. Born in Philadelphia in 1937, Shepp played alto saxophone and clarinet in school band programs, but his music career might have begun as a stroke of fate. He moved to New York after graduating from college in 1959, and he started taking jazz gigs to support himself while he sought acting and writing jobs. Within a year, and still as a beginner on tenor, Shepp was thrust into the center of the New York avant-garde as a member of the Cecil Taylor Quartet. In 1960, Shepp was still a weak player—his first recording, Taylor's *Air*, while a classic example of Taylor's early work with Buell Neidlinger and Dennis Charles, shows Shepp fumbling on his instrument, still working out his sound. But by the *Into the Hot* sessions a year later, Shepp had become comfortable, developing an assertive, throaty sound with a rhythm and blues rasp, and a penchant for short, spastic phrasing that borrowed equally from John Coltrane's extreme ranges and Horace Silver's blues-influenced hard bop. Shepp further developed his style as a player and composer as a member of the short-lived, poorly documented New York Contemporary Five, which also featured Don Cherry and Danish altoist John Tchicai (whose clean technique and occasionally bizarre musical ideas have served him well through a long and unjustly neglected career which continues today).

Like most saxophonists of his generation, Shepp developed a style largely derivative of John Coltrane. Shepp, however, did so under Coltrane's direction, joining Coltrane for a number of performances and recordings, including *A Love Supreme*, on which Shepp's playing was ultimately excised, and *Ascension*. As he did for Albert Ayler, Coltrane arranged a contract for Shepp with Impulse, and Shepp's first recording as a leader, *Four for Trane*, consists of four Coltrane compositions and one original work.

For Shepp, jazz is first and foremost black music, and his goal as a musician is to express the politics and struggle of black America. To the extent that something as abstract as instrumental music can express the concrete political situation of a given time, Shepp has been consistently successful, even becoming more conservative in the 1980s, as much of America did. Much of his 1960s recordings, on the other hand, are full of fire, taking titles like "Malcolm, Malcolm, Semper Malcolm" and "Pickaninny (Picked Clean-No More-Or Can You Back Back Doodleboug)." The recordings made reference to musical styles with political connotations, like minstrel songs, bossa novas, and Sousa marches. "Hambone," the first track on Shepp's 1965 album *Fire Music*, is a multi-themed composition, with solo sections based over clear, singable riffs, and shows a clear Ellington influence in the harmonically sophisticated, choral voicing of the opening theme. Perhaps it shows Ellington's influence on Cecil Taylor more than Ellington directly—the overall structure and simple riffs are reminiscent of Taylor's composing style in the early 1960s.

FREE JAZZ DRUMMERS

In a fashion similar to the first generation of bebop drummers, drummers in New York in the 1960s made many of the most radical stylistic changes in free jazz. Frequently, the drumming alone determines whether a performance is post-Coltrane modal jazz or free jazz. Wind players like Archie Shepp and Don Cherry could play the same style in the context of free jazz or hard bop, and they sometimes did. The elimination of timekeeping from the drummer's responsibilities, to a great extent, not only enables soloists to explore their style without hindrance of form and traditional rhythm; it defines free jazz as a genre.

Sunny Murray (b. 1936) was one of the earliest drummers to abandon time keeping for extended periods of time. After some more traditional work in the mid-1950s, Murray joined the Cecil Taylor Unit in 1959 (part-time at first, until Dennis Charles left permanently), and later joined Albert Ayler's group. In both bands, as well as others, Murray developed an aggressive style with a wide dynamic range, and no allusion towards regular tempo whatsoever—a very difficult task that even the freest of free jazz drummers have difficulty sustaining. In the place of regular time, Murray reacts to soloists with lightning reflexes, offering fills and accents in response to phrases, while still maintaining some stylistic ties to hard bop with a constantly ringing ride cymbal.

While his playing has been poorly documented on recordings until the late 1990s, Milford Graves (b. 1941) was a tremendously influential drummer on the New York free jazz scene in the 1960s, and as both teacher and performer, remains active and respected today. Graves began playing congas as a teenager, and he always took an interest in Asian and African percussion. His own playing, and even his setup, has been less beholden to the jazz tradition than most free drummers as a result. A master technician, Graves tends to use cymbals and gongs only occasionally for color, concentrating on busy work on drums instead.

Beaver Harris (1936–1991) had a relatively late introduction to music. He did not begin to play drums until he was nineteen or twenty, but the Pittsburgh-born drummer developed quickly into one of the most versatile drummers in jazz, and he was able to maintain working relationships with Sonny Rollins, Thelonious Monk, Albert Ayler and Archie Shepp with equal success. Like Shepp, with whom he recorded frequently in the 1960s and 1970s, Harris enjoyed synthesizing jazz styles from the past, and capably went from Max Roach-influenced hard bop playing to Murray-like accents and rumbles one moment to the next. He led the unfortunately neglected group 360 Degree Music Experience throughout his career, applying his eclectic and swinging style to a large ensemble.

OTHER FREE JAZZ MUSICIANS

After leaving Ornette Coleman's quartet in the 1960s, *Don Cherry* initially worked as a side man for both Sonny Rollins and Albert Ayler. As a band leader, he made three of LPs for Blue Note that expanded Coleman's concepts, producing side long suites of compositions and improvising segues between themes. As his career progressed, Cherry, who had something of a reputation as Coleman's trumpet playing doppelganger, developed his interest in internationalism (the Blue Note albums were made with a global group, and *Symphony for Improvisers* used jazz musicians from Argentina, France, Germany and New York). By the end of the 1960s, Cherry was a solid and creative multi-instrumentalist, playing African and Asian flutes and stringed instruments in addition to trumpet. He continued to blend free jazz with Asian and African melodies and styles until his death in 1995.

The trombone had almost disappeared from small group jazz after the technical demands of bebop put the music out of reach for all but the most technically skilled trombonists. In the meantime, the collective improvisation of free jazz reminded critics and listeners alike of similar ideas in New Orleans jazz of the 1910s. *Roswell Rudd* was one of many trombonists who saw an opportunity to make trombone viable again as a solo instrument in jazz, and with a background in Dixieland revival jazz, he carried over the tailgate style of playing to free jazz successfully. Rudd has made precious few recordings as a leader, but he appeared throughout the 1960s on the work of Cecil Taylor, Steve Lacy and Archie Shepp, and was a member of the New York Art Quartet with John Tchicai. In recent years, he has shown an interest in folk music of other cultures, and his 2003 CD *MALIcool* features the unusual and surprisingly successful collaboration of Rudd's rough-and-ready trombone with traditional musicians from Mali.

In Europe, the extended stay of Albert Ayler had a tremendous impact on musicians. A new generation of musicians, inspired by Ayler, sprang up throughout Europe, but especially in Germany and the United Kingdom. While the English improvisation scene developed quickly into music that is less apparently related to free jazz, German musicians like bassist Peter Kowald and tenor saxophonist *Peter Brötzmann* kept stylistically closer to their inspiration. Brötzmann's early LPs for his own FMP Records are masterpieces of chaotic noise. The spiritual ecstasy of Ayler is replaced by a chilly, almost nihilistic violence on 1968's *Machine Gun* and 1969's *Nipples*, both of which featured some of the best English, German and Dutch free jazz musicians (who were also some of the best in the world). Brötzmann has performed with just about everyone who has been involved in free jazz from the late 1960s until today, While he now tends to work in smaller ensembles, his lean, muscular playing is still powerful enough to cause temporary hearing damage without amplification.

THE 1960S, PART III
Chicago

Since Eddie Condon first named his band "the Chicagoans," the Midwest's largest city has always strived to distinguish its jazz culture from that of New York. In the 1950s, when New York's music scene concentrated on the fiery playing of hard bop musicians like Art Blakey and Sonny Rollins, Chicago musicians focused on more moderate tempos and the relaxed swing of pianist Ahmad Jamaal and tenor saxaphonist Von Freeman. Even the oddness of Sun Ra seems moderate in the face of Cecil Taylor's blinding tempos.

Similarly, in the 1960s, when the New York free jazz scene modeled itself after previous communities in New York, keeping the small combos and clubs that were a part of the jazz tradition, the Chicago avant-garde created a formal organization that included a school of music, and sought out alternative venues for performance. And while New York free jazz in many ways extrapolated John Coltrane's music with increased energy, dissonance and volume, the Chicago scene usually went the other direction entirely, working with long silences, static forms and occasionally arch-conservative performance styles.

In 1961, when Sun Ra left Chicago and took many of Chicago's best avant-gardists with him, pianist Muhal

Richard Abrams formed a rehearsal band of his own, the Experimental Band, to explore new ideas about music and to fill the void in Chicago left by the Arkestra. Abrams, born in 1930, had already established himself as a solid hard bop pianist and had developed working relationships with Max Roach and Dexter Gordon, and as a member of the Chicago-based quintet MJT +3, released an LP in 1958 that featured several of his compositions. In 1965, after years of difficulties finding appropriate places to play, the Experimental Band morphed into the Association for the Advancement of Creative Musicians (AACM), a formal non-profit organization. With state registration, the AACM became a support group for African American avant-gardists in Chicago who were eligible for grants, provided a school and other support, and sought new venues for performances. As the eldest member of the organization by a good ten years, Abrams acted as a figurehead and mentor, and helped to develop a few common aesthetic ideas among the other members.

In seeking out non-commercial means of support, the AACM was a first in what had previously been considered a pop genre. By receiving non-profit status, the members of the AACM acknowledged that their music would not be commercially viable. It was an explicit statement of what had been suggested twenty years earlier in New York: that jazz was now serious art, rather than entertainment. And as such, the AACM claimed entitlement to the same financial and artistic support from governments and universities that had been keeping the European art music tradition alive in America since World War II. The experiment in organization was very successful. The AACM still thrives in Chicago, and maintains a close relationship with Chicago's Columbia College, and affiliated artists, including the flagship Art Ensemble of Chicago, performing worldwide. They also served as a template for similar, locally based organizations in other cities—the most successful of them, St. Louis, Missouri's Black Artists Group, had a sister organization relationship with the AACM, and collaborations among musicians from both circles are common.

Under Abrams's guidance, the younger members of the AACM developed, if not a common aesthetic, certain common guidelines and ideas behind their approaches. As a whole, the musicians of the AACM shy away from the emotional and spiritual intensity of free jazz, replacing the wails and screams of Ayler and colleagues with a chilly, intellectually rigid approach to sound. Frequently, performances by every member of the AACM feature long stretches of single sounds played in isolation; whether the sounds are simple, single notes or long stretches of percussive noise, they are usually surrounded by silence on either side. It is an approach to time that avoids any sense of regular pulse, swing, or forward motion. Most AACM members also strive for maximum contrast within individual performances, following up sparse lists of odd sounds with mid-tempo swing, and playing several instruments, so that within a single solo, a saxophone note might be followed by a small bell or a whistle. Often these contrasts are used to demonstrate the odd sense of humor among the musicians: for instance, Roscoe Mitchell's "The Maze" for nine players uses a massive percussion set-up that is visually imposing and takes a good two hours to build on stage, but with nine people and several hundred instruments, the work is quiet and sparse in the extreme, with long stretches of silence followed by single strikes of an instrument.

While the sparse angularity of the AACM aesthetic (as well as their organized approach to administration) finds common ground with the academic avant-garde of European art music, the rhetoric, theatricality and use of percussion reflects Afrocentrism as inspired both by Sun Ra's previous example and by the political spirit of the 1960s. By using Eurocentric means to assert Afrocentric perspective, the AACM reflects not only the uniquely African American problem of culture transported and destroyed (i.e. the strength of African culture can not be fully appreciated by European standards, and must be adapted in order to receive equal treatment); they also reflected the unusual racial politics of Chicago, the most racially segregated large city in the North.

THE ART ENSEMBLE OF CHICAGO

Formed by members of Muhal Richard Abram's Experimental Band, the Art Ensemble of Chicago (AEC) was initially the best known and best documented representation of the AACM to the rest of the world. Over the course of 1969, the beginning of their recording career, AEC had recorded and released at least ten LPs, relocated to Paris, and established themselves as international leaders of the jazz avant-garde.

Four members of the group had already performed and recorded together, both as members of Abrams's Experimental Band, and as members of saxophonist Roscoe Mitchell's sextet (all musicians in the AACM are multi-instrumentalists, and this chapter will refer to their primary instruments only), who recorded the first AACM release, *Sounds*, in 1967. Together with Mitchell, saxophonist Joseph Jarman, trumpeter Lester Bowie, and bassist Malachi Favors, joined by percussionist Don Moye within a year or so, announced themselves as representing the AACM at concerts, and played in African costume and face paint (except for Bowie, who wore a scientist's lab coat, once again confounding the African and European academic traditions) in front of a banner with the mottos "Great Black Music" and "Ancient to the Future."

Although the Art Ensemble's initial burst of activity was entirely with the support of small Chicago and Paris based independent labels, by 1973 the group had garnered enough critical attention to earn them a contract with Atlantic Records, who had a reputation for signing avant-garde musicians with popular appeal since the Ornette Coleman recordings of 1960.

Art Ensemble performances are multimedia affairs. Beyond costumes, face paint, and a stunning variety of musical styles, the group (until their most recent performances) always incorporates elements of dance, theater and poetry into their presentations, reflecting both the influence of Sun Ra and the wide range of interests among the AACM members. Musically, they demonstrate a thorough knowledge of the traditions of Africa, America and Europe. *Baptizum*, their first Atlantic LP is a typical live performance from 1973. Over the course of a forty-five-minute set, the ensemble starts with a traditional sounding African drum quintet, segues into a dramatic parody of country blues and work songs by way of a brief shouting match with the audience, moves to a lyrical Mitchell composition (somewhat reminiscent of Miles Davis's "Flamenco Sketches," although a good deal more abstract with the typical frozen-in-time rhythmic feel), turns into another Mitchell composition that might be called up-tempo but is based largely on the extended repetition of a single note, then becomes an extended trumpet solo by Bowie. Bowie's solos were a staple of AEC performances, and Bowie specialized in running through a large number of styles in a brief period of time—in this case, a combination of Bubber Miley, blues, experimental techniques and military bugling over a ninety-second span. After an intense, free jazz-like Joseph Jarman composition, the group closes the set with "Odwalla," a simple descending riff that is played as the horn players process off stage.

The Art Ensemble continued to receive positive critical attention and success throughout the 1970s and 1980s and toured with the benefits of tour busses and label support (after their contract was up with Atlantic, the group began their own label for a brief period of time before signing with ECM records) that most New York free jazz musicians forwent. Attention dwindled in the late 1980s, as it had for most outside musicians, and the group performed less frequently, concentrating on other projects as individual band leaders (Roscoe Mitchell, the most austere member of the group, was most successful, with his alternations between sparse textures and showers of rapidly played saxophone scales). Joseph Jarman left music nearly completely. Instead, he ran a Buddhist dojo in New York and performed only rarely. Upon Lester Bowie's death of cancer in 1999, the Art Ensemble returned to performing as a trio.

ANTHONY BRAXTON

Alto saxophonist Anthony Braxton, born in Chicago in 1945, spent his teenage years obsessed with the unusual combination of science fiction, John Coltrane, and Paul Desmond (the saxophonist in the Dave Brubeck group). In many ways, his entire body of work synthesizes his childhood interests, combining the rigid intellectual systems of science fiction with Desmond's purity of tone and Coltrane's intensity and extended technique. Braxton's unbridled creativity as a performer and composer, combined with the stunning complexity of his ideas, has made him at once an inspiration to younger musicians, a leader in his own right, and an inimitable player whose convoluted mix of styles serves as a means to its own end.

Braxton's first group as a leader was the Creative Construction Company, formed with fellow AACM members Leroy Jenkins on violin and Wadada Leo Smith on trumpet. The unusual instrumentation with no rhythm section allowed Braxton to explore his strong interest in the European style avant-garde, and his willingness to experiment with sounds in a way only tangentially connected with jazz. Among other works, he composed a piece for four amplified shovels for the group, which often used either Muhal Richard Abrams or bassist Sirone to fill out a quartet. CCC earned him an early reputation as a musician better aligned with Karlheinz Stockhausen and John Cage than Miles Davis and Sun Ra—a perception that he still fights to shake.

In 1968, Braxton released the landmark album *For Alto*, a two LP set comprising well over an hour of unaccompanied alto saxophone. It had been a requirement of the AACM school of music to prepare and perform a set's worth of solo music, but to record a solo saxophone project of such a scope was unprecedented (perhaps the last thing left to do first in music). Each side of the album is a different composition, and the four works are further divided into a total of eight different sections, each with a different approach to the instrument, and each dedicated to a different person. The result is a record with far more variety than one might expect from a single musician on a single instrument, from the angry growling of "To Composer John Cage" (Braxton, while deeply influenced by Cage's music, was highly critical of his ideas about jazz, and publicly accused Cage of racism) to the whispered lyricism of "Dedicated to Ann and Peter Allen."

Braxton's titles for compositions are uniquely unprintable. As a rule, each composition receives three titles: one, to be used for rehearsal purposes that is not publicly stated, a second graphic title, consisting of a diagram that might show some aspect of the composition or other personal meaning, and third, a number which does not necessarily reflect the time at which Braxton completed the work. For instance, the four compositions on *For Alto* are compositions 8a, 8b, 8c and 8d—Braxton retroactively assigned the number eight and collected them with his other solo saxophone compositions.

Throughout his career, Braxton has chosen to return again and again to separate but related strands of his musical thought. In addition to the small ensemble compositions for which he is best known, he has repeatedly composed large

scale works for large, and occasionally impractical ensembles
(Composition #19 for 100 tubas was premiered in New York
on June 4, 2006, although only 70 tuba players were available). He continued to explore solo performance, and he developed free improvisation with no planning whatsoever on
a series of duets with musicians like guitarist Derek Bailey
and Max Roach. Braxton also recorded his own takes on jazz
standards, starting in 1974 with the two- volume *In The Tradition* (which displays Braxton's absurd sense of humor in
his rumbling, goofy playing of Charlie Parker's "Ornithol-
ogy" and Miles Davis's "Donna Lee" on contrabass clarinet
at speedy tempos that make the slow speaking instrument
completely inarticulate). Braxton is additionally committed
to education, and has held a post as professor at Wesleyan
University since 1992—many of his students at Wesleyan,
such as accordionist/pianist Ted Reichman and violist Jessica
Pavone, began their professional careers as members of the
ensembles Braxton has led through the 1990s.

Braxton has spent the bulk of his career working with
musicians outside the AACM, and despite his debt to the organization for many of the musical and philosophical ideas
that Braxton holds, he never adopted the racial separatism
that is occasionally observable in long standing members of
the group. What many fans consider the best work of Braxton's career has been his quartet of the mid-1980s, featuring
three white musicians who share Braxton's interest in both
jazz and the European avant-garde. Because he worked with
bassist Mark Dresser, pianist Marilyn Crispell, and drummer Gerry Hemingway for longer than any other group,
Braxton was able to bring even more complexity to his own
Classic Quartet than he had already been showing in individual compositions. The recordings made with the quartet
during a 1985 tour of England are Braxton's masterpieces.
With the stunning creativity, technique, and interactivity
of the quartet, Braxton began performing collages of his
works, sometimes playing two or three pieces at the same

time. The net effect of so many parallel ideas is information overload—the listener is better served if she approaches the performances as if they were freely improvised (which, in parts, they are), while admiring the quick-change textures, and the ability of the group, almost in spite of the strangeness of the music, to swing as hard as Count Basie.

HENRY THREADGILL

Although he was not a founding member of the AACM, alto saxophonist and flutist Henry Threadgill (b. 1944) had gone to college with Joseph Jarman and Roscoe Mitchell and played in the Experimental Band before service in the Army took him to St. Louis, just in time to miss the formation of the AACM. For Threadgill, who had been trained as a classical clarinetist at the American Conservatory of Music, jazz is only one among many styles and genres from which he can draw in his work as a composer and band leader.

Threadgill's first major project as a leader, Air, began in a way that illustrates his typically eccentric approach to musical tradition. Like many AACM members, Threadgill was an active participant in Chicago's theater and dance scenes, and made his early living providing music for theatrical productions. Commissioned in 1971 to provide arrangements of Scott Joplin's music for a production that could only budget for three musicians, Threadgill did not make the obvious choice of hiring a pianist. Instead, he assembled a trio with AACM drummer Steve McCall and bassist Fred Hopkins. Threadgill played saxophone, flute and hubkaphone, (a self-built percussion instrument made from automobile hubcaps). Seemingly unfit to perform the harmonically oriented, piano-based music of Joplin, Threadgill used the group's weakness as its chief strength. McCall and Hopkins did not function as a regular rhythm section, instead playing as co-soloists with Threadgill. The combination of free jazz textures and openness with older styles was remarkably successful, and the group re-formed in New York in 1975, when they released around a dozen albums (1979's *Air Lore*, their most successful album, consisted of Threadgill's open and loose arrangements of music by Joplin and Jelly Roll Morton) before McCall returned to Chicago in 1982. With some personnel changes, Air continued to perform, eventually renamed New Air, until 1986.

Even before the breakup of Air, Threadgill has been writing for and performing with larger groups with unusual instrumentation, blending genres and using unique formal ideas that re-order short phrases into long, unpredictable composed sections. With his Sextett (sic), actually a seven-piece group, but so named because the two drummers function as a single voice in Threadgill's compositions, he began to concentrate on long compositions. One of the byproducts of Threadgill's interest in unusual timbre (the Sextett included a cello, for instance) was a new kind of musical conservatism. Threadgill uses long, non-traditional forms and unusual changes from chord to chord, but he works with recognizable and traditional elements, even if he is more likely to draw from the calypso or tango traditions than from mainstream jazz.

Over the course of the last twenty years, Threadgill has led a number of different ensembles—his reluctance to become routine in his music has led him not only to disband groups at the height of their success, but to re-compose music just before performances. His main group from the 1990s, the Very Very Circus, consisted of a double trio of tuba, guitar, and either saxophone or French horn, backed by a single drummer, although the two trios work together, and the music is less chaotic than its name and instrumentation might imply. Through the use of long melodies over riffs and short, repeated sets of changes, Threadgill can and does rearrange the elements of his compositions at will, and no two performances of individual works are the same.

18

POSTBOP PIANISTS

The five pianists discussed in this chapter share little in common except the instrument they play and activity during the 1960s, 1970s, and 1980s. After about 1965, even the vague stylistic divisions of inside and outside begin to break down; individual musicians' recordings become subgenres in themselves, and in order to organize the tremendous variety of ways that people define the jazz tradition for themselves, arbitrary classifications are often made, and instrument is as good a classification as any.

With the removal of the piano from the standard jazz combo by Ornette Coleman and most outside musicians after him, pianists with an interest in stretching beyond hard bop were left to their own devices. And while McCoy Tyner spent the 1960s redefining accompaniment with his power and speed, pianists like Bill Evans and Paul Bley were developing the piano as a trio instrument with a lighter touch and a new balance and interaction with the bass and drums.

For Chick Corea, an early interest in Cecil Taylor and outside playing proved to be a dead end. After a few excellent albums strongly influenced by Taylor's outside piano, Corea, with few colleagues in his genre and an interest in populism fueled by religion, turned back inside, and then to rock. For Paul Bley, who had been the closest thing to a compatible pianist Ornette Coleman had found between the 1950s and the 1990s, a light and lyrical touch was not incompatible with avant-garde styles, and the Canadian-born Bley straddles the line between inside and outside, working with extended techniques, dissonance, and modal lyricism in equal measure. Andrew Hill had been developing his own style independently from the beginning of his career, without much regard to the work of other post-bop musicians, while Keith Jarrett's long-winded but conceptually solid improvisations were formed in the repetitive, jam-oriented contexts of Charles Lloyd's and Miles Davis's groups.

BILL EVANS

Pianist Bill Evans had already made a permanent mark on jazz as a member of the Miles Davis Quintet before his own trio became the model for post-bop piano. The contributions Evans made to *Kind of Blue* were well beyond those of an accompanist; he provided ideas of mood, arrangement, and in at least two instances, composition. He claimed to have written "Blue In Green" alone, based on a suggestion of two chords from Davis (they are generally co-credited today), and "Flamenco Sketches," while based on a set of modes decided by Davis, was based largely on introduction of Evans's own "Peace Piece," which he had recorded the previous year. Evans took the same idea of using sophisticated means towards romantic, accessible ends to his own remarkable trio the following year, thereby establishing himself as the standard against which other pianists have been compared since 1959.

Evans, born in New Jersey in 1929, was a talented but unmotivated pianist in his youth by his own admission. He attended Southeastern Louisiana University on a classical piano scholarship, then after his mandatory service in the Army moved to New York City, where he made one or two recordings with dance bands. In New York, he made the acquaintance of composer George Russell, with whom he made a few recordings for RCA in the mid-1950s. The association with Russell led him to the salon meetings at Gil Evans's apartment and his brief but important tenure with Miles Davis in 1958. The recording of *Kind of Blue* had the effect of solidifying Evans's style—he had previously played an adventurous brand of bebop influenced by the Tristano school—and, as association with Davis did for most of his sidemen, placed Evans at the forefront of critical and popular attention to jazz.

Evans shied away from larger ensembles his entire career as a soloist, preferring to work with a trio of piano, bass, and drums with occasional solo performances and recordings. His classic trio, formed in 1959 with the brilliant young drummer Paul Motian and the equally brilliant and even younger bassist Scott LaFaro, was not the first such professional group by any means, but the popularity the group held among musicians, critics, and casual listeners alike established the piano trio as a standard ensemble. While the trio in its initial lineup lasted only a few years— LaFaro sadly died in a 1961 automobile accident at the age of twenty-three just as he was beginning to redefine bass playing—their LPs for the Riverside label stand as landmarks and models for the modern piano trio.

Critics and historians, in an effort to explain the brilliance of the Evans Trio, especially on two LPs made from performances at the Village Vanguard in Manhattan, *Sunday at the Village Vanguard* and *Waltz for Debby*, have made fairly sweeping statements about single elements of the group's style. It has been said that the trio introduced elements of European art music to post-bop jazz, that they made the piano, bass, and drums equal partners without the usual melody/accompaniment divisions, and that Evans pioneered opening up the rhythmic feel of the group by avoiding downbeats. All of these assertions speak to the creativity and novelty of the trio, and all are exaggerations. LaFaro played with virtuosic technique, often soaring up to the upper register of the bass for long solos, and often opting to play countermelody instead of a traditional walking bass line. And Motian is a colorist more than a clock; while he only rarely strays from a standard tempo, he is more likely to add light brush work and cymbal washes than a straight and steady ride cymbal. For the most part, however, chorus structures remain intact, and solos remain solos, even if the interaction of the group sometimes obscures things. What is perhaps most novel about Evans's own playing had been an established part of his style by the time he joined Miles

BILL EVANS TRIO, "SOLAR," *SUNDAY AT THE VILLAGE VANGUARD*

"Solar," recorded during a stand at the Village Vanguard in New York less than two weeks before bassist Scott LaFaro's death, exemplifies the kind of freewheeling interactivity for which the Evans trio is best known. Working with an already unusual and difficult to follow head by Miles Davis – "Solar" is harmonically derived from the first 12 measures of the standard "How High the Moon," and is unusual in containing no melodic or harmonic repetition to mark its structure – the trio constantly confounds the listener, adding unusual accents and eliding solos to the extent that following the structure of the performance is a difficult task at best.

The nine minute performance can be heard as roughly divided into three equal sections. First Evans solos, then at approximately 3:30 on the recording, LaFaro, and finally a more interactive section in which Evans trades phrases with LaFaro and Motian. But throughout the performance, LaFaro plays like an excited and defiant young man, occasionally storming up the neck of the bass into countermelody and steadfastly refusing to play a steady, walking bassline throughout.

Davis: his unusual chord voicings, often featuring chords based on fourths instead of thirds. What made the Evans Trio with LaFaro successful was a combination of these elements with the creativity and spontaneity of three musicians at the top of their game.

Following LaFaro's death, Evans hired bassist Chuck Israels, an accomplished musician in his own right, but much in the tradition established by LaFaro and thereby overshadowed. Evans continued to play largely in a trio format for the rest of his career with few exceptions, like the notable *Conversations with Myself*, which saw Evans playing in a trio alone, laying down three piano tracks with overdubbing. The other members of Evans's trio in later years could not always match the level set by Motian and LaFaro. Bassist Eddie Gomez, for instance, took up the style that LaFaro had left behind, but where LaFaro is interactive, Gomez is often overbearing—an effect enhanced by excessive reliance on electronic amplification. Despite a few lackluster efforts that resulted from depression and substance abuse, Evans maintained a high level of playing himself, and his last trio with bassist Marc Johnson and drummer Joe LaBarbera began to touch on some of the chemistry that his first trio had demonstrated. Evans died in 1980 at the age of fifty-one, having been plagued throughout his life with addictions to drugs and alcohol.

PAUL BLEY

Born in Montreal in 1932, Paul Bley developed the reverse side of the free jazz coin from Cecil Taylor. In place of Taylor's fire and dissonance, Bley uses lyricism and long modal stretches while still throwing away traditional ideas about form.

Initially a capable bebop pianist, his debut recording as a leader featured Art Blakey and Charles Mingus in a trio

setting. Bley shows a competent technique and a clear interest in some of the harmonic stretching that Lennie Tristano
and Dave Brubeck had been using in their own music. In
1955, Bley settled in Los Angeles, where he was among
the first musicians to take an interest in Ornette Coleman,
who sat in with Bley at occasional gigs (apparently against
the wishes of club management). For Bley, Coleman's open
approach to soloing was a revelation, and upon returning
to New York around 1960, he found himself working with
another similarly influenced musician in clarinetist Jimmy
Giuffre. Giuffre had been an accomplished swing player,
and then a cool jazz experimentalist with a well established
career years before he first encountered Coleman at the
Lenox School of Jazz in 1959, and was encouraged by Coleman to break out of the strict structures he had been using
previously. With bassist Steve Swallow, the Jimmy Giuffre
3 continued to play the folk influenced proto-modal jazz
that had been Giuffre's forte, but they also explored atonal-
ity and sparse structures. On their 1961 LP *Free Fall*, Bley
barely plays at all; the group concentrates on nearly solo
performances, with occasional bursts of sounds from the
other players. And, unlike the non-tonality of free jazz, the
Giuffre Trio explored properly atonal jazz—rare and difficult to pull off—playing clear melodies based on intervals
that do not offer a sense of a tonal home.

After playing with Giuffre and establishing his own
style with clarity, Bley became an organizing force among
New York's most radical musicians. He co-founded the Jazz
Composers Guild in 1965, on similar principals to those
that guided the AACM, but on a less government sanc-
tioned (and less successful) level. He has also recorded
prodigiously, releasing four or five LPs a year on various
small labels, with rare breaks, right into the twenty-first
century. Such a large volume of recorded work, in a great
variety of contexts, can be counterproductive; it is difficult
to get a handle on Bley's breadth, and to pick examples as

typical. On his 1969 LP *Closer*, Bley works with a trio of Barry Altschul on drums and Swallow on bass, and runs through a surprising number of different approaches over the twenty-nine minutes of the recording. Within the first two tracks, both written by his ex-wife Carla Bley (an accomplished and significant jazz composer who deserves far more attention than space will allow in this book), Bley jumps suddenly from the folksy, relaxed "Ida Lupino" to the nervous "Start," and proceeds to play all manners of styles in between on subsequent tracks, which combine the creative interactivity of the Bill Evans Trio with the tempoless drumming of free jazz.

ANDREW HILL

Perhaps because his style is easily described, pianist Andrew Hill has often been relegated to status as an also-ran in the world of post-bop jazz. Hill applies the dense, odd harmonies and stop-start phrasing of Thelonious Monk to modal jazz, and discussion of his career can and often does end with that statement. But while his style might be high concept, and not particularly influential—he seems to develop those elements of bebop and hard bop that were the first to be abandoned by free jazz musicians—the harmonic and rhythmic complexity and distinctive melodies of Hill's music merit serious attention, and his large body of work shows an iconoclastic sense of development that is ignored by such brief discussion.

Hill, who was born in Chicago in 1937, made his strongest impact with a series of LPs made for Blue Note between 1963 and 1967, where his challenging but accessible compositions fit in perfectly with Blue Note's not-quite-free jazz aesthetic and roster. *Point of Departure*, the 1964 LP that is often considered his best, features strong performances from a typical mid-1960s Blue Note lineup: Kenny

Dorham, Eric Dolphy, Joe Henderson, Hill, bassist Richard
Davis and Tony Williams. The performances are structured
as standard hard bop performances, with a series of solos
that follow the structure of the head, followed by the head
a last time. What distinguishes Hill's music is the unusual
structural ideas, disguised by flowing melody, that serve his
compositions. For instance, "New Monastery" is a theme
of twenty-two measures in a comfortable tempo that does
not sound nearly as strange as it is. The highlight of *Point
of Departure* is the ballad "Dedication." Again an unusual
form—a 28-bar AA'B structure in which the final phrase
is only four measures long—the simple, dirge-like melody
and countermelody are stated by Henderson and Dorham,
while Dolphy soars over the rest of the band on the bass
clarinet. Towards the end of his tenure with Blue Note, Hill
switched camps. He had already had a hit as a composer
with "The Rumproller" as played by Lee Morgan, and on
the 1968 LP *Grass Roots*, Hill combines his unusual melodic
sense with Horace Silver styled hard bop.

As years went on, Hill became less active as a performer,
preferring to teach to support his own music rather than
take gigs as a side man. By the middle of the 1970s, Hill had
embraced the timeless drumming of free jazz while leaving
his harmonic approach more or less unchanged. On his 2006
release, *Time Lines* (once again on Blue Note), Hill seems
to suspend time altogether on tracks like "Malachi," while
saxophonist Greg Tardy summons the spirit of Eric Dolphy
with brilliant bass clarinet playing. Hill died in 2007.

CHICK COREA

Born in 1938 in Chelsea, Massachusetts, Chick Corea
brought some of the fire and percussive quality of McCoy
Tyner to the piano trio format, along with healthy doses of
Latin jazz and Cecil Taylor's dexterity and strangeness.

Corea's father was a gigging musician, and as a child, Corea was surrounded by jazz and Latin music. He transcribed solos by Bud Powell and Horace Silver and still reflects their influence on his own playing. As a young adult, Corea played piano in the Afro Cuban bands of Mongo Santamaria and Willie Bobo. The pianist's role in such music was largely dependent on playing the *montuno*, a riff, usually played in octaves, that reflects the *clave*, the syncopated rhythm that serves the purpose that a steady beat serves in other music. Corea does not necessarily depend on the rhythmic bases of Afro Cuban music, but the insistent, percussive lines in octaves became a trademark stylistic element.

In 1964, Corea joined the quintet of hard bop trumpeter Blue Mitchell, who recorded a few of Corea's compositions, including "Tones for Joan's Bones," which Corea later recorded himself as the title track of his debut LP as a band leader. While Corea's playing for Mitchell fell soundly within the Horace Silver style of blues- inflected hard bop, a few of his solos feature both the rapid, chromatic lines and the frequent repetition of the tonic of a chord (another feature of the *montuno*) that infuse his playing regardless of the year or style of his performance.

Corea made his own major contribution to the piano trio repertoire in 1968, the same year he replaced Herbie Hancock in the Miles Davis Quintet, with the brilliant LP *Now He Sings, Now He Sobs*. With the energetic and assertive playing of drummer Roy Haynes and bassist Miroslav Vitous, Corea's trio seems to owe more to the early trio recordings of Cecil Taylor than to Bill Evans, although harmonically, Corea is more likely to use the fourths and strong bass of McCoy Tyner than Taylor's denser voicings. As Taylor had done on his first LP, Corea opens *Now He Sings* with a blindingly fast 12-bar blues, and like Taylor's strange introductions, the head to "Matrix" obscures the meter with a highly syncopated melody played in octaves.

Other compositions on the album are more typically complex than a standard blues form—the title track, for instance, is based on a long, complicated head with several sections and mixed meter.

Corea's interest in Cecil Taylor would become more apparent to listeners in 1970, when he and bassist Dave Holland both left Miles Davis to form a trio with drummer Barry Altschul. As a trio, Corea, Holland and Altschul began to incorporate ideas from free jazz into their own complex compositions, and Corea began to experiment with extended technique, reaching inside the piano to pluck strings by hand and to strike harmonics. With the addition of Anthony Braxton on reeds, the cooperative quartet named themselves Circle. In February of 1971, Circle recorded and released *Paris Concert*, a live performance of over ninety minutes that might be described as post-free jazz. With all the musicians at their peak, Circle performed a wide range of music, from a particularly intense version of Wayne Shorter's "Nefertitti" to freely improvised duets to a Braxton composition, listed on the album as "73° Calvin (Variation -3)" but announced from the stage as "73, 506 Kelvin, 8." Unfortunately, Circle had a short life. That year, Corea, who had just embraced Scientology, disbanded the group in an effort to focus on more accessible music capable of attracting a larger audience—Braxton has claimed Corea's turn from the avantgarde was directly requested by the cult's leaders. The three remaining members of Circle went on to record Holland's stunning LP *Conference of the Birds*, replacing Corea with tenor saxophonist Sam Rivers. Corea's own later work will be discussed in the next chapter.

KEITH JARRETT

Keith Jarrett, a contemporary of Corea's who shared keyboard duties with him in Miles Davis's group in 1969, has been a somewhat controversial figure in jazz. A child prodigy who began playing piano at age three, Jarrett drew his greatest attention with long solo performances that entranced his fans and struck others as self-indulgent and boring. Regardless, his phenomenal technique as a pianist is difficult to deny, and in ensemble contexts, where other musicians keep his indulgences in check, Jarrett stands as one of the most significant voices of post-Evans jazz piano.

Jarrett was born in Bethlehem, Pennsylvania, in 1945, educated at the Berklee School (now College) of Music, and hired into Art Blakey's Jazz Messengers briefly in 1965. He received a great deal of popular attention between 1966 and 1969 as a member of the Charles Lloyd Quartet. Lloyd, who played tenor saxophone in a kind of light, laid back version of John Coltrane, was able to perform in large rock venues and had some crossover appeal with young audiences. The Lloyd Quartet specialized in sustaining simple riffs for extended periods, appeasing a popular taste for extended jams that were common among psychedelic rock bands.

Following his eighteen-month stint with Miles Davis (the only extended period that Jarrett's purism allowed him to play electric keyboards), Jarrett recorded prolifically, both as the leader of a quartet and solo. As a solo artist, Jarrett seemed compelled to release every note he played in concert or a recording studio in the 1970s—for years, the *Sun Bear Concerts,* his ten-LP boxed set of performances from a tour of Japan, held the record of longest album recorded by a single artist. Combined with a fairly standardized method of improvisation, in which a slow introduction segues into a simple ostinato figure over which he might play for an hour, and the vaguely sexual movements and vocal noises that indicate intense concentration to some listeners and generate annoyance to others, the volume of Jarrett's solo recordings gave many the impression that he was self-absorbed, limited in creativity, and had trouble editing himself. At the same time, those qualities fit in nicely with the sexual revolution and "me generation" rhetoric of the 1970s, and his solo albums, especially *The Köln Concert*, sold remarkably well to fans as enthralled as his critics were derisive.

The popularity and consistency of Jarrett's solo performances might give a false impression of his range as a pianist, however. His 1970s quartet, with bassist Charlie Haden and saxophonist Dewey Redman, both former Ornette Coleman sidemen, and drummer Paul Motian from the Bill Evans Trio, was in some ways the sum of its parts, exploring the open forms and folksy ideas of Coleman in combination with the subtlety of touch and harmonic ideas of Evans. Jarrett is neither afraid to stretch outside nor ignorant of past styles, and in more recent years, his "Standards Trio" with Gary Peacock and Jack DeJohnette has been called the greatest piano trio since Evans's by more than one critic.

19

FUSION

Since the 1950s, rock had been vying for the position of America's preeminent musical genre over jazz. Ironically, it was the British Invasion of 1964 that sealed the deal. Jazz audiences shrank dramatically in the second half of the 1960s, and only a handful of jazz musicians like Miles Davis and Stan Getz were able to sell significant numbers of recordings. By the early 1970s, clubs were closing, record labels were folding, and jazz writers were complaining far more often than they were paying compliments. When musicians began to take up the electric instruments, straight eighth-notes, and backbeats of rock and funk, creating what they called "jazz rock," "jazz/rock fusion," or more simply "fusion," many jazz purists cried foul. Their complaints of sellout often had good evidence behind them. Freddie Hubbard, for instance, was openly bitter in interviews in the 1970s, and made some genuinely bad albums in an effort to cash in on rock's freely spending audience.

At the same time that older musicians felt forced to include rock elements in their music to ensure sales, many of the most creative musicians of the 1970s had grown up around the music, and the Beatles were as available to inspire as Louis Armstrong had been. Tony Williams, for instance, was sixteen years old when he made his first recording in 1962, and as a teenager and young adult in the 1960s, he grew up surrounded by the music of British invasion bands the same way every American of his generation did.

Anyway, if jazz musicians were selling out to rock, rock musicians had been buying into jazz before that. In the United States, the psychedelic rock of bands like the 13th Floor Elevators and Jefferson Airplane began featuring long jams and noisy freak-outs that owed no small debt to Albert Ayler and John Coltrane in the mid-1960s. Guitarist Carlos Santana formed his eponymous band in 1966; by the time he played at Woodstock in August of 1969, his Afro blues-Cuban-rock hybrid featured long, virtuosic guitar solos that dwarfed the amount of singing in his performances. And on the fringes, Don Van Vliet, performing as Captain Beefheart, led his Magic Band in music that might best be described as an application of Ornette Coleman's ideas to the blues, predating Coleman's own Prime Time by a few years with a similar sound.

In England, where rock felt less of the stylistic influence of rhythm and blues, the late 1960s saw the development of "art rock." Bands like King Crimson and Yes combined the volume of rock with complex forms and harmonies borrowed from Miles Davis and Wayne Shorter. And in the meantime, many rock musicians had developed a technical virtuosity and penchant for solos that caught the ears of young jazz musicians. Formed in 1966, the power trio Cream featured the same kind of interactivity and flashy solos in their electric blues that the Bill Evans Trio had been demonstrating in a quieter and more harmonically sophisticated fashion.

With the sole exception of the Soft Machine, who worked independently to create their own version of fusion all of the groups discussed in this chapter contain former members of Miles Davis's groups. Davis's 1969 albums

In a Silent Way and *Bitches Brew* brought a substance to the idea of using electric instruments and rock elements in music with a jazz sensibility. Just as jazz has always borrowed from contemporary popular and art music styles, elements of rock and rhythm and blues had been in use in jazz long before *Bitches Brew*. However, the financial success of the album, and Davis's unusual approach to the use of electronic instruments and solid-bodied guitars allowed his younger sidemen to properly synthesize the music in which they had trained with the rock that was the unavoidable soundtrack of America since 1964.

THE SOFT MACHINE

Although they were marketed, and are still usually discussed, as a rock band, the Soft Machine were among the first and most successful groups to combine elements of jazz and rock thoroughly enough to blur the divide and become fusion. The members of the trio, drummer Robert Wyatt, organist Mike Ratledge, and bassist Hugh Hopper, had all been schoolmates in Canterbury, England, and frequently met at Wyatt's home to improvise and listen to jazz records. Tapes of their childhood jam sessions show less than successful attempts at ambitious and sophisticated goals—they attempted to improvise in the styles of Cecil Taylor, Thelonious Monk, and European avant-garde composers like Karlheinz Stockhausen and Pierre Boulez—and Wyatt was the only member to show obvious talent from an early age. With bassist Kevin Ayers and guitarist Daevid Allen, Wyatt and Ratledge formed a psychedelic rock band called Wilde Flowers, and when Allen, an Australian, was denied a visa to return to England after a trip to Paris, the three remaining members called themselves the Soft Machine. Allen stayed in Paris, where he continued to lead various eccentric projects, all called

Daevid Allen's Gong, and worked with members of the AACM, among others.

The Soft Machine received their first big break in 1968, when they were hired as the opening act for a tour of the Jimi Hendrix Experience; they went on to record their first LP, *Volume One*, over a period of four days in New York. The album demonstrated some of the jazz harmonies and long solos of jazz, but included some old material from Wilde Flowers. The following year, with *Volume Two*, the Soft Machine stretched out further. With Hugh Hopper replacing Ayers on bass, the band recorded two long suites of songs performed without interruption (including a direct thanks to the Jimi Hendrix Experience for what little public exposure they received, quirkily and typically mentioning the Experience by name). On tracks like "Hibou, Anemone and Bear," Ratledge's distorted electric organ, Hopper's often-distorted and unusually melodic bass, and Wyatt's powerful drumming and singing propelled the band through long stretches of odd meters, post-bop harmonies, and avant-garde influenced solos.

With their extreme volume, absurd lyrics, and penchant for experimentation, the Soft Machine solidified their self-imposed alienation to both both rock and jazz fans. It did not help matters that they frequently argued and thus changed personnel often, sometimes including a horn section, sometimes including no original members. But the band was deeply influential, and formed the core of a group of closely related bands from Canterbury that retained a unique sense of melody and strong jazz influence. Robert Wyatt has been most successful since he left the group in 1970 as a songwriter. Unfortunately, a freak accident in 1973 (mistaking a French door for a bathroom door, he fell from a fourth story apartment, breaking his spine) left him a paraplegic and he no longer drums or performs publicly, but still releases fascinating albums.

TONY WILLIAMS AND JOHN MCLAUGHLIN

Tony Williams (1945–1997) had met English guitarist John McLaughlin (b. 1942) through Miles Davis before Williams left to lead his own band in 1969. McLaughlin, who had been performing in both jazz and rock contexts with similarly oriented musicians like bassist Jack Bruce and drummer Ginger Baker, both from Cream, set the template for fusion guitar with Davis. In it, he combined the harmonic sophistication and dissonance of post-bop jazz with the extreme volume, distortion, and virtuosic single-note solos of Jimi Hendrix (or, perhaps more directly, English blues and rock guitarists like Jeff Beck and Eric Clapton who had inspired Hendrix). With organist Larry Young, McLaughlin and Williams formed Tony Williams' Lifetime in 1969. Around the same age as McLaughlin and Williams and equally talented and adventurous, Young took the lead, as he would in most organ trios, only occasionally, preferring to concentrate on bass and harmony in the guitar driven Lifetime.

While Miles Davis found his inspiration in the funk and soul of Sly and the Family Stone and James Brown, Williams' busy, non-repeating style was better aligned with English rock drummers like the Who's Keith Moon, Robert Wyatt, and the Jimi Hendrix Experience's Mitch Mitchell Lifetime's first LP, 1969's *Emergency!*, had little of the funk influence on *Bitches Brew*. In its place is raw power and a creative blend of rock pounding plus the light, rapid swing for which Williams had previously been known. Part of the power was the accidental by-product of poor production: a cynical engineer used to recording mainstream jazz recorded the band carelessly, allowing the tape to distort, unintentionally adding satisfyingly raw edges to the album. But from the opening drum roll of the title track, through Williams's corny, Hendrix-inspired vocals on "Beyond Games," *Emergency!* synthesized the best elements of free jazz, modal jazz, and British rock, and added a rhythmic complexity in tracks like "Via the Spectrum Road," a blues of sorts in the unusual time signature of 11/8.

Lifetime's second album, 1970's *Turn It Over*, seemed even less related to Williams' past in post-bop jazz. McLaughlin had switched guitars and developed a darker, fuzzier sound than he demonstrated on *Emergency!*, and the guest appearance of Jack Bruce on bass and vocals transformed the group into a fairly standard psychedelic rock band, if an unusually technically sound one. The inclusion of John Coltrane's "Big Nick" might have indicated a link to the jazz tradition, but a healthy squeal of feedback from McLaughlin within the first minute of the performance made the intentions of the group clear. Unfortunately, Williams suffered from his own fame: although still in his mid-twenties (an age at which most jazz musicians still have not made their first mature recordings), his work with Miles Davis and on Blue Note had established him firmly as a jazz musician, and Lifetime alienated his jazz purist fans. The group disbanded after 1971.

After leaving Lifetime, John McLaughlin, who had recently become a devotee of Transcendental Meditation guru Sri Chinmoy (also known as Mahavishnu), formed his own fusion group, the Mahavishnu Orchestra. With the powerful but less tricky drumming of Billy Cobham and the unusual choice of violinist Jerry Goodman, McLaughlin turned up his guitar even more, but composed tunes with more clarity than Lifetime had used. On *Birds OF Fire*, his first LP with the Mahavishnu Orchestra, McLaughlin explored the rhythmic complexity he had hinted at in Lifetime, and expanded his role as a lead voice.

RETURN TO FOREVER

If Lifetime was a talented rock band that is called fusion because of its personnel, Chick Corea's Return to Forever was a talented jazz band that is called fusion because of its use of electric instruments. Following the breakup of Circle, Corea formed Return to Forever with bassist Stanley Clark, tenor saxophonist and flutist Joe Farrell, Brazilian percussionist Airto Moreira (who often uses only his first name), and Airto's wife Flora Purim on vocals. On two LPs, an eponymous debut and *Light as a Feather*, Corea led the band at the electric piano, playing in a slightly distilled version of the post-bop style he displayed on *Now He Sings, Now He Sobs*, through performances which were deeply influenced by the samba and bossa nova of Airto's native Brazil. With Airto's hand percussion replacing the relatively heavier drum set, the band had a light and breezy sound, and gained popularity quickly. Much of the success of the band lay behind the flashy technical playing of Clark, who plays rapid sixteenth-note solos with the flexibility and assuredness of a pianist. He eventually switched to electric bass guitar, and became a successful leader on his own in the late 1970s and 1980s.

In 1973, Return to Forever took on a slightly harder edge, when Airto was replaced by drummer Lenny White, who had drummed on *Bitches Brew*, and guitarist Bill Connors was added. As a quartet (Flora Purim had left the band as well), the group had a decidedly more intense approach even to the light material. After Al Dimeola replaced Conners, Return to Forever enjoyed a healthy career until Corea broke the band up in 1975. Since then, Corea has returned to acoustic piano and run both electric and acoustic bands as separate, parallel projects.

HERBIE HANCOCK

Most Miles Davis alumnae in the 1970s seemed to take Davis's music as permission to explore contemporary pop music, but they took their inspiration from John

McLaughlin and the blues and art rock of Great Britain. Herbie Hancock, who had written the funky "Watermelon Man" in 1961, found his greatest inspiration in the funk of Sly and the Family Stone, and found it easy and successful to transfer his riff based compositional style of tunes like "Watermelon Man" and "Cantaloupe Island" to the more contemporary rhythms and synthesizers of funk.

As a leader, Hancock had begun using synthesizers and electric piano almost as soon as he left Miles Davis. His first LP after leaving Davis in 1968, *Fat Albert Rotunda*, already made his interest in funk clear— the title track is as driven by electric bass and percussion as anything Curtis Mayfield might have recorded. Hancock had picked up from Davis a willingness to use recording and editing techniques as part of the compositional process, and through albums like *Sextant* and *Mwandishi*, Hancock created a blend of funk rhythm and free jazz dissonance, not unlike Sun Ra's music, full of overdubs, editing, and electronic effects.

With the release of *Headhunters* in 1973, Hancock seemed to have made the transition from jazz pianist to funk synthesizer keyboardist complete, and he emphasized his point with a transformation of his own "Watermelon Man" on the album. The album opens with "Chameleon," a fifteen minute long jam based almost entirely on a two-measure bass riff. There is a nominal head, but the driving force behind the performance is the contrapuntal funk textures supplied by bass, drums, Clavinet (an electronic harpsichord of sorts, already familiar to most listeners in the 1970s from Stevie Wonder's use of the instrument) and guitar. Hancock's synthesizer solo on "Chameleon" is a masterpiece, in which he blends rhythmic complexity and chromatic lines he had used in Miles Davis's group with the new noisemaking possibilities of the synthesizer and electronic effects such as tremolo, echo and ring modulation (an effect in which two different pitches are electronically combined, creating a complex aggregate of tones). The album was a big hit, reaching number thirteen on Billboard's pop charts and eventually going platinum.

Hancock continued to record in the same style as *Headhunters* well into the 1980s, and kept his ears open to the latest developments in pop music the entire time. In 1983, Hancock had his biggest pop hit yet with the album *Future Shock*—the lead single, "Rockit" was a massive hit on a level that music without vocals almost never achieved in the 1980s. Produced by Bill Laswell, who will be discussed in Chapter 21, Hancock, in place of a band, worked in the studio with drum machines and sequencers, as well as Grand Mixer D.ST manipulating records, and he created a mechanized, danceable album that exemplifies both the robotic pop of the age and the old school hip-hop that was just beginning to capture the American attention at the time. Hancock and Laswell hired a wide array of musicians from the New York rock, hip-hop and avant-garde scenes to assist on the album, and in doing so, Hancock created a fusion of 1980s pop and hip hop with jazz in a manner that was much more successful than his mentor Miles Davis would attempt a few years later.

WEATHER REPORT

Formed in 1970, Weather Report managed to sustain a much longer career than most first generation fusion bands, releasing albums for a full fifteen years. In their first incarnation (they went through several personnel changes, retaining only keyboardist Joe Zawinul and saxophonist Wayne Shorter from their beginning to their end), the band was started by Zawinul, an Austrian pianist who already had a significant legacy in Cannonball Adderly's hard bop groups through the 1960s. It also included Wayne Shorter, and bassist Miroslav Vitous, with drummer Alphonse Mouzon and percussionist Airto Moreira. The connection to

Miles Davis was clear even without hearing their music—
Zawinul had appeared on *In a Silent Way* and composed the
title track—and the first two albums made no effort to hide
their inspiration. Both the eponymous debut and *I Sing the
Body Electric*, their second LP, focused on the coloristic,
lyrical elements of Davis's early proto-fusion albums, both
are more memorable for texture and mood than any specific
melodies or grooves.

By their third album, 1972's *Sweetnighter*, Weather Report had begun putting the emphasis on stronger, funkier
grooves (much as Miles Davis had also done). Shorter's
style as a soloist also changed dramatically No longer the
harmonically tricky Coltrane disciple, Shorter played soprano saxophone more frequently, and tended towards
shorter, simpler phrases that often played rhythmic counterpoint to the snare drum, busier between hits and pausing
on accented beats. While formally, performances still had
something of the timeless sprawl of the first two LPs, the
band sounded more incisive than they had, sacrificing some
of their sonic variety and sense of adventure for a stronger
beat and more memorable melodies.

Weather Report had their greatest success with *Heavy
Weather* in 1976, and much of the credit for their popularity
went to their new bass player, Jaco Pastorius. Pastorius, who
had joined the band the previous year, was something of a
maverick. He had stunning technical skills on the fretless
bass, and was among the first musicians to exploit the possibilities of the instrument that were absent on the double
bass, or in the presence of frets. He also had a cocky, flamboyant manner on stage (and off), and more often than not
served the function of a lead instrument with Shorter, while
bass lines were provided by Zawinul's synthesizer. "Bird-
land," the lead track on *Heavy Weather* and a tune popular enough to become a standard among high school bands
within a few years, is a typical Zawinul composition from
the period. In what at first sounds like a haphazard con-

trasting fashion, short themes are stated with long, modal interludes between them. Pastorius plays the first theme, but the most repeated melody comes later in the composition, repeated with increasing volume and harmony. It is a thrilling and catchy performance—more so in the context of the album, where it is followed by the frankly sappy "A Remark You Made."

Pastorius left Weather Report in 1980 to form his own band, and his flamboyant playing began to take on the sheen of the new generation of guitar "shredders" of the early 1980s, of whom Eddie Van Halen was among the first and best known. And in the same way as Van Halen, often Pastorius's reputation as a technical ideal for aspiring young bassists belied of surprisingly creative compositions and arrangements, such as those on the live 1981 LP *The Birthday Concert*. Sadly, Pastorius likely suffered from mental illness, and exacerbated it with drug abuse; by 1984, he was beginning to destroy his own career with public breakdowns, and his death in 1987 came after a beating that was likely related to his attempt that night to force his way onto the stage of a performance.

In the meantime, Weather Report headed further away from their unpredictable, sprawling sound, and Shorter made progressively less impact on each album until he finally left the group in 1985, ending their tenure.

20

THE 1980S AND NEW CONSERVATISM

Jazz criticism took a pessimistic turn in the early 1980s. Most of the best musicians of the 1960s had spent the past several years reacting to a shrinking audience, either playing at tiny shows in loft spaces for a few dozen people on a good night (and usually taking non-musical day jobs to support themselves), or selling out to audiences with fusion, which had approached elevator music in style and seriousness throughout the 1970s. With few exceptions, jazz purists, offended by the perceived indignity of fusion even at its most creative level, lamented the impending death of jazz at the hands of rock, which many believed signaled a dumbing down of American culture. Rare positive reviews of albums released by jazz musicians under age forty or so portrayed the albums as a diamond in a sea of coal, and *Down Beat*, one of the only jazz magazines still in print by 1980, seemed to be searching for a savior for jazz.

Critics had reason to be confused about the fate of American culture; around the 1980s there was a wholesale change in the politics and taste of the generation that had brought about the cultural revolution of the 1960s. Apparently jaded by their inability to sustain the societal changes they had

helped to bring about, "yuppies" (young, urban professionals) who had participated in protests and listened to *A Love
Supreme* in the 1960s voted en masse in the 1980 presiden-
tial election for Ronald Reagan, a conservative Republican
who had represented the counter culture's biggest enemies
fifteen years earlier. Where youthful idealism was replaced
by materialism, the Baby Boom generation, who constitut-
ed the largest age group in the Unites States, left the mark
of their political shift on all forms of popular culture. In
cinema, the predicament of the self-obsessed, aging former
hippie found its best voice in the popular 1983 film *The Big
Chill*, in which former college classmates were brought together by the death of a friend that clearly represented their
revolutionary past. On television, one of the most popular
programs of the 1980s, *Family Ties*, followed the traditional
sitcom trope of family dynamics and generation gaps; the
comedic twist is that the children were conservative Repub-
licans interested in financial gain, while their aging hippie
parents represented the revolutionary old guard. And while
radio stations that followed the so-called "Album Oriented
Rock" format began changing the name to "Classic Rock,"
MTV, which had started broadcasting in 1981, was literally
changing the face of popular music to a more attractive one,
bringing attention to both physically attractive acts and
otherwise unpopular bands that had had the foresight to
make music videos when there was still a limited selection
available for broadcast.

In this new, conservative cultural atmosphere, the ec-
centricities and indulgences of jazz musicians who had developed their style in the 1960s and early 1970s remained
interesting only to a small and rapidly diminishing audience. There were a few musicians around 1980, however,
who were able to avoid both obscurity and fusion bands.
Guitarist Pat Metheny had a large and enthusiastic fan
base by 1980. A passionate and devoted jazz fan as a child,
Metheny took up the guitar at age thirteen, and released

his first album as a leader by the age of twenty-one. His first recordings showed a great deal of creativity and the strong influence of Keith Jarrett and guitarist Jim Hall. By the mid-1980s, the Pat Metheny Group, featuring the synthesizer work and compositions of Lyle Mays, was regularly releasing easy going, almost flavorless fusion At the same time, Metheny has regularly stretched himself in side projects like the surprising *Song X*, recorded in 1985 with Ornette Coleman, and he has maintained respect from jazz purists and avant-gardists while continuing to indulge the cornier side of a passionate yuppie fan base.

A good deal of hope was also placed in the World Saxophone Quartet, or at least in the members of the group that formed in 1976. The four original members, Oliver Lake, Julius Hemphill, David Murray, and Hamiet Bluiett, as well as alto saxophonist Arthur Blythe, who later replaced Hemphill, all played with technical surety (which conservative jazz listeners often thought was lacking among free jazz musicians), a thorough understanding of jazz history, and willingness to stretch into non-tonal soloing in nearly any context. David Murray had created a masterpiece with his 1980 album *Ming*, scored for his octet, which for a time showed promise as a recession-era alternative to the big band. As a composer and performer, he and the other saxophonists associated with WSQ seemed to be able to synthesize the multiple styles of post-1960 jazz. He mixed sophisticated arranging with the energy of free jazz and the R&B rhythms of fusion. The World Saxophone Quartet itself was remarkably successful throughout the 1980s, even, more often than not, without benefit of a rhythm section..

As it had happened before, and will surely happen again, the rumbling in the press over the death of jazz was comfortably silenced by the mid-1980s. But in a manner unique in jazz history, the inevitable resurgence of interest in jazz was accomplished not by finding the next new style, but by looking backwards to the last time jazz had a healthy

audience. While several musicians from the bebop generation and before experienced resurgences in their careers in
the 1980s (some, like Dexter Gordon, looked and sounded
as if they had been hired from the grave to make new albums), a new generation of musicians came of age. Most of
these musicians had received formal education in jazz and
showed a new, academic respect for jazz history. They approached the music as if there were a sacred canon of compositions and performance styles for the first time. It was
a simultaneous reinforcement and destruction of the jazz
tradition, a declaration that doing something new was the
old way of things.

WYNTON MARSALIS
AND THE YOUNG LIONS

Trumpeter Wynton Marsalis has been the center of controversy and had the attention of the jazz press for nearly his
entire life. When he released his first, self-titled jazz album
as a leader in 1982, it came with a massive push from Columbia records. He came from a prominent musical family
in New Orleans (his father, Ellis is a jazz pianist and was a
well-known educator before his son's debut), attended Juilliard Conservatory for a brief period, and dropped out to
join Art Blakey's Jazz Messengers. Marsalis was still debat-
ing whether to pursue a career as a jazz trumpeter or as
a classical soloist at the time, and he made recordings in
both genres through the mid-1980s. Marsalis was the perfect figure at the perfect time: young, handsome, talented,
and most importantly, black and committed to acoustic jazz,
which made him a rare and highly desired commodity.

His first albums showed a clear debt to Miles Davis circa
1965. Working with a quintet made up of his contemporaries, including his older brother Branford on tenor saxophone, Marsalis wrote modal compositions of some quality,

but little novelty. As a soloist, however, Marsalis was extremely capable from the very beginning, playing with a pure, dark tone with no vibrato that was reminiscent of Miles Davis, but technically much more consistent and without the cracked notes that Davis turned into expressive ornamentation.

At times, discussion about Wynton Marsalis in jazz circles has overshadowed his work. In 1985, when Branford left Wynton's quintet to tour with rock musician Sting, a feud between the two brothers was played out publicly, and Wynton's purist stance against working in any rock context brought to the public's awareness his conservative musical perspective. There is significant irony to the rift between the two brothers: Sting, in an effort to assert his independence from his old band, the Police, marketed his practice of hiring young jazz musicians, and his band also featured Wynton's pianist, Kenny Kirkland, and Weather Report drummer Omar Hakim—so the crossover act was a deliberate act of alienation on both sides of the jazz-rock divide.

In the meantime, the still young Wynton developed his style away from what many criticized as an overdependence on Miles Davis. On 1984's *Hot House Flowers*, the best album of his early style, Marsalis played a number of older compositions, such as Hoagy Carmichael's "Stardust" and Duke Ellington's "Melancholia" with a full orchestra in arrangements that owed a great debt to Gil Evans. As the 1980s progressed, Wynton, often under the guidance of writer Stanley Crouch, developed a strong interest in early jazz, especially Louis Armstrong and early Duke Ellington. By 1990, Marsalis was writing in earlier styles as well, infusing much of his music with elements of early blues and jazz. A glance at Wynton's discography makes the issue clear—starting in 1988 with the release of *Majesty of the Blues*, he may have used the word "blue" in more album titles than any other jazz musician after 1970.

In 1991, he became the artistic director of Jazz at Lincoln

Center, and has used its funding, prestige, and relationship with public television to ably advance the public awareness of jazz history. The Jazz at Lincoln Center program evolved out of the Lincoln Center Jazz Orchestra—a big band that followed the post-1980 trend of jazz repertory ensembles, and specializes in playing older works by mostly deceased composers and arrangers. With the broader program of Jazz at Lincoln Center, Marsalis has promoted the cause of developing a jazz canon. While such a goal has given a museum quality to the public concept of jazz, it has also gone further to bring more interest to the music than fusion had previously, and has become the common way of discussing jazz. Rashied Ali has spent the 1990s taking a similar approach to free jazz. His group Prima Materia has re-recorded works such as Albert Ayler's "Bells" and John Coltrane's "Ascension" in an effort to bring the same kind of scholarly attention to free jazz that more conservative styles have enjoyed since 1990.

Wynton Marsalis might have been the center of attention in the 1980s, but he was just one of a generation of musicians that were playing acoustic instruments in older jazz styles throughout the 1980s. Most of the Young Lions, as did just about every jazz musician born in the 1960s, had the benefit of a formal college education in jazz. With up to four years dedicated to practice and study of the music, many musicians from this generation, still in their early twenties, were able to outplay their inspiring predecessors. . Branford Marsalis and drummer Jeff "Tain" Watts, both members of Wynton's quintet through the mid-1980s, have maintained their connection with modal jazz, especially John Coltrane's version, since breaking ranks. Branford, after a brief flirtation with fusion, has released a number of engaging albums with a sound and compositional approach halfway between Coltrane and Ornette Coleman, while Watts, less productive as a bandleader, has worked in a variety of contexts and has released two albums of his own

featuring his still immature but very promising compositions. Other notable members of the generation, who have
all retained a connection with inside jazz from the 1960s
(although with varying interests in outside styles) include
saxophonists James Carter and Joshua Redman, trumpeter
Roy Hargrove, pianists Kenny Barron and Marcus Roberts,
and vocalists Kevin Mahogany and Kurt Elling.

CAREER RESURGENCES
AND THE RISE OF THE BOXED SET

The Young Lions and their respect for musicians past were
not the only influence on the increased conservatism of
the jazz world in the 1980s. The first major attempts of
the recording industry to push the compact disc as a new
format occurred in 1982. While tape formats preceded CDs
in the 1960s and 1970s, they were essentially designed for
portability and never replaced the LP. Using promises of
improved sound quality and permanence, manufacturers
and record labels attempted, and eventually succeeded, to
convince the public to replace their record collections completely with compact discs. As added incentives to persuade
collectors to replace their LPs, and to take advantage of the
expanded capacity of CDs, labels raided their back cata-
logues, adding "bonus tracks" of alternate and incomplete
takes from older sessions, and began to collect musicians'
entire recorded works on boxed sets.

The increased availability of older jazz recordings
brought about a resurrection in the careers of many older
musicians, while others revisited the material and style of
their earlier records. Herbie Hancock, who had reunited
in 1976 with the rest of the Miles Davis Second Quintet
(with Freddie Hubbard taking their former leader's place),
enjoyed parallel careers in the 1980s, pleasing popular
audiences with the synth-pop of *Future Shock* while he

maintained a central role in the jazz scene with VSOP, as the band was now called. Their recordings, as well as the 1981 album *Quartet*, which featured the Davis rhythm section with Wynton Marsalis, were more conservative than they would have been had they revisited their music from fifteen years earlier. While the group still featured some of the best living jazz artists, and their sound was immediately recognizable, VSOP never threatened to pull apart the forms with which they worked, as they had with Davis.

In a fashion similar to VSOP, the band Old and New Dreams comprised Charlie Haden, Ed Blackwell, and Don Cherry, all alumni from Ornette Coleman's first quartet recordings, with tenor saxophonist Dewey Redman, a later frequent collaborator with Coleman. The group specialized in playing the same repertoire that they had first recorded some twenty years earlier, in much the same way. At the same time, their albums were among the freshest and most vibrant recordings of the 1980s.

Tenor saxophonist Dexter Gordon also enjoyed popularity at the end of his life nearly as great as he had had at his peak in the 1940s. In 1986, Gordon starred in the film *'Round Midnight*, playing a character that combined the biographies of Bud Powell and Lester Young. He was nominated for an Oscar for his work, and Herbie Hancock's score, which featured Gordon, won awards in both the United States and France. Although he was well past his prime as a soloist, the recordings he made, with a rough sound and behind-the-beat phrasing, were quite popular. A similar kind of attention was brought to Eubie Blake; the pre-jazz pianist was celebrated in a Broadway musical, *Eubie*, in 1978, performed on the television show *Saturday Night Live*, and attended his one hundredth birthday celebration shortly before his death in 1983. It featured a host of musicians, all blissfully ignorant of the fact that he was born in 1887.

21

THE GENRE BUSTERS

Fusion was neither the first nor the only possible music that combined jazz with other genres in a way that was confusing and frustrating for purist audiences. In a sense, the history of jazz has been as much about the adulteration of a tradition as it has been about the preservation of one. The act of begging, borrowing, and stealing whatever materials might help a given work have been a part of all the arts, and if a rule exists for creative artists, it is not that stealing is wrong, but that the artist should steal from the best.

If, as this book argues, jazz is defined less by musical and technical features than by consensus, then it follows that as American culture inevitably changes, so does the definition of jazz and the canon of its great musicians. Certainly, after World War II, when jazz musicians increasingly acted on their own personal ideas about jazz without clear guidelines from colleagues and audiences, a number of musicians fell through the cracks in tradition, while others have worked in entirely nontraditional fashions that became developments instead of aberrations. The phenomenon might have been more frequent and apparent after 1960 or so, but jazz has never existed in a vacuum. Singers such as Frank Sinatra, early rhythm and blues musicians like Louis Jordan, and country musicians like Chet Atkins and Bob Wills all trod a thin line between jazz and other American popular music genres; some, like Atkins (who saw no contradiction in playing Django Reinhardt-influenced renditions of "Tiger Rag" at the Grand Ol' Opry), have been put squarely into their genre by history, while others, like Sinatra continue to be topics of debate.

The conservative atmosphere of the 1980s may ultimately have been a short term backlash against the cultural revolutions of the 1960s, but by then a new paradigm of creativity had already developed among artists, who saw the increased individualism and experimentalism of the arts as the death of genre altogether. In a sense, Marsalis reinforced the same assertion. For many artists, including jazz musicians, anything that could be done within the confines of a specific genre had already been done by the end of the 1960s. While Marsalis, among others, reacted to the cultural dead end by turning back to earlier styles, others looked to the intersections and gaps between jazz and European art music, or between novels and biographies, or between documentary and comedy. Yet a third school of thought, best represented in jazz by alto saxophonist John Zorn, turned to collage and juxtaposed previously segregated genres for the sake of irony or novelty.

The degree to which the musicians discussed in this chapter have had an impact on jazz varies greatly, as does the degree to which they take their inspiration from the jazz tradition. All of them, however, share the fact that, intentionally or not, their music subverts standard concepts of jazz in some way.

IMPROVISATION IN THE UNITED KINGDOM

In the United States, free jazz was often mistaken for free improvisation; the lack of formal structure, tonality, and steady tempo sounded to most audiences like a lack of any restrictions at all. In fact, free jazz developed into a fairly strict style in a fairly short period of time, and avoidance of some traditional aspects of jazz became as necessary to free jazz as the maintenance of other elements, like instrumentation, head-and-chorus structure, and the division of groups into wind sections and rhythm sections. By contrast, the musicians involved in the improvised music communities that sprang up in large cities throughout Europe in the 1960s, of which London is perhaps the best known, had different cultural conventions to break, and their own versions of free jazz developed into identifiable styles of their own.

In England, improvisers generally begin performances with as few preconceived musical ideas as possible, and often work to eliminate any connection with established genres whatsoever. Among the first such groups in London was AMM (not an acronym, but a meaningless list of letters), initially the trio of guitarist Keith Rowe, drummer Eddie Prevost, and saxophonist Lou Gare. AMM makes frequent use of chance and indeterminate processes (acts whose outcome cannot be predicted or controlled, like dropping coins on a drum head), which, to some extent, reduced the possibility of influence on their music even from their own taste and intent. Rowe, especially, has found new ways to approach the electric guitar, using radios, small motors, knitting needles, and almost anything except traditional technique to create and manipulate sound while leaving the guitar lying flat on a table top. The use of indeterminacy, as opposed to a kind of improvisation in which sounds are conceived and then executed according to plan, aligned AMM with the European and American academic avant-garde, who had been working with chance since John Cage's *Music of Changes*. The often changing personnel of the group also included avant-garde composer Cornelius Cardew and several classically trained musicians like pianist John Tillbury (who, with Prevost and Rowe completes the present incarnation of the group). At the same time, Eddie Prevost had a background in jazz and frequently cites Elvin Jones as a primary influence on his playing—although Prevost tends to play at glacially slow tempos with a lighter touch than Jones, he also brings a sense of swing to AMM's performances, as if he were playing every hundredth note on a Coltrane Quartet recording.

AMM quickly inspired a number of young musicians in London, particularly jazz enthusiasts, and most of them at one time or another played in drummer John Stevens's Spontaneous Music Ensemble. Over the twenty-five years of the group's existence, SME ranged from a duo to a twenty-piece orchestra, all guided by Stevens's quiet, pointillistic aesthetic. His intention was to keep the group's work within at least a passing relation to the jazz idiom, but still strictly improvised from first note to last. For the most part, regardless of the instrumentation, SME's music was steadfastly quiet and sparse, with each musician in the group more focused on ensemble sound than on his own playing. The 1973 recording *Face to Face*, for instance, features a series of duets in which each player focuses their attention the other and all playing is incidental to the observation, with the hope that the entire performance springs from the subconscious.

Many of the former members of SME carried out notable careers as soloists and (usually nominal) band leaders, including bassist Dave Holland, who later joined the Miles Davis Quintet. Guitarist Derek Bailey (1930–2005) was among the most popular and the most puzzling. Bailey had been a professional guitarist since the 1950s, with a background in jazz and popular music and a steady supply of gigs in dance bands in Sheffield. In 1963, he formed a trio named Joseph Holbrooke (after an obscure late Romantic composer whose music the trio never played) with drummer Tony Oxley and bassist Gavin Bryars; the group began as a fairly traditional jazz combo, with an interest in John Coltrane (a ten-minute rehearsal tape was briefly available on CD, in which the group plays a quiet, lyrical interpretation of Coltrane's "Impressions").

In 1966, he moved to Europe and joined SME, and ceased playing jazz heads for the remainder of the twentieth century. Bailey's distinctive approach to the guitar arose out of an interest in the concept of pure, non-idiomatic improvisation. To achieve his goal, he studied a variety of music that allows for improvisation; in his 1980 book *Improvisation: Its Nature and Practice* (which stemmed from a BBC radio series of the same name, and was further developed into a television series for Channel 4 for the second edition in 1991), he explores the use of improvisation in flamenco, Indian classical music, and jazz, among other idioms, before Bailey writes about his own brand of free improvisation. Bailey's distinctive, angular playing is best heard on number of solo recordings, mostly on his own Incus imprint. A technical master, Bailey seems to change styles with every note, jumping from dense harmonies to rapid, dissonant solo lines to unusual harmonics within a single second. He also collaborated with a great many other musicians in a variety of contexts, and organized Company, an irregular, moving festival of improvisation that assembled a number of creative musicians and presented their first performances together.

At the end of his life, Bailey began to explore genres again, beginning with *Guitar, Drums 'n Bass* in 1997, in which he improvised over dance tracks provided by DJ Ninj. Bailey began to allow himself to fit within a traditional texture (while maintaining his own inimitable style), rather than transform it into something new. He seemed to perfect the new approach with *Mirakle*, recorded in 2000 with bassist Jamaaladeen Tacuma and drummer Calvin Weston, who both have backgrounds with Ornette Coleman's Prime Time as well as more traditional funk. Bailey recorded standards for the first time in 2002; the peculiar CD *Ballads* features old-timey tunes like "Melancholy Baby," in which he played solo on an old acoustic guitar in poor playing condition Bailey somehow managed to place the melodies, played traditionally, in the context of his solo improvisatory style in a strange, but not disconcerting way. His last album, *Carpal Tunnel*, documents Bailey's struggle with the disease (no longer able to hold a pick, Bailey chose to learn guitar technique again from scratch), In the months following the recording, it was discovered that his difficulties were the first symptoms of a misdiagnosed motor neuron disease, which eventually took his life on Christmas day, 2005.

Whereas Bailey used jazz techniques and harmonies as only one element among many in his improvisations, a number of English improvisers have maintained stylistic connections to free jazz. Saxophonist Evan Parker, while he frequently pulled at traditional frameworks and explored free improvisation, developed his playing largely as an extension of John Coltrane's style. Parker often borrows phrases from Coltrane, and has mastered the use of multiphonics to stunning degree. He tends to play with three distinct styles: pointillistic (quiet bursts of sounds), powerful Coltrane-like lyricism, and long phrases of rapidly alternating multiphonics. Parker's multiphonic torrents benefit from his ability to circular breathe (a technique that allows the player to expend air from the mouth while inhaling, thus creating single notes or phrases of theoretically limitless duration): best featured on the 1989 CD *Conic Sections*, Parker sustains long, rapid phrases for as long as twenty-five minutes at a time, with enough control to present two or three independent lines at once.

DOWNTOWN NEW YORK: NO WAVE AND THE KNITTING FACTORY

In New York in the late 1970s, while mainstream jazz was at its nadir, the most vibrant musical community in town was only tenuously associated with jazz. While Harlem and midtown still hosted jazz performances, the area below 14th Street hosted the visual arts community as well as a growing underground rock movement, at clubs like CBGB's and Max's Kansas City. While most musicians in downtown New York developed the well-publicized and often-discussed punk rock movement, a small scene was developed, cynical about the possibilities of pop song structure and traditional harmony as it was found even in punk. The No Wave was named as a combination of "New Wave," as much pop music was called at the time, and *No New York*, the title of a compilation LP that featured many of the central figures in the movement. No Wave bands specialized in deliberately amateurish, confrontational noise produced on instruments that the musicians often refused to practice or learn to play traditionally.

In their effort to make a nihilistic statement, the downtown New York underground rejected even the rebellion of punk—which was a kind of conservative movement of its own before long, replacing the excesses of disco and pop with older forms of rock, albeit played more aggressively and louder than earlier bands. Many New York bands embraced what they considered the subversive elements of disco and dance music. James Chance, a Wisconsin-born saxophonist who had moved to New York to join the free jazz scene, led an unusual and abrasive funk band that performed off-kilter versions of James Brown grooves, while Chance shouted and played out of tune saxophone, and frequently started fist fights with audience members. By the early 1980s, the underground had also embraced the band Defunkt. Led by trombonist Joseph Bowie (younger brother of AACM trumpeter Lester), Defunkt played energetic, danceable music that incorporates elements of free jazz, funk, hip-hop, and occasionally No Wave style noise.

By 1987, the No Wave movement, by now petered out, had attracted all number of experimental and unusual

musicians to downtown Manhattan, and they found a meet-
ing place at Michael Dorf's music club on Houston Street.
The Knitting Factory's eclectic booking policy involved
hosting performances by musicians from a wide variety
of backgrounds, including free jazz, academic composition,
rock, and several styles from other countries—often, all on
stage at once. Most of the musicians working at the Knitting Factory, even when their connection to jazz has been
only tangential, have found their CDs for sale in the jazz
bins at most record stores.

While the older London-based scene was intent on strip-
ping music of association with any genre or idiom, downtown
New Yorkers reveled in juxtaposing and recontextualizing
genres. John Zorn, especially, gained international fame
from his rapid- fire genre hopping, both as a composer of
his own works and a player/arranger of older music. His
band's second, eponymous CD, Naked City, which serves as
the best introduction to the Knitting Factory scene, would
treat soundtrack music from film and television (especially the spaghetti western soundtracks of Italian composer
Ennio Morricone, who was an early obsession of the often-
obsessed Zorn) through a variety of styles. For instance, two
bars of a country tune, three seconds of free jazz, a heavy
metal burst and a cocktail piano arrangement might all find
space to appear within five seconds of a typical performance.
Zorn has treated his own career in a similar fashion, leap-
ing between long-term projects with ease, from his "game"
series of compositions whose rules for performance were
based on sports and games, to soundtracks, to No Wave (his
early LP Locus Solus, featuring the untuned guitar of Arto
Lindsay is a primary document in the history of pitchless
noise in New York), to his series of tribute albums to jazz
composers (of which Spy vs. Spy, covering the music of Ornette Coleman with punk rock speed and volume, is one of
his greatest triumphs). The result of such a varied and busy
career is a recorded legacy of over 250 CDs.

NAKED CITY, "YOU WILL BE SHOT"

Naked City, Track 3

Clocking in at a typically brief one minute and thirty seconds, "You Will Be Shot" is a fairly simple exploration of rapid genre hopping. At the same time, it also demonstrates a somewhat traditional, jazz derived approach to structure. The entire performance, which contains no solos and only four or five notes played by Zorn, consists of three repetitions of a three-part structure that parallels the repeated question and single answer phrasing of the 12-bar blues. In the case of "You Will Be Shot," however, harmonic structure is replaced by stylistic structure. The "A section" begins with a brief, rhythmically complex phrase in the style of the theme music for the James Bond films, and is followed with a noisy, pitchless moment of the radically sped up polka rhythm that forms the basis of hardcore punk. Following a repetition of these two sections, the band jumps immediately into about five seconds' worth of a country shuffle, and a final burst of hardcore. As is typical for Zorn's work of the time, there is no development of ideas, although the three-section theme is repeated twice. In the context of Zorn's music, the interest is derived not from the music itself, but from the collaging of surf guitar, hardcore punk, and 12-bar blues into an easily recognizable, and distinctly new idea.

Guitarist Bill Frisell, who worked with Zorn in Naked City, has probably exerted the greatest influence on the jazz mainstream among downtown New York musicians. Born in Baltimore, Maryland in 1951, raised in Denver, Colorado, and educated at Berklee School of Music in Boston, Frisell came to New York in the 1980s with his career already established as a side man on several albums on ECM records. While his early music is largely in the vein of other ECM artists like Pat Metheny, Frisell distinguished himself from the beginning with a unique tone and a strong interest in country, blues and bluegrass. His composition "Rag," for instance, which he performed frequently and recorded at least twice, is more often a waltz than a rag, but with quirky pauses built into the head, he ably hops among rag, country and jazz styles in a fashion that John Zorn would use if he were transplanted into a Bowery saloon in 1923. Frisell makes frequent use of signal processors, especially delay, looping and reverb, to help him achieve timbrally what Zorn achieves stylistically. Over the course of a solo, Frisell might sound at first like a pedal steel guitar, with a light attack and swelling chords. Before long, he might kick in distortion and use feedback for a single note. Frisell also liberally bends the neck of his guitar, causing a dip in pitch—his warbling, swelling chording has been rapidly replacing the traditional dark sound of Wes Montgomery as the standard jazz guitar tone over the course of the 1990s. With the release of *Nashville* in 1997, Frisell began to make the country and bluegrass influences on his playing more explicit, and his subtle but adventurous music has found a popular audience.

SMOOTH JAZZ

Around 1989, several commercial-minded radio stations adopted a new format known as smooth jazz. Designed to provide relaxing background music to office work and dinner dates, smooth jazz allowed for music from a variety of popular music styles, but provided specific restraints for what could be played: moderate tempos of eighty to one hundred beats per minute, a maximum of approximately 50% tracks with vocalists, major keys and a minimum of dissonance and dynamic variation. Play lists at smooth jazz radio stations have generally consisted of a mix of pop singers like Sade, Celine Dion, and Lou Rawls with slower, quieter fusion records and R&B ballads. But while the radio format itself has little to do with jazz, it has also provided a name for a particular brand of commercially oriented fusion that has its own history, and its own poster child in soprano saxophonist Kenny G.

Born Kenny Gorelick in Seattle, Washington, in 1956, Kenny G had some experience in fusion and stage shows (he dropped his last name while working with a touring Barry White show) before he signed a contract with Arista in 1981. With his fourth album, 1986's *Duotones*, Kenny G reached an unparalleled level of success as a saxophonist, especially for the slick, repetitive and largely uneventful single "Songbird." He has continued his popularity with a string of seventeen CDs, including an anthology, with barely any distinguishing characteristics among them—most of his recordings end with a fade out, rather than subject a listener or grocery shopper to the distraction of a final chord. Generally playing against a fully synthesized background, Kenny G plays simple melodies and rapid but simple solos that largely consist of scales up and down the instrument that might be a warm-up for other musicians. But while he has been a source of frustration and comedy among critics and jazz enthusiasts, his albums have consistently sold in the millions, dwarfing the sales of mainstream jazz artists by a factor of ten. For most Americans, who had long ago lost track of developments in jazz, Kenny G became the primary figure in post-fusion instrumental music.

Purist critics, however, have ignored some stylistic developments themselves in an effort to point out Kenny G's limitations as a musician. As much as anyone with more than a passing interest in jazz might be loathe to admit, Kenny G is part of a tradition of jazz that finds its origins in *Charlie Parker With Strings*, and continues through the more commercially oriented recordings of guitarist Wes Montgomery and the genuinely talented saxophonist Grover Washington, Jr. That Kenny G is an uncreative, technically limited musician with a cloying sound that would have difficulty managing the harmonic complexity of a Wayne Shorter composition is nearly impossible to deny. His 1999 recording *Classics in the Key of G*, featuring bland mid-tempo renditions of jazz standards, serves to reinforce this impression, even as it was likely an attempt to silence jazz critics. At the same time, he and stylistically similar musicians like saxophonists Najee and David Sanborn (both of whom are far more capable musicians) have taken up a tradition as it was established in the last recordings of Miles Davis.

The most common reaction among jazz critics and fans upon hearing Kenny G's name (most do their best never to hear his music) is thorough dismissal with the statement, "that's not jazz." But to deny Kenny G's connection to the jazz tradition and his importance in falsely defining that tradition to an audience far wider than most jazz musicians will ever enjoy, is to change the very definition of jazz itself, adding the requirement that it must be musically engaging at all times. Kenny G's music may be bad jazz, but it is jazz nevertheless. His career only demonstrates that jazz, like any other musical tradition, can produce terrible music, and that on occasion, terrible music can be very popular.

22

LATELY

Development in jazz over the past one hundred years has been additive rather than linear; for every young musician who innovates and still calls his music jazz, there are a dozen other musicians who prefer earlier approaches. Compound that phenomenon with the fragmentation of styles after bebop, and there is a dizzying number of different kinds of music that lay claim to the descriptor "jazz," much of which seems to have nothing to do with other jazz styles.

On May 6, 2006 (a Saturday night), the following performances were scheduled to take place in New York, according to the *Village Voice*: trumpeter Dave Douglas and his quintet at the Village Vanguard, playing a Miles Davis influenced mishmash of free jazz, bebop and early fusion; Wynton Marsalis at Lincoln Center paying anachronistic tribute to New Orleans's Congo Square with a set of early jazz and Ghanian percussion; odd vocalist Andy Bey, whose feminine voice has made a surprising comeback at the end of his career, with a quartet at the Jazz Standard; the David Gilmore Group, a blues/fusion act, at the Jazz Gallery; and first generation free jazz bassist Henry Grimes, who had disappeared from the public eye for nearly forty years as he battled mental illness and homelessness, performs at the Center for Improvisational Music in Park Slope, Brooklyn (a likely sold-out performance). Add to this list dozens of unadvertised concerts in smaller clubs throughout the five boroughs, and consider that after each of these performances, audience members are likely to discuss the jazz scenes in Chicago, Los Angeles, Philadelphia, London and Berlin over a drink.

With such a wide array of music vying for public attention, it is difficult, if not impossible, to assess the importance and popularity of any given jazz sub-style in the twenty-first century. A few common points generally apply, however. Jazz is alive and well, and is still growing in popularity since its nadir in the late 1970s—even if the audience has become fragmented to the point that financial success as a jazz musician is unlikely for most. Jazz has received its most positive break since 1990 with increased emphasis on jazz in education. The creation of jazz departments at nearly every music school and university in the United States has brought about an entirely new way for musicians to learn their instruments and to develop their styles. Nearly every jazz musician under the age of forty now has formal training, and the concentration of what was once years spent at jam sessions into four years in classrooms and practice rooms has produced a generation of technically facile musicians.

In the 1980s, fueled by the twin controversies of Wynton Marsalis and Kenny G, jazz communities seemed to be divided in to three warring factions of traditionalists, fusion devotees and avant-gardists. The contentious tone of letters to the editors of jazz magazines seems to have cooled, as mainstream jazz looks to figures formerly regarded as avant-gardists as the new torch bearers for the constantly changing jazz tradition. Trumpeter Dave Douglas first came to prominence as the leader of the Tiny Bell Trio with guitarist Brad Shepik (née Schoeppach) and drummer Jim Black, with playful renditions of Balkan folk music with elements of fusion and free jazz. In 2001, Douglas signed a contract with RCA and has been their flagship jazz artist ever since—he has not changed his downtown New York polystylistic approach to music; his audience, however, now includes a large number of mainstream jazz listeners who might have ignored his approach twenty years earlier. In the meantime, John Zorn has spent the last ten years concentrating on a single, remarkably conservative project. *Masada* consists of hundreds of short melodies largely derived from Jewish folk music. While the tunes have been performed in a variety of contexts by ensembles that occasionally do not even feature Zorn's playing, he has most frequently performed on alto saxophone with a piano-less quartet, also called Masada, that sounds for all the world exactly like the Ornette Coleman Quartet of 1960, with the exception of the predominance of Middle Eastern modes.

Free jazz has made a considerable resurgence in popularity since 1990, developing a new audience, mostly culled from aging fans of punk rock and indie rock. The annual Vision Festival, started in 1995 on the Lower East Side of Manhattan, has grown steadily throughout its history (sold out concerts are the norm even though they have moved several times to progressively larger venues) It has presented long programs of free jazz, with many older musicians from the first generation of free jazz, like saxaphonist Sam Rivers and trumpeter Bill Dixon, younger musicians that joined the New York free jazz scene in the 1970s and 1980s like bassist William Parker and multi-instrumentalist Daniel Carter, and an even younger third generation of musicians, like the gifted percussionist Susie Ibarra and the John Coltrane-inspired saxophonists Andrew Lamb and Ras Moshe. On Sunday evenings at ABC No Rio, a former squat in the gentrified Lower East Side, Blaise Siwula hosts a weekly gathering of free improvisers featuring a scheduled performance followed by impromptu jams. These performances attract free jazz and improvisation enthusiasts of all ages from all walks of life. Strangely, while most musicians involved in free jazz are still working with ideas and concepts conceived forty years earlier, they continue to call themselves and their music avant-garde, and the term has changed its meaning within jazz circles to refer to all outside music.

Although in 1985 it seemed that fusion had transformed into the banalities of smooth jazz, after 1990 it became apparent that, for musicians born after the British Invasion of 1964, the music of Miles Davis after *Bitches Brew*, as well as Tony Williams's Lifetime and other fusion bands from the first half of the 1970s, provided an untapped source of inspiration. Jim Black's Alas No Axis, a quartet with clarinetist Chris Speed, guitarist Hilmar Jensson and electric bassist Skuli Sverrisson, has incorporated harmonies and textures from indie rock bands like Sonic Youth and Pavement into its music, while Black's virtuosity and creativity at the drum set has kept him the clear leader of the band through their guitar-and electronics-driven sound. On the West Coast, guitarist Nels Cline has been a remarkable and creative fusion musician in his compositions, playing, and career choices. He has released several albums of solo guitar, and as the leader of a trio, showing tremendous stylistic flexibility, he combines Bill Frisell's style with free jazz rhythm on some tracks and plays long, dissonant jams in the style of Sonic Youth on others. He has also worked frequently with post-punk bassist Mike Watt, and is well featured on Watt's 1997 CD *Contemplating the Engine Room*, which approaches a new style of jazz rock on its own in long instrumental tracks with extensive improvised solos. At present, Cline is a member of indie rock band Wilco, and still leads his own groups when time allows.

In more traditional circles, a number of younger musicians have been able to find new approaches to old forms and develop individual voices without sounding derivative. Pianist Brad Mehldau has been a favorite among critics, taking an approach that echoes the Bill Evans Trio with his subtle touch and interactivity, but he has developed a more contrapuntal style, and toys with the concept of the jazz standard, mixing renditions of old standards like "Bewitched, Bothered and Bewildered" with popular rock tunes like Paul McCartney's "Yesterday." The Philadelphia based collective known as M-Base has also been prodigious and successful. The members of M-Base, led by alto saxophonist Steve Coleman (although informally, they have been associates since the mid-1980s), have developed complex theories about the integration of funk, hip hop, and African musical elements into a mainstream jazz context. Coleman, alto saxophonist Greg Osby, pianist Geri Allen, and vocalist Cassandra Wilson all lead their own groups and support each other's projects, and have successfully and consistently challenged listeners with complexity and creativity while crossing over to larger audiences. Wilson, specifically, has been a remarkable crossover success. Whether her music now can rightfully be considered jazz, her deep, complex voice and loose, conversational phrasing have served her well on a number of critically acclaimed and financially successful albums.

While free jazz has found a new audience almost by default, as ex-punks turn to musicians like Cecil Taylor as a rite of passage, many other musicians have deliberately and more self-consciously sought crossover appeal among rock audiences. Many of the most successful crossover artists have rushed to fill the void left by the death of Grateful Dead guitarist Jerry Garcia, and joined touring acts like Phish at music festivals geared towards neo-hippie audiences. Medeski, Martin and Wood have been particularly successful. The organ trio, who had previously been involved in a fairly wide variety of post-bop projects, have adapted themselves for blissful dancing; drummer Billy Martin focuses on dance beats influenced by James Brown, and further influenced by the sped-up James Brown samples of electronic dance music, and the group sustains grooves for extended periods of time, often forgoing solos altogether —the repetitive but catchy results are trance inducing to fans and boring to jazz purists. Guitarist Charlie Hunter, a technically skilled and essentially conservative player, has attracted the jam band audience with his unusual technique of providing both bass and lead lines on his eight-string guitar. The Bad Plus has taken a novel approach to the concept of crossover: the piano trio dresses and packages their albums as any indie rock band of their generation would, and play creative and often humorous covers of older rock tunes like Queen's "We Are The Champions," as well as their own Ornette Coleman- and John Coltrane-inspired original compositions. Their music is more radical than it appears on the surface, however—within the camp of their disco covers and the power of their heavy rock beats is an interaction and creativity reminiscent of Paul Bley.

In 2000, documentary filmmaker Ken Burns, who enjoyed tremendous popularity for his marathon television miniseries *The Civil War* and *Baseball*, completed his trilogy of long films about American history with the 19 hour *Jazz*. First broadcast on PBS in January of 2001, the documentary strongly featured the opinions of Wynton Marsalis. Burns had not previously been a fan of the music, and as the primary consultant for the film, Marsalis infused the documentary with many of his controversial opinions and more than a few factual errors. While *Jazz* was not the most accurate and unbiased music documentary on television, it was one of the best publicized, and on the surge of interest brought by its broadcast, hopes were high among jazz professionals that the twenty-first century would be a busy one. So far, the short term effects have been somewhat disappointing: PBS has had much more success rerunning rock concerts than Burns's documentaries during pledge drives, and neither PBS nor any other network has followed through with additional jazz-related programming. But through a collaborative effort with Jazz at Lincoln Center, Columbia Records, and PBS, Ken Burns Jazz has developed beyond the scope of a television miniseries into a series of introductory CDs (most of which serve as excellent introductions to the artists they discuss) and an educational program (available on the web at http://pbskis.org/jazz). With a fully designed curriculum for grade school music courses, the PBS Jazz Kids program fills a void at a time when music programs in public schools in America have been reduced or eliminated outright across the country.

It would be foolhardy to attempt to predict what the generation of musicians currently learning from PBS's curriculum will create and market as jazz. Nearly every survey of music written before 1990 concludes with wildly inaccurate extrapolations of then-current trends. While the only surefire prediction about the stylistic turns jazz will make in the twenty-first century is that it will be unpredictable, a few trends have been in place and will likely continue. The self-conscious elevation of jazz from popular music to art music first posited by the bebop generation has continued. Since 1990, both the McArthur Foundation and the Pulitzer Prize have awarded jazz artists for the first (and, in the case of the McArthur "genius" grant, second) time, and the establishment of Jazz at Lincoln Center has given jazz a permanent home on the campus of Juilliard Conservatory. Rutgers University-Newark's Masters program is the first degree program devoted to jazz history; Columbia University's Center for Jazz Studies has been an active association of faculty since 2001, providing jazz study classes in the University's music department; and the University of Texas Center for American Music shows hope of following Columbia's model into jazz territory soon.. As jazz scholarship catches up with performance as a course of academic study, however, it remains to be seen how musicians will react. It seems unlikely that jazz musicians will take the direction that European art musicians have taken in the United States, where orchestras have decreased their interest in new music and composition has become almost wholly dependent on academic programs for support. However, jazz musicians are already faced with a changed audience—increasingly educated and increasingly white—and twenty-first century jazz audiences will surely respond to unpredictable changes in similarly unpredictable ways.

APPENDIX
Recommended Recordings

The following list of recordings ought not to be considered a ranked listing of the best jazz CDs on the market, although there might be a great deal of overlap between such a list and this one. Rather, the following discography compiles many of the individual tracks and LPs discussed in this book, and with some luck and a few points of contention, offers a fair survey of jazz styles. With a working knowledge of jazz styles, time periods, and artists, a studious listener will invariably discover his or her own favorite recordings and quickly develop preferences that will lead to a larger collection. For many jazz fans, developing a collection of recordings quickly becomes an obsession, and the hunt for the newest, or oldest, or most obscure recording by a favorite artist can become daily activity.

While our understanding of jazz history and sub-styles is necessarily dependent on sound recording, the best way to experience the music and gain understanding remains live performance. Beyond the reasons discussed in Chapter 1, a live jazz performance provides the opportunity of time spent in a room full of people with similar interests and varying degrees of expertise, and especially given the dwindling audiences that jazz musicians have experienced over the last twenty or thirty years, most fans are excited at the chance to discuss a performance, recommend a recording, or carry on about jazz in general. And with only the possible exception of remote parts of Alaska, there is probably no place in the United States, Japan, or Europe that is more than two hours' travel away from a worthwhile jazz performance.

For the most part, discussion of these recordings can be found throughout this book and any number of other surveys of jazz history or recordings, and discographical information is provided without comment unless necessary. At press time, all catalog numbers and specific CD issues are in print and available at most record stores, although not necessarily in stock—compact disc retailers receive deliveries several times a week, however, and usually have little difficulty processing special orders. Recently, the new medium of Internet music services has settled after a few years of legal issues and shows signs of stability. Services such as eMusic, Real Rhapsody, iTunes, Yahoo Music, and Napster provide a reliable source of music for non-audiophiles, and with the likelihood that a monthly rate for unlimited downloading or streaming of recordings will become the norm, such services will probably become the most common method of acquiring recorded music in the near future. At present, licensing issues, the youth of the medium, and somewhat low demand still limit the availability of jazz recordings online, sometimes in surprising ways. Of course, recordings downloaded or streamed from the Internet come without benefit of documentation, and compact disc liner notes in many cases contain some of the best writing about jazz in print. Issues of sound quality, however, are exaggerated by passionate collectors who sometimes become more concerned with sound quality than with the music constructed from the sounds in question. Compact discs remain the most widely available permanent format for recorded sound, and they are far more reliable than computer hard drives. Until the development of a medium as sonically rich as live performance, robust as vinyl LPs, and cost effective and convenient as online services, they remain the best choice for a permanent collection of sound recordings.

A NOTE ON RECORDINGS
MADE BEFORE 1930

Anthologies of early jazz are plentiful and often confusing, aided by passionate collectors and confusing copyright laws. Different countries have different standards on when sound recordings enter the public domain, and while there is a current effort to create an international standard, many European labels take advantage of the current obscurity of international copyright laws to release collections of music first released as recently as fifty years ago without seeking permission or paying royalties. Often, small labels provide excellent and well-researched anthologies of superior sound quality, but nearly as often, sloppy, poorly mastered, and barely documented CDs reach the market at unreasonable prices. It can be difficult to distinguish between small, boutique labels run by conscientious music fans and opportunistic fly-by-night operations run on the cheap; sticking to established labels and attractive jewel cases might not be the most thorough guarantee of quality, but it is a good general practice until interest in a specific artist or style leads to more thorough knowledge of available recordings.

Fortunately, one of the best sources of early jazz recordings is available without cost on the Internet. Redhotjazz. com, a collaborative website run by Scott Alexander, is an impressive database of information on jazz recordings made before 1930 (and some after), and provides a carefully organized and easy-to-navigate collection of recordings in RealAudio format for listening purposes. While the recordings available on redhotjazz.com are not collectible, they provide a valuable resource for the listener interested in developing a collection of early jazz recordings.

A NOTE ON BOXED SETS

The number of sets of complete recorded works by individual artists and jazz sub-styles grows on a weekly basis, as labels reorganize and make available every note they can find on tape. While interest in complete documentation has been a boon for serious collectors and devoted fans, large, expensive boxed sets can be intimidating for new jazz listeners. Consistent, high-quality performance by artists such as Miles Davis and Ornette Coleman is rare, and the possibility that the first a listener hears of an otherwise worthwhile jazz musician are that musician's first tentative fumbling on tape is significant. In this discography, I have made an effort only to include large sets that contain generally acknowledged "classic" recordings. *Holy Ghost*, the nine disc set of recordings featuring Albert Ayler released in 2004 by Revenant Records, for instance, while it is a valuable and high-quality collection, is omitted because of the original obscurity of the recordings collected. In every case, I have indicated large, multi-disc sets with the letter B in parentheses following the title in this discography; while they are a valuable resource and often worth owning even for a new jazz collection, the reader is advised to avoid the expense of especially large collections unless interest in the contents is already strong.

RECOMMENDED RECORDINGS

The CDs below are listed roughly in the order in which they are discussed in this book. Any commentary in this appendix is specific to recordings in particular, and the chapter in which the music is discussed is indicated in brackets as the last item in each entry.

Various Artists. *Ken Burns Jazz* (B), Columbia/Legacy 61432 [Introduction]

Joplin, Scott. *Greatest Hits*, RCA 60842 [2]
>   Note: Mostly performed by pianist Dick Hyman.

Smith, Bessie. *The Collection*, Columbia/Legacy 44441 [2]

Original Dixieland Jazz Band. *1917–1923*, EPM Musique (France) 158492 [3]

Morton, Jelly Roll. *The Complete Library of Congress Recordings* (B), Rounder 1888 [3]
>   Note: While a limited edition package, this four CD set of Alan Lomax's recordings of Morton in interviews and performance are a landmark, and are accompanied by well over one hundred pages of Grammy-winning notes and articles.

Morton, Jelly Roll. *Jelly Roll Morton* (B), JSP 903 [3]
>   Note: JSP boxed sets are reliable, budget-priced sources of well-mastered early jazz recordings—this five disc set is usually available around the price of two full-priced CDs.

Morton, Jelly Roll. *Greatest Hits*, RCA 68500 [3]
>   Note: A more manageable single CD that serves as an excellent introduction.

Oliver, Joe "King." *Great Original Recordings 1923–1930*, Louisiana Red Hot 607 [3]

Bechet, Sidney. *Ken Burns Jazz*, Sony 61441 [3]
>   Note: While the issues in the *Ken Burns Jazz* boxed set have been discussed, the CD anthologies devoted to individual artists under the title *Ken Burns Jazz* are reliable, thorough compilations of high sound quality. For later artists like John Coltrane and Ornette Coleman, they are somewhat unnecessary, and it is a shame to forgo full albums recorded after the invention of the LP, but for jazz

before 1948, the *Ken Burns Jazz* compilations are highly recommended.

Armstrong, Louis. *Complete Hot Fives and Sevens* (B), JSP 100 [4]

> Note: JSP comes through again. There are better sound remasters and more attractive and well-documented sets of Armstrong's classic ensemble recordings, but with a street price around $20, the JSP set is an attractive package for recordings that are a necessary part of any CD collection.

Beiderbecke, Bix. *Volume 1: Singin' The Blues*, Columbia/Legacy 45450 [5]

> Note: Volume 2 from this two CD anthology is also highly recommended, and it is somewhat puzzling that the two discs have not been paired as a single set.

Johnson, James P. *Carolina Shout*, ASV Living Era 5355 [5]

Waller, Fats. *The Very Best of Fats Waller*, RCA 63731 [5]

Ellington, Duke. *The Essential Duke Ellington*, Columbia/Legacy 89281 [6]

Basie, Count. *America's #1 Band: The Columbia Years* (B), Sony 87110 [6]

> Note: At a budget price and with very little filler, this four disc set is among the rare large boxed sets that merits recommendation as an introduction to a specific artist's music.

Basie, Count. *The Complete Atomic Basie*, Blue Note 28635 [6]

Goodman, Benny. *The Very Best of Benny Goodman*, RCA 63730 [6]

Hawkins, Coleman. *Ken Burns Jazz*, Polygram 549085 [7]

Tatum, Art. *The Definitive Art Tatum*, Blue Note 40225 [7]

Gillespie, Dizzy. *The Complete RCA Victor Recordings: 1939-1949*, RCA 66528 [8]

Powell, Bud. *The Complete Blue Note and Roost Recordings* (B), Blue Note 30083 [8]

Powell, Bud. *The Amazing Bud Powell, Vol. 1*, Blue Note 32136 [8]

Parker, Charles. *Complete Savoy and Dial Studio Sessions* (B), Savoy Jazz 17079 [9]

> Note: Again, several different labels have licensed and released "complete" issues of Parker's recordings from the first and most productive years of his career. The Savoy set is more complete than most, with several alternate takes and recordings of Parker as a side man, and comes with excellent liner notes. Listeners with perfect pitch should be aware that a pressing of disc 4 from this set has been accidentally released at the wrong speed and plays slightly higher than a half step sharp of the original performances. Savoy will replace the disc, although by now every copy of the boxed set contains a corrected disc. Be aware that "Donna Lee" should be in the key of A-flat major, and make the somewhat personal decision as to whether it matters enough to mail the disc away for replacement.

Parker, Charles. *Best of the Complete Savoy and Dial Studio Sessions* (B), Savoy Jazz 17120 [9]

The Quintet. *Jazz at Massey Hall*, OJC 44 [8, 9]

> Note: Also available in SACD format, which generally offers tremendous sonic improvement over standard CD formats, but requires a different player.

Monk, Thelonious. *The Complete Blue Note Recordings* (B), Blue Note 30363 [10]

Monk, Thelonious. *Thelonious Monk Quartet with John Coltrane at Carnegie Hall*, Blue Note 35173 [10]

Clifford Brown/Max Roach Quintet. *Brown and Roach, Inc.*, Polygram 814644 [11]

Rollins, Sonny. *Saxophone Colossus*, OJC 291 [11]

Silver, Horace. *Horace Silver and the Jazz Messengers*, Blue Note 64478 [11]

Art Blakey and the Jazz Messengers. *Moanin'*, Blue Note 95324 [11]

Tristano, Lennie. *Intuition*, Blue Note 52771 [11]

Konitz, Lee. *Motion*, Verve 065510 [11]

The Dave Brubeck Quartet. *Time Out*, Sony 15562 [11]

Davis, Miles. *The Complete Birth of the Cool*, Blue Note 94550 [12]

Davis, Miles. *Bag's Groove*, OJC 245 [12]

Davis, Miles. *'Round About Midnight*, Sony Legacy 94750 [12]
> Note: Since the mid-1990s, Columbia Records (now a subsidiary of Sony) has been issuing the complete works of Miles Davis on Columbia in a series of boxed sets. All of them contain previously unreleased material and extensive liner notes, and complete takes, which were almost never heard on Davis's albums after around 1968. Anyone hoping to start a serious collection of jazz CDs would do well to start by collecting these.

Davis, Miles. *Sketches of Spain*, Sony 65412 [12]

Davis, Miles. *Kind Of Blue*, Sony 64935 [12]

Davis, Miles, *ESP*, Sony 65683 [12]

Davis, Miles, *Bitches Brew*, Sony 65774 [12]

Davis, Miles, *Live Around the World*, Warner Bros. 46032 [12]
> Note: During the 1980s, Davis's LPs consistently shocked and disappointed critics while earning high sales and frequent radio airplay. This LP demonstrates well that Davis's approach in the 1980s was more successful on stage than in the studio.

Mingus, Charles. *Mingus Ah Um*, Sony 65512 [13]

Mingus, Charles. *The Black Saint and the Sinner Lady*, Impulse 174 [13]

Sun Ra. *The Singles*, Evidence 22164 [13]
> Note: While most Sun Ra performances last considerably longer than three or four minutes, this collection of singles spans Ra's entire career. Although it may not include the very best recordings of the Arkestra, this two disc set offers a palatable and thorough introduction to Sun Ra's eclecticism.

Sun Ra. *The Futuristic Sounds Of Sun Ra*, Savoy Jazz 17259 [13]

Sun Ra. *Concert for the Comet Kohoutek*, ESP-DISK 3033 [13]

Taylor, Cecil. *Looking Ahead!*, OJC 452 [13]

Taylor, Cecil. *Conquistador!*, Blue Note 90840 [13]

Coleman, Ornette. *Beauty Is a Rare Thing: The Complete Atlantic Recordings*, Atlantic 71410 [13]

> Note: An extreme rarity among jazz boxed sets, this collection of the Ornette Coleman Quartet recordings made between 1959 and 1961 is consistently well performed and paced to have few moments of filler, and can be safely purchased as an introduction to Coleman's music. The Atlantic LPs collected here are all classics of early avant-garde jazz, and available as separate discs, as well.

Coltrane, John. *Giant Steps*, Atlantic 1311 [14]

Coltrane, John. *My Favorite Things*, Atlantic 1361 [14]

Coltrane, John. *The Complete 1961 Village Vanguard Recordings* (B), Impulse 232 [14]

> Note: A four disc set from which the LP *Live at the Village Vanguard* was culled.

Coltrane, John. *A Love Supreme*, Impulse/UMVD 589945 [14]

> Note: This "deluxe edition" reissue contains the original LP on one disc, as well as a second disc comprising alternate takes and a live performance of the entire suite. The original LP is also available as a single disc.

Coltrane, John. *Interstellar Space*, Impulse 543415 [14]

Nelson, Oliver. *The Blues and the Abstract Truth*, Impulse 1154 [15]

Getz, Stan and Joao Gilberto. *Getz/Gilberto*, Polygram 521414 [15]

Smith, Jimmy. *The Sermon!*, Blue Note 24541 [15]

Dolphy, Eric. *Out to Lunch*, Blue Note 98793 [15]

Albert Ayler Trio, *Spiritual Unity*, ESP DISK 1002 [16]

Shepp, Archie. *Mama Too Tight*, Impulse 248 [16]

Brötzmann, Peter. *Machine Gun*, FMP 400024 [16]

Art Ensemble of Chicago. *Bap-tizum*, Koch Records 8500 [17]

Braxton, Anthony. *For Alto*, Delmark 420 [17]

Braxton, Anthony. *Quartet (London) 1985*, Leo Records 200/201 [17]
Note: Braxton's quartet performed brilliantly throughout their 1985 UK tour, and released several albums of performances with similar titles. Any one of them is worth owning, and although the music may be an acquired taste, once the taste is acquired, all of the mid-1980s quartet recordings are worthwhile.

Henry Threadgill's Zooid. *Up Popped the Two Lips*, Pi Recordings 2 [17]
Note: At the time this book went to press, Henry Threadgill's recordings from the twentieth century are all out of production. This 2001 release is excellent, but the present state of Threadgill's catalog is regrettable; one can only hope for reissues.

Bill Evans Trio. *Sunday at the Village Vanguard*, OJC 140 [18]

Bley, Paul. *Closer*, ESP DISK 1021 [18]

Hill, Andrew. *Point of Departure*, Blue Note 99007 [18]

Hill, Andrew. *Time Lines*, Blue Note 35170 [18]

Corea, Chick. *Now He Sings, Now He Sobs*, Blue Note 38265 [18]

Circle. *Paris Concert*, ECM 1018 [18]

Holland, Dave. *Conference of the Birds*, ECM 829373 [18]

Jarrett, Keith. *Standards, Vol. 1*, ECM 811966 [18]

The Soft Machine. *Volumes 1 & 2*, Big Beat UK 920 [19]

Tony Williams' Lifetime. *Emergency!*, Polygram 539117 [19]

Return To Forever. *Light As A Feather*, Polygram 827148 [19]

Hancock, Herbie. *Mwandishi: The Complete Warner Bros. Recordings*, Warner Bros. 45732 [19]

Hancock, Herbie. *Head Hunters*, Sony 65123 [19]

Hancock, Herbie. *Future Shock*, Sony 65962 [19]

Weather Report. *Weather Report*, Sony 48824 [19]

Metheny, Pat and Ornette Coleman. *Song X: The 20th Anniversary Edition*, Nonesuch 79918 [20]

World Saxophone Quartet. *Plays Duke Ellington*, Nonesuch 79137 [20]

Murray, David. *Ming*, Black Saint 010 [20]

AMM. *AMMMusic*, ReR 9 [21]

Bailey, Derek. *Improvisation*, Ampersand 2 [21]

Parker, Evan. *The Needles*, Leo Records 348/349 [21]

Defunkt. *Defunkt/Thermonuclear Sweat*, Hannibal 571505 [21]

Naked City. *Naked City*, Nonesuch 79238 [21]

Frisell, Bill. *Live*, Hannibal 1517 [21]

Douglas, Dave. *The Tiny Bell Trio*, Songlines 1504 [22]

Zorn, John. *Masada: Live at Tonic 2001*, Tzadik 7334 [22]
> Note: Zorn's quartet recordings of Masada are numerous, excellent, and consistent to the point of redundancy. Any single Masada album is as good as any other, although the 2 disc live sets are usually a bit more energetic.

Other Dimensions in Music with Matthew Shipp. *Time is of the Essence; the Essence is Beyond Time*, Aum Fidelity 13 [22]
> Note: An excellent live performance by a premiere post-1990 free jazz ensemble.

Jim Black's AlasNoAxis. *AlasNoAxis*, Winter & Winter 61 [22]

The Nels Cline Singers. *The Giant Pin*, Cryptogramophone 600120 [22]

Mehldau, Brad. *The Art of the Trio, Vol. 5: Progression*, Warner Bros. 48005 [22]

The Bad Plus. *These are the Vistas*, Sony 87040 [22]

DeJohnette, Jack and Bill Frisell. *The Elephant Sleeps But Still Remembers*, Kindred Rhythm 1116
> Note: Released too recently to be discussed in this book, this excellent live set by DeJohnette and Frisell merits inclusion on the merits of its quality, and as a reminder to the reader to check regularly for new releases.

BIBLIOGRAPHY

For the purposes of further study, the following bibliography offers a number of works from various perspectives, arranged roughly in an order that parallels this book—of course, there is significant overlap among them. No effort has been made to offer support for the arguments made in this book; indeed there are works here that I find somewhat difficult to swallow, both as literature and scholarship, and, occasionally, as political and racial documents. However, no understanding of any kind of history is complete without an understanding of the contradictions and conflicts that surround it, and I leave it to the reader to develop his or her own opinions.

General Studies

Porter, Lewis, Michael Ullman and Ed Hazell. *Jazz: From Its Origins to the Present.* New York:Prentice Hall, 1983.

Szwed, John. *Jazz 101: A Complete Guide to Learning and Loving Jazz.* New York: Hyperion, 2000.

Early (Pre-Swing) Jazz

Berlin, Edward A. *King of Ragtime: Scott Joplin and His Era.* New York, Oxford University Press, 1995.

Giddins, Gary. *Satchmo: The Genius of Louis Armstrong.* New York: Da Capo Press, 2001.

Kirkeby, Ed. *Ain't Misbehavin': The Story of Fats Waller.* New York: Da Capo Press, 1975.

Lomax, Alan. *Mister Jelly Roll: The Adventures of Jelly Roll Morton, New Orleans Creole and "Inventor of Jazz."* Berkeley: University of California Press, 2001.

Sudhalter, Richard M. *The Lost Chord: White Musicians and Their Contribution to Jazz (1915–1945).* New York: Oxford University Press, 2001.

Schuller, Gunther. *Early Jazz: Its Roots and Musical Development*. New York: Oxford University Press, 1968.

The Swing Era and Bebop

DeVeaux, Scott. *The Birth of Bebop: A Social and Musical History*. Berkeley: University of California Press, 1999.

Gitler, Ira. *From Swing to Bop: An Oral History of the Transition of Jazz in the 1940s*. New York, Oxford University Press, 1994.

Gourse, Leslie. *Straight, No Chaser: The Life and Genius of Thelonious Monk*. New York: Schirmer, 1998.

Koch, Lawrence O. *Yardbird Suite: A Compendium of the Music and Life of Charlie Parker*. Bowling Green, Ohio: Bowling Green University Press, 1999.

Schuller, Gunther. *The Swing Era: The Development of Jazz, 1930–1945*. New York: Oxford University Press, 1991.

1950s and 1960s

Goldberg, Joe. *Jazz Masters of the 1950s*. New York, Da Capo Press, 2001.

Jost, Ekkehard. *Free Jazz*. New York: Da Capo Press, 1994.

Mingus, Charles. *Beneath The Underdog*. New York, Vintage, 1991.

Priestly, Brian. *Mingus: A Critical Biography*. New York: Da Capo Press, 1988.

Porter, Lewis. *John Coltrane: His Life and Music*. Ann Arbor: University of Michigan Press, 1998.

Rosenthal, David H. *Hard Bop: Jazz and Black Music 1955–1965*. New York, Oxford University Press, 1993.

Shim, Enumi. *Lennie Tristano: His Life in Music*. Ann Arbor: University of Michigan Press, 2007.

Sun Ra, Anthony Elms, John Corbett, Eds. *The Wisdom of Sun Ra: Sun Ra's Polemnical Broadsheets and Streetcorner Leaflets*. Chicago, WhiteWalls, 2006.

Szwed, John. *Space Is the Place: The Lives and Times of Sun Ra.* New York: Da Capo Press, 1998.

Since 1970

Nicholson, Stuart. *Jazz-Rock: A History.* New York: Schirmer Books, 1998.
Nicholson, Stuart. *Jazz: The 1980s Resurgence.* New York, Da Capo Press, 1995.
Whitehead, Kevin. *New Dutch Swing.* New York: Billboard Books, 1998.

INDEX

Christian, Charlie, 73
"Chronology," Ornette Coleman
    Quartet, 155, 156
Circle, 210
Clarinets, 4
Classic Quartet, 163–166
    Braxton, Anthony, 198–199
    A Love Supreme, 165–166
Cline, Nels, 248
Cole, Nat King, 170
Coleman, George, 135
Coleman, Ornette, 141, 153–158
    Atlantic Records, 155–157
    Bley, Paul, 206
    chorus, 153–154
    "Chronology," 155, 156
    classical ensemble compositions,
        157–158
    composers, 153–154
    electric instruments, 158
    Free Jazz, 156–157
    jazz recordings, 155–157
    Lenox Jazz School, 154
    pitch, 154, 155
    Prime Time, 158
Coltrane, Alice, 168
Coltrane, John, 159–168
    Ascension, 166
    avant-garde, 166–168
    Ayler, Albert, 184
    Classic Quartet, 163–166
    combining musical and
        spiritual, 159
    Davis, Miles, 133, 161–163
    duration of solos, 163
    early years, 160–161
    Giant Steps, 162–163
    impact on jazz, 159–160
    jazz recordings, 161–163
    Kind of Blue, 162–163
    A Love Supreme, 165–166
    Philadelphia, 160–161
    sheets of sound, 162
    Shepp, Archie, 185–186
    Thelonious Monk Quartet, 162
    worshipped, 159
Columbia Records, Davis, Miles,
    131

Commercial music industry,
    170–172
Compact discs, 231
Comping, 5
"Conquistador," Cecil Taylor Unit,
    152–153
Cool jazz, 111–112, 117–119
Corea, Chick, 201, 208–210
    Afro Cuban music, 209
    Latin music, 208, 209
    Now He Sings, Now He Sobs,
        209–210
    Return to Forever, 218–219
Cosey, Pete, 138–139
Cotton Club, 68
Creative Construction Company,
    196
Creole Jazz Band, 39, 40
    "Chimes Blues," 41
Crossover artists, 249–250
Crush tones, 7
Culture, jazz, 15
Cutting sessions, 75
    Kansas City, 75

D
Dameron, Tadd, 95
Dance music, 239
Dave Brubeck Quartet, "Take
    Five," 121
Davis, Miles, 111–112, 125–140,
    126–127
    apotheosis of cool, 125–126
    bebop, 127–128
    Birth of the Cool, 128–129
    Bitches Brew, 137–138
    book-length studies, 126
    Coltrane, John, 133, 161–163
    Columbia Records, 131
    composers, 127–128
    electronic instruments, 136–137
    Evans, Bill, 203
    Evans, Gil, 132–133
        reduced harmonic language,
            132–133
    First Quintet, 130–131
    focal point of new jazz substyle,
        125